The Education
of a Prejudiced Man

THE EDUCATION OF A PREJUDICED MAN

◄§ Joseph Gerard Brennan §► ,1910-

CHARLES SCRIBNER'S SONS / NEW YORK

Library of Congress Cataloging in Publication Data
Brennan, Joseph Gerard, 1910–
  The education of a prejudiced man.
  1. Brennan, Joseph Gerard, 1910–
  2. Philosophers—United States—Biography.
  I. Title.
  B945.B7444A33   191 [B]   77-4857
  ISBN 0-684-14915-X

1 3 5 7 9 11 13 15 17 19 V/C 20 18 16 14 12 10 8 6 4 2

PRINTED IN THE UNITED STATES OF AMERICA

ACKNOWLEDGMENTS

The Associate Alumnae of Barnard College, for quotation from Claude Levi-Strauss, "Structuralism and Ecology," *Barnard Alumnae,* Spring, 1972.

Basil Blackwell, Oxford, for quotation from *Collected Classical Papers of Gertrude Mary Hirst,* 1938.

An early version of portions of the Boston College chapters appeared in *Boston College Alumni News,* Fall, 1964.

Harcourt Brace Jovanovich, Inc., for permission to quote from "An Old Man," *The Complete Poems of Cavafy,* translated by Rae Dalven, copyright 1961, by permission of the publisher.

Harvard University Press, for quotation from Lionel Trilling, *Sincerity and Authenticity,* 1972.

Alfred A. Knopf, Inc., for permission to quote from Albert Camus, *The Myth of Sisyphus and Other Essays,* translated by Justin O'Brien, copyright Alfred A. Knopf, Inc., 1955; and from Jacques Monod, *Chance and Necessity,* translated by Austryn Wainhouse, copyright Alfred A. Knopf, Inc., 1971.

The Macmillan Publishing Co., Inc., for permission to quote from "Blood and the Moon," *The Collected Poems of William Butler Yeats,* copyright 1933 by the Macmillan Publishing Co., Inc., copyright renewed 1961 by Berthe Georgie Yeats.

The Macmillan Publishing Co., Inc., for permission to quote from Myles Connolly, *Mr. Blue,* copyright 1928 by the Macmillan Publishing Co., Inc., copyright renewed 1956 by Myles Connolly.

To Mrs. Merrill Moore for permission to quote from "Shot Who? Jim Lane!" originally published in Merrill Moore, *The Noise That Time Makes,* Harcourt, Brace, 1929.

The New Directions Publishing Corporation for permission to quote from "The Tomb of Akr Caar," Ezra Pound, *Personae,* copyright 1926 by Ezra Pound; and from "Ithaca," Gottfried Benn, *Primal Vision,* edited by E. B. Ashton, translated by Michael Hamburger, copyright 1971, New Directions Publishing Corporation.

The *New York Times* for permission to reprint my "Encounter: Getting to Know Sung Ae Park," copyright 1975 by the New York Times Company; and Francis T. Maguire's poem, "To a Dog Barking at Night," copyright 1968, the New York Times Company; both reprinted by permission.

Princeton University Press, for quotation from Judith Jarvis Thomson, "A Defense of Abortion," *Philosophy and Public Affairs* 1, no. 1 (Fall, 1971): 49.

Random House, Inc., for permission to quote from "Death's Echo" and "Miss Gee," W. H. Auden, *Collected Shorter Poems 1927–1957,* copyright W. H. Auden, 1964.

The quotation from V. Rev. Mother Marie de Saint Jean Martin O. S. U. is from her *Ursuline Method of Education,* Quinn & Boden, Inc., Rahway, N.J., 1946, copyright by the author.

Charles Scribner's Sons for permission to quote from Thomas Wolfe's *Of Time and the River,* copyright Charles Scribner's Sons, 1935.

Simon & Schuster, Inc., for permission to quote from Bertrand Russell, "A Free Man's Worship" in *Mysticism and Logic,* copyright Simon & Schuster, Inc., 1929.

An early version of a portion of the "Naples II" chapter appeared in *This Week* Magazine, August 11, 1946, as "Bosun's Chair."

Universal Edition (London) Ltd., music publishers, for permission to quote music and words from Zoltan Kodaly's "Hary Janos."

University of California Press, for quotation from Egon Schiele's diary, cited in Alessandra Comini, *Egon Schiele's Portraits,* 1974.

Warner Brothers Music, for permission to quote from song "Too Marvellous for Words," words by Johnny Mercer, music by Richard A. Whiting, introduced in the film *Ready, Willing and Able,* original copyright Harms, Inc., 1937.

Warmest thanks to Rear Admiral James B. Stockdale USN for permission to print his letter to me of November 24, 1975, and to Professor Alessandra Comini for sending me her "JGB Story." Thanks, too, to Thomas D. Burns for permission to quote from John Horne Burns, *The Gallery,* original copyright Harper and Row, 1948, and to quote from his brother's letter to me of July 10, 1947.

I am grateful to Emile Capouya and Oscar Schoenfeld as well as to David Pinkwas, Dorothy Stahl, and Joan Normoyle of Bethpage (N.Y.) Public Library for kind assistance.

I owe a special debt to Erik Wensberg whose including my "Fifty Years of *The Magic Mountain*" (herein revised as "Thomas Mann") in *The Columbia Forum,* Summer, 1975, helped this book find a home.

Above all, thanks to Patricia Cristol.

REMEMBERING

JOSEPH BRENNAN
1875–1949

NORA SHERIDAN BRENNAN
1882–1963

Contents

The Education
of a Prejudiced Man

PART

I

VALUE OF MONEY

᠎᠎ The first thing I learned was the value of money.

I was sitting on the curbstone looking through a piece of blue glass from a broken medicine bottle. This was Center Street, Roxbury, Boston, Massachusetts, and the traffic passing by was all lovely blue. The horses and wagons were blue, and the brewery auto trucks, piled with barrels, were blue. It was afternoon, maybe early fall, and I was about six years old. I had spent the morning quietly sliding down the stone sliding place between the two flights of red-brown stairs that led up to the doors of the three-family brick house where we lived. Then I had visited the trash dump in the back yard where I had found the blue glass. Now I was happy, for I could change the world from the firehouse to the old Unitarian church on Eliot Square into blue.

"Joe!" It was my mother calling me from the front window. I put the blue glass into my pants pocket and ran quickly over to her, for she could be cross if not obeyed promptly. She had black hair and gray-blue eyes. We called her Muzzie. That seemed quite natural to us, but it struck other children as odd. Most of them called their mothers Ma.

"I want you to go up to Beck's for a loaf of bread," she said, handing me a dime through the window. "Hurry now, and none of your dawdling. Listen to me, be careful of that money. Don't lose it, do you hear?" Not long before, I had lost fifty cents on the way to the store. Nobody took it from me. To this day, I don't think I dropped it. It was just that when I got to the store I did not have the fifty cents any more. My mother was very angry and said that I had been dreaming instead of having my mind on going to the store and doing my errand.

Another time, she had sent me for five pounds of sugar. On the way back I noticed a tiny white stream falling from the heavy bag onto the sidewalk. As the flow increased in volume and my bag diminished in weight, I stood staring in disbelief at the sugar pile on the sidewalk. Suddenly a swarm of hoarse-voiced Italian children issued from a dark alley known as the Court. They were armed with cups and spoons and with wonderful efficiency scooped up my sugar and ran. My mother was wild about the loss of the sugar, particularly about the Italian children getting it that way.

"I'll be careful," I said, clutching the dime, and set off for Beck's at an easy lope. Beck's was a pleasant store, with good smells and a large red-wheeled coffee grinder. Once at the age of four I had frightened Mr. Beck nearly out of his wits by quietly lifting his immense revolver from its hiding place back of the counter and pointing it at him. I had no intention of pulling the trigger. My older sister Eleanor quickly disarmed me and the incident was closed with no complaints.

When I got to the firehouse on Center Street, I stopped to look at the engines. They were bright-red-and-metal auto trucks. The old engines, and the splendid horses that pulled them, had been replaced a couple of years ago. The smell of horses hung on. I turned up Highland Avenue and climbed the hill. At Number 9 I stopped for a moment and looked up at the windows. Not long ago a little girl had died there of diphtheria. I moved on, but just before I got to Number 25 I crossed the street. Once a lady had called to me from Number 25. I went up the front steps to her and she offered me candy from a striped bag. Just as I was going to take a piece I remembered about kidnappers. I turned and ran down the steps, with her voice calling after me, "What's the matter, little boy, don't you want a piece of candy?"

At the top of the hill, on Highland Avenue, was an iron grating let into the sidewalk. This grating always absorbed my attention, although there was usually no more to be seen on the muddy bottom than a bottle cap or two. On this day I sat down beside the grating and put my nose to the bars. Today the mud floor (it was only a foot or so down) held four bottle caps and a bent spoon. I took the dime my mother had given me for the bread and very carefully balanced it on one of the bars of the grating. The bar was wide enough to support the dime, but as I shifted my position the grate moved a little and the dime fell through into the darkness below. I pressed my face to the bars. I could just make out the dime, white against the dark of the mud. I got up and looked around. Then I fetched a small tree branch from the gutter and poked at the dime through the bars.

All I succeeded in doing was burying the dime in the ooze. At that point I got up and ran home.

My mother had her white dust cap on her head, for she was cleaning house. She wanted to know where the bread was and I told her I did not get the bread.

"Didn't get it? Why on earth not?"

I told her I had lost the dime. Just lost it, that was all.

"Lost the dime!" She raised her mop and shook it at me. "Well now, you listen to me. You've been losing just too much money your father works day and night to earn! You march right out that door and don't you dare come back without the ten cents, d'you hear? The idea of you! Mooning and dreaming along the streets like a ninny. It's high time you learned the value of money. Get along with you now. And remember. Don't come back without that ten cents."

I walked slowly back down Center Street, climbed Highland Avenue once more, and sadly knelt down to the grate. Not a sight of the dime. At the curb nearby stood a half-filled trash barrel with an old curtain rod sticking out of it. With this I managed to turn the dime up from the muddy bottom so that half of it was visible. But the curtain rod could not pull the dime up through the grating. I tried to squeeze my hand through the bars, but it got caught and I freed it only at the cost of a long red scratch. I sat back and cried at that.

It was getting dark now. The yellow light of the street lamps (they were gas lamps, and the lamp lighter still came around with his long stick to light them), the smell of smoke from burning leaves, the chill of the darkening sky reinforced my despair. I cried some more.

"What's the matter, little boy?" A lady of indefinite shape and face, with a gentle voice, was bending over me. Catching my breath, I told her the story of my loss. I told her that my mother said never to come back home again, ever again, without that ten cents. My own sad tale moved me so that I began crying again. The lady opened her purse and handed me two nickels.

When I got home, it was quite dark. There was my mother standing at the front door looking down into the street. Her face was worried. "Where on earth have you been?" she said, staring at me. "I was just going out to look for you."

"You told me," I said, "you told me not to come back without the ten cents."

"Oh bother the ten cents," said my mother. "Come in the house now." But on the way to the kitchen she stopped and turned. "Did you find it then?"

I held my hand out, palm upward, to show the money.

"But that's *two nickels,* child." My mother pointed to the coins. "I gave you a dime. Where did you get that now?"

"A lady gave it to me," I replied with dignity. "A nice lady up on Highland Avenue. And she told me to tell you you are a very cruel woman."

My mother took the two nickels, looking hard at me. "Well, if you're not the Devil's darling!" she said grimly. "Come and eat your supper. March now!" She pushed me ahead of her gently into the kitchen.

At the kitchen table (it was covered with white oilcloth) sat my two older sisters Eleanor and Catherine. They had got home from their school, Notre Dame Academy, and were eating their supper. Catherine sometimes took me shopping with her, mostly at Timothy Smith's department store near Dudley Street. One cold winter day she bought me a hot chocolate at Drury's drug store. It came with a long spoon and whipped cream in a tall white cup with decorations around the rim. Eleanor was a little older than Catherine and talked less. She could play Schubert's "Serenade" on the piano in our parlor. She had seen *Madame Butterfly* and wanted to go to Japan.

That night I was allowed to have tea just like my sisters. This was a treat. I would dip my slice of plain bread (I disliked butter) into the teacup and let each bite dissolve harmoniously in my mouth. Even today the taste of a piece of bread dipped in tea, the madeleine of a poor man's Proust, starts from their hiding place memories of things past.

HAYNES PARK: ST. JOSEPH'S

Our kindergarten teacher was Miss Studely, a tall gray-haired lady with a smile. Mornings we sat around on little chairs in the classroom, sang songs, and made things. We wove red paper strips into gray paper frames. We arranged pegs, little colored wooden pointed things about a half inch long. (I liked the purple and yellow ones best.) Mornings at ten-thirty we had milk with plain crackers.

One day Miss Studely said, "Children, this morning we are going to have a treat at milk and cracker time." Smiling, she produced a large bowl, a bottle of cream, and a beater. She ground her shining wheel into the bowl, while we, crackerless, held our milk in front of us and waited. Finally she announced that everything was ready and began to stick some white paste from the bowl on to the crackers and to pass them out to us.

"What is this stuff?" I remember rudely asking, staring at the defiled cracker before me.

"Stuff indeed, Joseph!" Miss Studely said, patting more on a second cracker. "That's no way to talk about butter. Good, rich, wholesome butter. That's our special treat. Today for milk time we have butter on our crackers."

"I don't like butter!" My kindergarten mates paused in their eating to look at me.

"But everybody likes butter," said Miss Studely. "It's the best thing in the world for you. So nourishing. See here, maybe you think because it's not yellow, it isn't the same. But it's just the same."

"I don't like butter," I said.

"Does your mother have butter at home?"

"Yes."

"Yes, what?"

"Yes, Miss Studely."

"Don't you eat butter at home?"

"No, Miss Studely."

"Why not?"

"I don't like the way it tastes."

"The trouble with you, Joseph," said Miss Studely as she handed my buttered crackers to a willing child beside her, "is that you are *spoiled*."

Kindergarten came to an end, and so did first grade. Now I was in St. Joseph's parochial school. We had moved from Center Street to another part of Roxbury. We lived in a gray wooden three-decker house in a little dead-end street called Haynes Park off Warren Street, not far from Grove Hall, a square on the border of Dorches-

ter. Green streetcars with sparking trolleys ran up and down Warren Street. We lived in the top flat (they were never called "apart-
ments") of Number 7. It was hot in the summer. Ivan, the iceman,
wiped sweat from his red-brown forehead when he came into our
kitchen after toiling up three flights of back stairs with a twenty-five-
or fifty-pound block of ice on his back for our ice box. Twice a week
Mr. Schwartz, the Jewish ragman, slowly drove his old horse and
wagon around Haynes Park to see if people had rags or bottles or
other things for him. He sang:

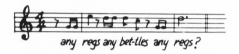

any rags any bot-tles any rags?

The whole area is now a black ghetto, and Haynes Park was
long ago bulldozed out of existence to make room for a public
housing project. Now they say it's a bad place, a high-crime area;
but when I strolled through there recently nobody bothered me and
I didn't see any rats. We had tremendous rats in Haynes Park,
though they stuck pretty close to Kenney's yard, where a couple of
Warren Street stores had their cellar entrances and kept their trash
barrels. We had none in the house.

In those days the neighborhood was still inhabited by "Yankees,"
as we called the lower-middle-class indigenous Protestant population.
But the Irish were moving in. Over on Blue Hill Avenue, a long
block away, the Eastern European Jews poured in. About a mile from
us the other way, on a hill known to older parishioners as "Tommy's
Rock," stood a very large Catholic church, St. Joseph's. The church
had a tall red brick tower in Romanesque style, and its great iron
bell rang the Angelus so loud in the morning it would wake people
far away. For some reason, the evening Angelus had a softer sound.
Here to St. Joseph's for Sunday and weekday Masses flocked the
Irish parishioners. Most of them were of the decent poor (the violent
drinking Irish lived in the South End and in South Boston) and
conscientiously sent their children to the parochial school hard by
the church. A few, to the pastor's indignation, allowed their little
ones to go to public school.

Like the church, St. Joseph's School was red brick, though of
coarser make. It stood three stories high with black iron fire escapes

all over the outside walls. The school building was erratically heated by a coal furnace (once a year the church took up a "Coal Collection") and the classrooms were pretty chilly in winter. On many mornings the ink at my desk would be frozen solid in its inkwell. Once when my hands were blue, Sister Margaret put her black woolen wristers on me and made me wear them until the room warmed up a little. But we weren't so badly off. There was hot soup every morning at ten, with a little meat in it, save on Fridays when we had cocoa in our tin cups. During Lent we had cocoa Wednesdays and Fridays.

About a block away from the school was a small bakery where we could buy cat pies for a cent apiece. A cat pie was two bits of pastry with mincemeat in between. There were large numbers of stray cats in the area, and it was believed that these cats furnished the material for pies. The bakery also sold candy from trays—dearos, dewey squares, mud bars, boston beans. For Lent, when we "fasted on" candy, there were coconut cakes that sold for a cent, as well as marshmallows. Neither counted as candy.

The nuns of St. Joseph's School were hard-worked women, genuinely concerned with our immortal souls. They took an intense personal interest in us, which may be another way of saying the same thing. But what struck me from the first was their violence, always colorful and often unpredictable. To us in the lower grades, the power wielded by the Sisters seemed directly backed by the super-natural. Their behavior seemed impulsive, unmotivated by external cause, springing from some deep inner necessity of their holy beings. I was quietly studying my catechism one day in second grade when Sister Marie Gabriel, a tense, pale nun of indescribable passion, called out my name. I stepped to the front of the room and she soundly whacked me twice on each upturned palm with her ruler. This was astonishing as well as painful, for I had done nothing to deserve punishment. I passed as a "good" boy, different from tough little pugilists like the Rogans or larcenous characters like the Finneys, whom the nuns battered daily out of sheer routine. Though my punishment was gratuitous, I bore Sister Marie Gabriel no grudge. To have protested would have seemed as senseless as arguing with a sudden ocean wave such as from time to time knocked me down when my mother took me to Revere Beach or Nantasket. Years later I heard that Sister Marie Gabriel had had a "nervous breakdown" and was no longer teaching.

Anyway, two whacks on the upturned palm of each hand was not so much. Most of the nuns fetched their disorderly charges businesslike cracks over the knuckles. The Sister Superior of St. Joseph's School (I think her name was Sister Therese of the Child Jesus) armed herself with a Homeric weapon she carried concealed in her capacious black sleeve. To me it looked like a large wooden plank, but I suppose it was really just a board of moderate size left at the convent by some carpenter after he had finished his work. Sister Therese was particularly stern with latecomers and sassers-back of nuns. Such was the reputation of her august arm and knuckleboard that tardiness at St. Joseph's was almost nonexistent and sassers-back of nuns a class of virtually no members.

I received corporal punishment at St. Joseph's yet one more time in the second grade. On this occasion the penalty was clearly merited. The music teacher, Sister Ambrose, visited our classroom three mornings a week, carrying her short black pointer, pitchpipe, and five-pronged chalk-holder for drawing staves on the blackboard. Normally she was good-humored, but one morning she encountered difficulty teaching us a hymn about the holy souls in Purgatory:

> *Holy souls in darkness pining,*
> *Pining for the blissful light;*
> *Waiting, longing, ever sighing*
> *To be free from sorrow's night.*

Trouble occurred at the following words—"Mercy, loving Jesus, mercy!"—where the melody suddenly went two-part. Our efforts were distinctly unmusical, indeed so much like the groans of the holy souls themselves, that we began to laugh. Sister Ambrose lost her temper, and opened her mouth wide. She had big horselike teeth. "I'm desperate, I tell you," she yelled. "Desperate!"

As in a dream, but with candor and clarity, I said aloud, *"Desperate Ambrose!"* Smothered screeches broke out all over the room, for the belligerent Ambrose was well known by his adventures in the funny part of the *Boston Post*.

"Come here, Joseph," said Sister Ambrose in a terrible voice. Mute and shriveled, I stood before her. "You have committed a sin, Joseph. You have been disrespectful to a nun!" The boys were still laughing, but the girls—now that it was a question of sin—looked on in prim silence. "Hold out your hand! No, palm down. Again."

After class Sister Ambrose came down to my desk, wiped my face a little with her handkerchief, and spoke kindly to me. I asked her whether what I had done was a mortal sin or a venial sin. She said she thought it was only a venial sin. I felt better after that.

According to Sister Margaret, who taught us in third grade, most children could not commit mortal sins before they had reached the age of reason, which was, in most cases, about seven years of age. But in rare instances, she said, a boy or girl could commit a mortal sin while still very young indeed. Once, she told us, there was a little boy hardly more than five years old. He lived with his parents and had a sister who was about seven or eight. This sister of his was very pious and would kneel for a long time before the Blessed Sacrament in church praying. But her little brother was very bad. He told deliberate lies, was disobedient, and used bad language. He did worse. He *blasphemed*. Blasphemy, Sister Margaret explained, spelling the fascinating word out on the blackboard, was a fearful sin in which one made fun of God or His Blessed Mother or of other sacred things. Now one day the little boy caught cold. Pneumonia set in and a few days later he died in the hospital. His parents were heartbroken, for they loved their little son, bad as he was. Afterward they used to speak of him as if he were an angel in Heaven.

One day the mother said to her pious little girl, the dead boy's sister, "Don't you ever think of your little brother who is in Heaven?"

The little girl gave her mother a long, sorrowful look. Then she said quietly, "He isn't in Heaven, mother. He's in Hell."

That was really a powerful story and Sister Margaret told it very effectively.

ON THE ALTAR

&> A pleasant thing in those days was to serve Mass as an altarboy. Somebody decided I should be "on the altar," and my father taught me the Latin responses. (I wonder if it's as much fun today with everything in the vernacular and simplified.) With a couple of weeks' drilling, I was a proper acolyte with black cassock neatly pressed, white surplice starched, ready for my first Mass. Ready as co-server, that is, for I was not yet prepared to serve Mass alone. For most Masses, two boys served, one taking the more difficult "Bell" side, the other the easier "Book." An experienced altarboy could serve Mass alone if he had to. My Mass was scheduled for six-thirty Monday morning, and my partner was a senior altarboy named Francis O'Connor. The celebrant was none other than Monsignor Michael J. Splaine, pastor of St. Joseph's.

Monsignor Splaine was for years a friend and traveling companion of our famed Archbishop of Boston, William Cardinal O'Connell. Monsignor had two sides to his personality, of which up to that time I had known only the first, his public personality shown typically on his state visits to our classroom. On these visitations Monsignor displayed a plump pince-nezed affability that helped soften the awesomeness of his visit. All the same, he was impressive. I remember in the third grade one boy copiously wet his pants (and the floor) when Monsignor appeared in the room for a chat. Sister was furious. Afterward she gave us an angry talking-to, telling us that we should see to our "needs" before coming to the classroom. Monsignor cheerfully ignored the incident.

"My dear little angel boys and girls!" he would say by way of greeting, then address some complimentary remark to the Sister standing by, all nervous smiles. "Ah, the Catechism, dear Sister, the Catechism," he would exclaim as he fingered the purple-lined buttonholes of his soutane. "Could we hear the Catechism, Sister, just a wee bit of it?" Sister would open the Catechism book and call on Rita Dowd, who had a perfect memory, or myself, who could repeat the lines "with expression."

"Why did God make us? Rita!"

"God made us to love Him, to serve Him in *this* world, and to be happy with Him in the *next*."

"What are the conditions necessary for a mortal sin? Joseph!"

"There must be a grievous matter, sufficient reflection on our part, and full consent of the will."

Monsignor would manifest complete satisfaction, then talk to us a little, exhorting us to be good, obey our parents, be obedient to the dear Sisters, study hard, love God, and pray to His Blessed Mother. Last of all he asked us to pray for "a very special intention" of his own. (Grownups said this intention concerned Monsignor's desire to be bishop of Portland, Maine, a wish that I don't think was ever fulfilled despite his friendship with Cardinal O'Connell and their trips to Rome together.) Then, after a cheery word to the boys about baseball and to the girls about their dolls, Monsignor would take his smiling departure, nodding to Sister on the way out, reminding her to take good care of his dear little angel boys and girls.

At six-thirty Mass, however, I discovered that Monsignor was another man. His early-morning self loomed taciturn and withdrawn. When Francis O'Connor and I rose to our feet as Monsignor entered the sacristy with "Good morning, Monsignor," he only muttered curtly and donned his brocaded sweet-smelling vestments in silence. (My favorite colors were the rose ones used only on Laetare and Gaudete Sundays, mid-Lent and mid-Advent.) For that first Mass of mine, O'Connor and I preceded Monsignor, with our hands folded, to the foot of the altar where burned the two candles I had lighted with a wax taper a few minutes before. It was a low Mass, the congregation sparse, but devout. Kneeling on Monsignor's left (the "Book" as opposed to the harder "Bell" side), I listened intently for the opening words of the Mass—

"Introibo ad altare Dei"

—to which I was prepared to respond:

"Ad Deum qui laetificat juventutem meam."

I never heard the words. Monsignor was saying the Latin to himself inaudibly and at great speed. Not a syllable could I hear from his lips as cue for my beautifully memorized responses. When, for decency's sake, I began to recite the *Confiteor,* Monsignor had already darted up the altar steps, leaving me with nearly my whole first batch of Latin unsaid.

Silently Monsignor flicked through the Epistle. O'Connor had to hiss fiercely at me from the "Bell" side to get me to rise to move the book. Genuflecting on the run, I shot around to the right side of the altar, where I snatched the great illuminated missal that lay open on its heavy wooden stand and worried it over to the Gospel side of the altar. Monsignor was standing there waiting. When the book was heaved up before him, he simply glanced at it, then nipped back to the center of the altar. On general principles, I said, *"Laus tibi Christi,"* and returned to my place at the foot of the altar, watching the priest as a retriever its master. Monsignor was obviously getting through large chunks of the Mass. Not to be left out entirely, I recited the *Suscipiat:*

"*Suscipiat Dominus sacrificium de manibus tuis, ad laudem, et gloriam nominis sui, ad utilitatem quoque nostrum, totiusque Ecclesiae suae sanctae.*"

But now I was aware that something was wrong. Looking around, I saw to my horror that O'Connor was being quietly sick to his stomach in a corner of the sanctuary. Then he exited, leaving the service of this particular reenactment of Calvary's sacrifice wholly in my inexperienced hands. The Offertory was upon me. I dashed to the little side table on which reposed cut-glass cruets of water and wine. I proffered the little bottles to Monsignor, noticing too late that I had neglected to take out the glass stoppers. The pastor seized the stopper of the wine cruet, intending, as it turned out, to draw it. But, under the impression that he wanted to take the entire cruet from my hand, I let go the handle. The little bottle bounded to the altar carpet, spouting wine like blood. Monsignor's expression was indescribable. Unfreezing, I dived for the floor, grabbing up the cruet, in which a little wine was still left. Monsignor firmly took both water and wine vessels from me, and set them before him on the altar. Then he poured out his own water and wine.

The next problem was the bell, which I had not been trained to ring. It was a great gold-plated affair like an oversized dish-cover within which nested three separate sets of small bells. When the whole array was lifted up by its handle and shaken, it jangled robustly, making a far braver noise than the weak sentimental chimes that later became fashionable. At this Mass, somebody *had* to ring the bell, so I knelt fearfully beside it, watching Monsignor and straining my ears for the sound of his voice. I tried to follow him as he raced through the Preface to the *Sanctus,* when I should have rung three times and did not ring at all, for he was already near the Consecration, at which I should have rung once and didn't. Puzzled, I watched his back as he bent over the altar and made rapid gestures with his hand. (A little Protestant boy I knew said his grandmother told him that when the priest made motions like that he was really controlling the movements of a crab on the altar in front of him.) There was no mistaking the solemn elevation of Host and chalice, and there I got my jangling in on good time. The next bell should have been at the celebrant's words, "*Domine non sum dignus,*" but

I rang it early, startled by the unexpected distinctness with which Monsignor pronounced the words *"Nobis quoque peccatoribus."* When the *"Domine non sum dignus"* finally came, I did not ring the bell.

"The bell!" said Monsignor in a low, cutting voice, "the bell!" I set up a feeble jangling and the congregation's communicants straggled up to the altar rail.

In the sacristy after Mass there was no sign of Francis O'Connor, save cassock and surplice flung on a bench. He had gone home. Monsignor said not a word to me but divested himself of chasuble and alb in silence, his lips tight closed. I was grateful for his silence. Later, when I had served Mass for him many times, I came to esteem the grim wordlessness of his early mornings more than the genial volubility of his angel-boy-and-girl performance.

The best time of year to serve on the altar, particularly if you had the six-thirty weekday morning Mass, was during the month of May. It was Mary's month, and in Roxbury the lilacs were in blossom, investing the morning air with their lovely scent. On those May mornings when you entered the sacristy of the church basement to reach down the wax-spotted cassock and surplice from the wooden wardrobe, you were aware of no sharp break between the fragrance of mayflowers and lilac drifting through the half-open windows and the odor of old incense, polished wood, and gilded vestments, tended by old Sister Clare, the sacristan.

BOSTON LATIN SCHOOL

໖ The nuns of St. Joseph's had me in their keeping until the end of the sixth grade, at which time I left parochial school for Boston Latin. The teacher of that grade, Sister Agnes, was a pale disciplinarian inseparable from her burly leather-bound *Lives of the Saints,* which she would read aloud or throw at disorderly boys with equal passion. One of her most effective methods of intimidating class hooligans was to describe, with admirable feeling for detail, the death of a former pupil of hers in the electric chair, at State Prison in Charlestown. Her unfortunate alumnus, she told us, made a full confession to the prison chaplain at the end, and died with the Holy Name on his lips.

Sister Agnes's gloomy views on the nature and destiny of man would have entitled her to a considerable position at the court of Philip II of Spain. At the same time, long before progressive education had even been heard of in Roxbury, she gave students freedom to work during class time at special tasks of their own design, provided it was in some way related to what we were studying. For many weeks at the blackboard I labored over an elaborate chalk map of South America, using a package of colored chalk that Sister Agnes gave me for my exclusive use. Brazil I colored a lovely leaf-green, Argentina an ardent cerise, while Chile—ah, Chile—shone softly in rich violet that blurred its beauty all the way down the west coast of the continent to Tierra del Fuego.

For reading and writing, Sister Agnes put boys and girls in alternate rows, each named for local Catholic colleges, male and female: Boston College, Emmanuel, Holy Cross, Regis. Sister then pitted the rows against one another in spelling bees, reading contests, and Palmer Method drills. In arithmetic we corrected each other's papers. Competition was keen, but despite some uncertainty in square roots and an irremedial weakness in penmanship ("Oval, oval, oval! Up, up, up!"), I ranked second in the class at the end of the year. Rita Dowd was first.

All this pleased my mother, but she had higher things in mind for me. Although she was a good Catholic and respectful toward Cardinal O'Connell's views on the importance of Catholic education, it was not her plan for me to jog peacefully along with the nuns of St. Joseph's forever. I must go to Boston Latin School. How else was I to get to Harvard and be a doctor? My father gently agreed, although he was not so ambitious for his children as his gray-eyed wife. My dark, slender father serenely handed out letters to the public from the General Delivery window of the main Boston Post Office on Milk Street. He looked like Eamon de Valera, but he had no iron in his soul. He had dark, curly hair, and loved to read his one-volume encyclopedia and improve his crystal radio set by winding new coils with wire. Yes, he said, Boston Latin was a very fine school.

Boston Latin School was the most prestigious public school in the United States. Had not its lads thrown snowballs at General

Gage's Redcoats on Boston Common in 1776? Every poor boy in
Boston who wanted to get into Harvard tried for Boston Latin. Admission procedure was simple. Boys from both public and parochial
schools were admitted to the first year (seventh-grade) level, if they
passed an entrance examination. I had no trouble with the exam,
but it was just about the last success I had in connection with Boston
Latin School. I was lost in the big new building on Louis Pasteur
Street near Harvard Medical School and the Boston Lying-In Hospital on Longwood Avenue. Lost in the great noisy cafeteria with its
malodorous cheese-ridden "hot plates," its crowd of pushing, shoving
boys who screamed, *"Pay for it!"* when somebody dropped and broke
a dish. Most hopelessly, I was lost in the classroom. Accustomed to
the nuns' intense interest in their pupils, I was puzzled by the dry
detachment of the Latin School masters. I tried half-heartedly to
keep up with the driving competitive pace of class- and homework,
but soon fell behind, surrendering myself to idleness and dreams. In
class I used to watch the minute hand of the electric wall clock move
forward with tiny jerks (years later, reading Bergson, I knew exactly
what he meant by saying that mathematical time is made up of little
isolated bits) and silently prayed that the bell ending the hour would
clang before I was called on. My only moments of peace were at
lunchtime, when I would escape from the cafeteria to a corner of
the gymnasium balcony, deserted at that hour save for rehearsals of
the fine school orchestra. It was lovely there: peace, harmony, a good
varnishy smell, my sandwich brought from home, and no one to
bother me. But, alas, in twenty minutes, the clamor of the bell would
send me back to some dreaded master with my lesson badly prepared
or not at all.

The Latin class was the worst. Mr. Lally, the master, wore
glasses of black horn under his heavy dark hair; his hollow windy
voice sounded like a bass clarinet. He had a pack of class cards on
each of which was written a pupil's name together with an accumula-
tion of marks and notations. He would shuffle those cards with terrible dexterity at the beginning of each class, then call out the name
on the card turned up. Woe to the wretched boy who was unpre-
pared; better for him that he had never been born.

"Brennan!"

There is something in us all that resents our being called by
our last name. Scholars tell us that our surname is not really our

name at all, but something superadded, a historical accretion tacked on in the course of centuries to distinguish us from others of the same first or "Christian" name. Today, when I am in Europe visiting friends, one of them—thinking it the English manner—calls me by my last name. All the same, I wince at it.

"Excuse me, Mr. Lally?" I would say weakly, the walls of my stomach collapsing.

Mr. Lally had the patience of the Holy Office. "The sixth sentence, Brennan, the sixth sentence from the top of page twenty-three of that book in front of you."

"The general . . . the army . . . from the camp . . ." Of course it was hopeless.

"Brennan," Mr. Lally would say, frowning his Assyrian frown, "will you tell me why it is that when you recite—or, I should say, *try* to recite—you always sound as if you were going to burst into tears?"

That would amuse the class. I might try again despairingly, but it always ended by Mr. Lally blocking out a remorseless *F* under my name with his silver pencil.

Latin School rewarded good scholars with weekly pasteboards called "Approbation Cards," while the idle and disorderly were punished by "Misdemeanor Marks." Every Friday afternoon in homeroom, Mr. Goodenough would give out the approbation cards, certifying to a week's excellent scholastic record in a particular subject. In my year and a half at Boston Latin I received only one of these cards: it was in Physiology and Hygiene, a minor subject. But some of my classmates got one or more nearly every week. One well-spoken Jewish boy named Wolf—his father owned a prosperous clothing store in Boston—had not missed a weekly approbation card in sixteen months. Wolf was really very bright. Sometimes I would ask him to help me with a Latin construction or a math problem. He would always oblige, accepting my thanks with a deprecating gesture, a courteous grown-up smile.

The misdemeanor marks were serious. You could get one for talking in class, failing to turn in a homework assignment, using a trot in Latin, and so on. One misdemeanor mark brought down the Deportment grade on your report card from *A* to *B*, two lowered it to *C*, and so on down the scale. If you were luckless enough to accumulate a total of six misdemeanor marks within a given period, you were forthwith struck by that arrow of God, the "Censure." Since I tended to be on the timid side, my Deportment was good. Although I had only that single approbation card to cover my academic nakedness, I did not have any misdemeanor marks. But the Furies who pursued me in those days remedied that lack in their own good time and in full measure too. For at length I committed an offense so frightful that it was dealt with by the ghastliness of Instant Censure.

For some time now my grades had been deteriorating. They had never been better than barely passing, except for the freakish 90 in Physiology and Hygiene. Now red-inked failure grades began to appear on my report card: a 50 in Latin, a 55 in Math, with the other grades no higher than 60s or low 70s. Those poor grades distressed my mother terribly. Daughter of an Irish father who had settled in Dumbarton to work on the boilers in the ships along the Clyde, she had early acquired (perhaps from her native Scottish mother) the passion for advancement through higher learning that flourished in Scotland. There, every poor mother's dream was to see her son a scholarship boy at the "Univairsity." My mother simply could not understand these report cards. Had not her son been an honor student with the nuns at St. Joseph's? Had he not ranked second in the class in the sixth grade? Was he not a great reader, poring over the big green and blue volumes of *The Book of Knowledge* until he had to be chased outdoors into the sunshine? He could not expect to go to Harvard and be a doctor unless he improved his marks. Did he want to be a penny clerk when he grew up? In her hurt and anger, she coldly averted her face from me. My father saw the report cards late at night when he came home from the post office, and next morning shook his head over them sadly, saying I'd have to learn to apply myself. Then he signed his name to the horrible things in his neat oval hand.

I knew the last report card before Christmas of that year was going to be disastrous, and weeks before it fell due I felt sick over the prospect. Yet I did nothing to help myself. Letting homework and class assignments drift where they would, I withdrew via my sisters' Lucille Montgomery books to the mild and pleasant world of Prince Edward Island, where I followed red-haired Anne Shirley from Green Gables through peaceful Avonlea until at last, with Gilbert Blythe (who became a doctor), she found her House of Dreams and an unbelievable number of children. But inexorably the grim afternoon arrived when Mr. Goodenough handed out the report cards just at the end of the school day. I drew the pale yellow rectangle from its manila envelope and stared at it. I remember the involuntary moan it dragged from me. I had a 40 in Math, a 35 in Latin. Nothing else was much above the 60 (pass) level except a 70-something in English. After school, I did not go home but spent the whole late Friday afternoon wandering in a sick daze around the Fenway where little Muddy River meanders by the Museum of Fine Arts until it finds it way to the broad Charles moving steadily toward Boston Harbor. On a creek flowing into Muddy River a mother duck was sailing along with her little ones following her like a train of yellow cars. I was thinking hard and crying and very scared. They could not comfort me.

Suddenly I had a brilliant idea, a plan that would relieve the torment, take away for a day at least the vision of the awful scene waiting for me at home. I tucked the report card into my Latin book and hurried the four miles home on foot. I could have gone via the trolley cars, Huntington Avenue to Massachusetts Avenue to Dudley Street Station by way of Washington Street, then home by transfer to the Warren Street–Grove Hall car. I had a little book of cheap student-fare tickets. But the trolleys were slow and crowded, and I tended to get carsick on them. Besides, I liked to walk. That weekend I played baseball with some of the Haynes Park boys in Kenney's yard with a rubber ball. We were forbidden to use the cheap baseballs known as "nickel bricks" for fear of broken windows. After supper I read *Quo Vadis* (my favorite character was Petronius) and on Saturday night listened to the Boston Symphony concert on our crystal radio, the earphones tight to my head.

Monday morning at school, I waited anxiously for lunch hour, then sought my hideout, the balcony of the deserted gym. I took the report card out of the Latin book and went to work on it with an ink eraser. At the end of ten minutes, I had pretty well scrubbed out the red ink of failure. Then, with the point of a fountain pen filled with blue-black ink I inscribed in the erased areas two passing grades, not high. The result was a little rough, but on the whole it did not strike me as noticeable. My head light and my stomach contracted to a ball, I went back to class.

When I got home that afternoon, I found my mother sewing at the dining room table. She was sitting in her usual chair, a high black rocker with a cushion on the seat. I handed the report card to her.

"Passed everything!" I tried to make my voice sound glad.

"Oh, I'm so happy," she said, putting on her glasses to examine the card. Slowly my heart climbed up into my throat and distended it. I was afraid she would notice the ever-so-slightly blurred ink on the altered grades for Latin and Math. But she handed the card back to me to place on the mantelpiece so my father could see it when he came from work. "You passed. Dad will be so pleased. You see what you can do when you apply yourself."

Nothing to fear now. My father would sign the card without hesitation. Ink-blurred figures would carry no implication of wrong to that gentle mind. So it turned out. All was well. Next morning I took my signed card back to school and returned it to Mr. Goodenough.

For about a week I knew a sort of peace, although I found myself waking before daylight unable to go back to sleep. Then one morning in Latin class, Mr. Lally called me to his desk. The other boys were writing.

"Brennan!" His voice hollow as a tomb. "What did you do to your report card?"

"My report card?" I remember gasping in an almost soundless voice. "Nothing!"

"Nothing. Very well. Take your seat."

So far had I removed myself from harsh reality that I walked home that afternoon without particular fear. Mr. Lally, the horrible card, Boston Latin School, all were four miles back there to the north and west. I was not thinking of them. They did not exist. But the merciful narcosis was short-lived. My mother was waiting for me at the door with a letter in her hand.

"You changed your report card!"

Let's forget what happened then, the words that were said then.

Next morning at school I was informed by my homeroom teacher that a Censure had been lodged against me, that I must report forthwith to the headmaster's office. I walked down the marbled corridor, panting with distress. A woman secretary, who wore a hair net, admitted me directly to the awesome presence of the headmaster, Mr. Patrick Campbell, all gray-haired worth and dignity. He asked what I had come for.

"I . . . I changed my report card."

"Oh dear, you're *that* boy." He shook his head in shock and sorrow. "Oh dear, that's a sad thing, a terrible thing."

I managed to choke out that my father was coming to school that day to see him. Mr. Campbell seemed relieved, said he was glad to hear that, and sent me back shaking to my classroom. Later I heard that he was very nice to my father when he came. Everyone was nice to my father. All the same, I was thrust forth from Boston Latin School. I never went to Harvard (not to the college, anyway) and I never became a doctor—at least of the medical sort.

For weeks my mother barely spoke to me, but my father, after one ineffectual scene, made no more of it but went back to reading his one-volume encyclopedia and improving the crystal radio set, singing softly to himself airs he had learned in Ireland. One of his favorites was about a destitute fisher boy befriended by a nobleman's daughter:

> *She begged of her father*
> *To find the boy employment.*
> *She begged of her father*
> *No more to let him roam.*

> *By his friends he was neglected,*
> *He was poor and dejected,*
> *The poor little fisher boy*
> *So far away from home.*

BOSTON: SYMPHONY

ào Apart from school, Boston was a good place to grow up in. The city itself was small enough for a good walker to get from one end to the other in no great time. Although Roxbury was not part of the downtown area (it was a separate community until 1862), it bordered conveniently on "Boston Proper" on the south side of the city. My father liked to walk and would take me with him on fine Sundays on a three-mile stroll from our house to Huntington Avenue, where the Museum of Fine Arts looked out through its rear windows on the Fenway. In the museum we would amble around comfortably, studying the pictures. My favorite was *Watson and the Shark,* Copley's enormous canvas showing a man who had fallen from a boat and now lay struggling in the water, naked and terrified, long hair streaming, as the monster jaws of the shark gaped fearfully beside him. Leaving the museum, we might pause at the entrance walk to look at *The Appeal to the Great Spirit,* Daniel Chester French's bronze equestrian statue of a Plains warrior, head flung back, arms to the sky. My father would remark how wonderful it was that all people, as indeed the Indians, had knowledge of God. We would walk along Huntington Avenue in silence for a while. Then my father might say, "The Mohammedans worship the true God. But in the wrong way." Another silence as we turned off in the direction of Mrs. Jack Gardner's house, since 1920 the Isabella Stewart Gardner Museum.

"Atheists say there is no God," my father would remark. "Agnostics say we don't know whether there is a God or not." Then we would stroll into Mrs. Jack's palazzo for a quiet tour of her Venetian splendors. My favorite picture there showed a lady in a short black jacket and full white skirt dancing to the music of two guitar players whose heads were bent over their instruments at exactly the same angle. My father said it was by Sargent, a famous portrait painter who knew Mrs. Jack. Sometimes on Sunday afternoons there would be music and the sound of strings or flute would mingle with the plash of fountains in the inner court. Years later I read that Henry James once complimented Mrs. Jack on the melodies of her toilet; he was referring not to her musical plumbing but to her costume.

I knew my way around the business district of Boston pretty well. When I was eleven years old I got a summer job as an office boy with the Boston law firm of Tyler, Eames, Wright, and Hooper, and held it for four summers. Every day I hand-delivered letters to the State Street Trust and the New England Trust and law firms like E. Sohier Welch and Ropes, Grey, Boyden and Perkins, a name so sacred that proper Bostonians, they said, did not utter it but only thought about it. My errands often took me to the Union Club on Park Street, where parchment-faced gentlemen sat on black leather chairs and smoked cigars brought to them by respectful attendants in red-and-black–striped vests. Founded during the Civil War by a group of Bostonians who wanted a place where gentlemen could spend the evening without hearing Copperhead talk (as at the Somerset Club), the Union included among its early members Ralph Waldo Emerson, Oliver Wendell Holmes, and James Russell Lowell. Most of the senior members of Tyler, Eames belonged to the Union Club.

Occasionally in the course of my duties I would be summoned to the presence of Mr. Charles T. Tyler himself, a bald, tall, irascible lawyer with fringes of white hair around his ears. His rages were legendary. (Annie Bannin, his fiftyish telephone operator, would quote bowlderized bits of them to her friends on other phone lines: " 'G. D.-it!' he said, 'J. C.!' ") In Mr. Tyler's great office, lined with model ships, I would receive instructions for taking the train to his feudal manor near Pride's Crossing. It was lovely to escape the summer Boston heat, to sniff the cool Atlantic air of the North Shore, and to pet Mr. Tyler's prize English setters after delivering my package. More often my sea-smells were confined to the hot roast coffee scents of downtown India Street when I would rush something to a firm member taking the New York boat at 5:00 P.M. from the wharf at Atlantic Avenue. With the quarter given to me for my trouble, I would go back up State Street past the Old State House to Thompson's Spa on Washington Street where, at the marble standup counter, they served the most delicious chocolate ice cream sodas in heavy squat glasses.

From time to time I was sent to pick up or return a book at the Boston Athenaeum, sacred private library of the Brahmins. The reading room was dusty brown (the wood) and yellowed white (the marble busts), and the air smelled of old cloth and leather bindings. An ageless functionary gently saw to it that I did not disturb the books on the shelves while waiting for Mr. Ellis's copy of *Shore Birds of Maine*.

For my own reading purposes I could go to the Boston Public Library on Copley Square. Like so many cultural institutions founded by old Bostonians, the great library was inspired by the patrician-democratic wish to provide open access to cultural riches to all, including the foreign-born and their children: Irish, Italians, Russian Jews, and the rest. Since 1895 the library had been housed

in a large building, elegant and odd (now supplemented by a new
ten-story annex), constructed with utter lack of economy on the plan
of a Renaissance palace—courtyard, fountains, and all. Sargent, Abbey, and Puvis de Chavannes did the interior murals. The Boston
Library housed all kinds of good books, but sometimes they were a
little hard to extract from the venerable circulation apparatus. Early
in my high school years I became a Thomas Hardy freak, and got
nearly all his novels and poetry out of my Roxbury branch library.
The poetry puzzled me, though years later I came to prefer it to
most of his novels. What soul in moments of self-pity could fail to
find solace in the beat of:

> *Let him in whose ears the low-voiced*
> *Best is killed by the clash of the First,*
> *Who holds that if way to the better*
> *there be, it exacts a full look at the Worst,*
> *Who feels that delight is a delicate growth*
> *cramped by crookedness, custom and fear,*
> *Get him up and be gone as one*
> *shaped awry; he disturbs the order here.*

Anyway I couldn't locate *Jude the Obscure,* the novel of Hardy I
wanted most to read, since my English teacher told me the novel had
caused a scandal when it first appeared in Victorian England. There
was extramarital sex, denunciations of monogamy, and little children hanged at the end. So I put in for *Jude* at the main library in
Copley Square. Fifteen minutes passed before I was summoned to
the main desk by a worried-looking library gentleman who held my
slip in his hand.

"Library rules," he told me, "do not permit copies of this book
to be taken out of the library. If you really wish to read it, you must
read it here and in the presence of a librarian."

Doggedly I made my way through the gloomy tale, distracted
by various library persons, male and female, passing my table at frequent intervals, checking (I supposed) to see whether I was doing
anything indecent. To this day odd survivals of old New England
taboos can be found in the Boston area. I have always been particularly fond of the unconscious Puritanism of a sign I noticed once at
a beach near Rockport:

DRESSING, UNDRESSING, AND OTHER
OBJECTIONABLE PRACTICES STRICTLY FORBIDDEN

But my absolute pet Boston institution was the Symphony. At the age of twelve, I was taken to a young people's concert at Symphony Hall with a group from Norfolk House, a Roxbury settlement house on Eliot Square. The Boston Symphony Orchestra was then still under the baton of Pierre Monteux. I could not believe that such gorgeous sound could exist on this earth: the orchestra sounded like a great golden organ. With the Introduction to Act III of *Lohengrin* there began for me an affair with music, rising to a love (in romantic Nietzsche's way of putting it) of a man for a woman he does not trust—passion with a thorn of doubt in it. In high school my obsession with music extended to my playing hooky from school on Friday afternoons in order to line up for the Symphony rush seats available for a quarter—later raised to fifty cents. We lined up on the broad, flat steps of the Huntington Avenue entrance and in winter stamped our feet before they froze entirely. At one o'clock they let us in to an area where one could buy coffee and brownies while waiting for concert time to come around. One could go to one's seat early and spend a fascinating half hour listening to a harpist tuning his demanding instrument, a lonely violinist fingering a difficult passage, a percussionist softly stroking his kettledrums, laying an anxious ear over their heads. Then the flood of musicians —there was the principal cellist Jean Bedetti, flutist George Laurent, the contrabassoonist Boaz Piller (his cleaning woman called him "Bozo"), Richard Burgin, the concertmaster, and finally the conductor, Serge Koussevitzky himself, all elegance and command. The oddly dressed Boston ladies applauded with just the right mixture of enthusiasm and well-bred reserve. None of the vulgar shouting one hears these days at the end of a passable performance of Brahms's Second Piano Concerto or Mahler's Eighth Symphony. The older ladies' hats had that institutional character celebrated in the legendary reply to a question concerning their origin, "My dear, we do not *buy* our hats, we *have* our hats."

Gods would appear at Symphony—not just their music, but the composers themselves in unbelievable flesh. Rachmaninoff himself played his piano concerti, Stravinsky conducted his Psalm Symphony, Respighi his Roman Pines, Schönberg his Transfigured Night. Ravel came when I was a junior in high school. He was a very little man, nervous and *raffiné;* he almost fell off the podium (that was before they had rails) into the lap of—was it Mrs. Rantoul?—in the first row. Then he led the orchestra through his *Rapsodie Espagnole,*

In high school I became addicted to critic H. T. Parker's Homeric reviews of Symphony concerts in the Boston *Evening Transcript.* Tyrannical editor of the monstrous music-and-drama section of the venerable newspaper, Parker liked to brighten up the pages with pictures of Garbo (caption: "The Clear Garbonic Glow") and Joan Blondell in a tweed coat ("The Rough and the Smooth"). I once sent him something after a concert:

> *At the rattling end of the rattling Scherzo*
> *Of the symphony by Mr. Berezowsky,*
> *The gentleman behind me,*
> *Well groomed and fed*
> *In his good wife's ear*
> *Unmetrically said—*
> *"These fellers all try to imitate Tchaikowsky."*
>
> *But the gentleman beside me*
> *Who was serious and critical*
> *(Who was writing on the program*
> *All the things he should)*
> *At the end of the symphony*
> *Rubbed his chin thoughtfully*
> *And noted down carefully—*
> *"Modern, but good."*

It was bad verse, but Parker printed it, and I could say that I had something of mine in the *Transcript.* He was a cross little man, inseparable from his jacket of brown Harris tweed and a stout cane. In his seat in the first row of the first balcony just to the right and above the orchestra he perched, as someone said, like a small and bitter gargoyle above the Brahmin sea. Parker applauded Continental fashion by banging his cane straight down on the floor. He once brought it down on the august toes of Mrs. Jack Gardner, with whom he was sharing a box at the Opera. Her remarks were said to have been unforgettable.

In those days the old Chicago Opera Company came to town. I heard Debussy's original Mélisande, Mary Garden, sing in their production of *Pelleas;* she was getting on in years, but who cared?

My first *Tristan* was a Chicago Opera offering. Frida Leider was Isolde, and I forget who sang Tristan. Next morning I woke up with that ache known as *"Tristan* hangover." Opening the *Transcript,* I found that Parker too had succumbed:

> In all the music of the theatre, perhaps in all the music man ever wrote, who has written with such sustained and manifold intensity? Underneath, to be the well to every memory, the source to every vision, the multivoiced orchestra. Yet the human tones for once have prevailed over it, until it proclaims the ship and Isolde, only to be hushed over the dead Tristan. The Chicagoans detail no fight for the castle. The sooner the better to Isolde and the orchestra transfiguring and culminating the ecstasies of the garden. Exaltation sublimates her song into a beauty forever wordless. Mme Leider, singing, touches more than the fringes. To the last piercing, longing note the house listened stirless. For there is that in Wagner's music which transcends mortality; while there was that in last night's performance that set it free.

Nearly half a page of Parker's baroque prose had preceded this, and at the top of his piece on this forgotten *Tristan,* he set a characteristic head:

BOSTON HAS NEVER KNOWN ITS FELLOW

How did I know contrabassoonist Boaz Piller's cleaning woman called him Bozo? From Elford Caughey, a member of the orchestra who befriended me. He came from Pittsburgh and was the youngest man in the orchestra—the second harpist. No human I have ever met had more kindness and charm than El. He gave me books and records, introduced me to other people in the orchestra, took me to innumerable concerts and plays. Taking a taxi from his book-lined apartment in the Fenway, he would often come to supper at our flat in Roxbury. With his grace and humor, he completely captivated my mother and sister Catherine. (Eleanor had long since become a Maryknoll nun and lived far away in Japan.) El introduced me to the world of painting, of which I knew next to nothing, took me to exhibitions, opened my eyes to color and form. I knew nothing of dance, until he took me to Mary Wigman, nothing of English music until we went to hear and hear again Cuthbert Kelley and his

English singers who sang the madrigals of Dowling, Weelkes, Morley, and Byrd, and sometimes a contemporary piece like Peter Warlock's haunting carol "Corpus Christi."

El carefully kept the homosexual side of his life hidden from us. Not until years later, when I had left Boston, did I know about this and how lonely his life had become. By then he had fallen upon evil days; when someone with whom he was living left him, El became an alcoholic and had to leave the orchestra. For years he lived in and out of institutions. He dragged out the last months of his life in a room at the Hotel Hemingway near Symphony Hall, a block away from where my sister Catherine was living at the time. Every day she brought him milk shakes, for toward the end those were all he could get down past his inflamed throat. He died of cancer of the tongue.

Toward the end of Richard Strauss's tone poem *Ein Helden-leben,* the battle music dies away and, over quiet sustained strings, the two harps the score calls for play a meditative figure in which the second harp delicately echoes the first. El was always nervous when Koussevitzky placed this number on the program; it put the second harpist on the spot. By chance just the other night I turned on a telecast of Ozawa leading the Boston Symphony. They were near the end of *Heldenleben.* I found myself looking for the conductor's cue to the harps at that place in the score, watching as anxiously as El when he knew Koussevitzky's seignorial eye was upon him.

CALIFORNIA "VOYAGE"

క్రు Most boys who flunked out of Latin School found themselves in English High, prisoned in a gloomy pile of red brick sprawling the length of a bare street in Boston's seedy South End. So I joined the sons of Italians, Syrians, Jews, Armenians, Chinese, blacks, and Yankees who crowded by thousands into the disinfectant-smelling corridors at eight in the morning and poured out past Daniel Chester French's statue *The Spirit of Alma Mater* at two thirty-four in the afternoon. It wasn't a bad school. I had an excellent physics course and a couple of good English teachers. For my exertions in literary composition I won a couple of prize books. One of them was a presentation copy of *Moby Dick* from which the editor, one of our own faculty, had cut out all "those morbid and unnecessary philosophical passages that serve only to obscure what is essentially a good whaling story." Sometimes I think he was right about that.

It was Melville who put the idea of going to sea in my head. I was obsessed with *Typee* and its sequel *Omoo*. (*Mardi* was too much for me.) I couldn't make it all the way to the Marquesas, though. I had to settle for a summer on a ship that sailed back and forth from New York to San Francisco, via Havana and the Panama Canal, stopping at various ports of call en route. I signed on the *California* as an engine-room wiper, a job that came by way of a Scottish engineer from Dumbarton. Though I was just past seventeen and underweight, the company doctor in the Panama Pacific warehouse on the dock at Fifty-seventh Street stamped my wrist with green ink to certify that I was as physically fit as all the naked giants there assembled. I was immediately put to work in the engine room, but before we had been twelve hours at sea I was unspeakably sick. My boss, Paddy the storekeeper, let me stay a day in my bunk, then dragged me up to the forecastle deck. There he made me remain all day, walking ten paces and sitting down alternately, eating crackers every once in a while. By sunset I had recovered and was hungry once more. Next morning I was back in the engine room, a hellish steel-yammering lower world over which Mr. Ritchie, the first assistant engineer, presided as sovereign. The chief engineer was rarely seen, for all he did (said his Scottish juniors) besides keeping figures on the fuel oil was to draw his breath and draw his salary. Mr. Ritchie was the real boss, a dark, handsome Glaswegian who wore three gold stripes on the shoulderboards of his beautiful dress whites. One day early in the voyage, Paddy the storekeeper ordered me into the fire room to work at something with a handful of waste. I rebounded from the 135° temperature that hit me in the face and respectfully approached the elegant "Furrst" standing god-like in his white coveralls by a main turbine, surveying his domain.

"Mr. Ritchie," I yelled above the clamor of the engines, "I can't stay in that fire room. It's too hot!"

Mr. Ritchie stood stupefied. In the first place, my addressing him at all was completely out of order. In the rigorous caste system of the engine room, a wiper was an untouchable. Second, what I had said to him was so unworthy of belief that he had no simple way of responding to it, even if protocol had allowed him to hold parley with a wiper. Later in the day Paddy told me that Mr. Ritchie had decided that I was probably subject to fits and ordered my removal from the engine room forthwith. An order came assigning me to pot-washing and garbage disposal duty in the engineer officers' mess topside, where I could have my fits in the suitable company of the "goo-goos," that is to say, the Filipino messboys. (The familiar expression "gook" is a variant of "googoo.") I was the only Caucasian on duty in the engineer officers' mess.

The duty turned out to be very pleasant. The engineer officers' pantry was on the boat deck, and a cool breeze always blew in there, except when we were anchored in Havana or San Diego, or crawling through the canal. (For that I had to go on deck and turn on the ventilators.) The food was good and ice cream available in vast quantities. My Filipino mates were very friendly, although they had occasional frightening brawls with one another and cut each other with the big galley knives. They loved music and we sang a lot. One and all of them looked forward to going ashore at Balboa, where their destination was Coconut Grove, the red-light district of old Panama. Here rows of open lighted cubicles facing the street awaited them at night, each with a brass-fitted bed and a heavily painted Oriental girl sitting on it. My mates went off to this sulphurous place like happy children dressed for a birthday party. They wore handsome light suits, pastel-tinted shirts, and glowing silk ties.

Chappie the cook bossed the pantry. While there was work to be done, little Chappie exacted excellence. My weakness was to leave scum and grease on the pots. I was particularly unreliable with pots that had held melted cheese. These Chappie would hand back to me with a "Joe, if anyt'ing wort' doong, wort' doong *raight!*"

But when the galley had been tidied up and the last pots and pans were ready to be put away under the steam table, Chappie would invite me to join him in singing symphonic bits to the accompaniment of percussion on the pots. Our most effective number was Ippolitov-Ivanov's "Procession of the Sirdar." One day after dinner we formed an impromptu sirdar-parade joined by two smiling messboys beating on the pans. We battered our pots with soup ladles, winding our way through the pantry, across the alleyway, into the (we thought) empty officers' messroom screaming, "Da-da-di-dah!" (tumpety-tum-tum), "Da-da-di-*dah!*"

"WHAT THE FOOK?"

We stopped dead. There at the table sat the chief, Mr. McElhose himself, alone, glowering. This gloomy, massive son of the Clyde almost never came to the engineer officers' mess, preferring to take his meals in the Ahab-like solitude of his cabin, where he figured his fuel consumption and reserves. But there, unbelievably, he was now, his black eyepatch standing out against his gray hair and brick-red face. He rumbled to his feet, towering over us, a Caledonian Polyphemus in his wrath.

"AH SAID WHAT THE FOOK?"

Paralyzed we stood before him, pots and ladles hanging limply at our sides, while he blasted at us a maniacal polemic on the subject of this desecration by googoos (I was an honorary googoo) of the engineer officers' messroom. Every other word was "fook" or its adjectival derivative "fooken" or (less frequently) the noun form "fookers." This frightening harangue in broad lowland Scotch roared over our heads for some awful minutes until at last Mr. McElhose foamed past us out of the messroom. As he made his way through the long passage to his quarters at the end, we could hear his thundering "fooken . . . fooken . . . fookers . . . " until, like the single final detonation at the close of a fireworks display, there rolled down the alleyway one last booming, definitive "FOOK!"

Everybody had a down on everyone else on that ship. The engineers loathed the deck people, the deck people hated the stewards ("flunkies"), and both engineers and deckhands lay in wait to beat up the masters-at-arms who had beaten them up the night before, and the stewards beat up the googoos. It was a little like the world.

For peace, I liked to retreat to the boat deck, where I had a hiding place between two lifeboats. There I would sit and watch the sea, letting my feet dangle out over the water fifty feet below. Now, on our way back to New York, we were passing Haiti on the starboard side. Flying fish skimmed in and out of the indigo swells. Contentedly I ate a grapefruit—there were loads of them in our pantry locker. Looking up, I studied the white-streaked stack over my head, still carrying the salt deposited there by the fearful seas that smashed over us the week before in a hurricane off lower California.

From the forecastle deck I had seen the black wall of cloud coming at us from the horizon. Stunned by a fall, I lay out the storm in my bunk, dimly feeling the jolt of the seas, as if the ship were hitting some great log over and over. The sea water came pouring in from the alleyway to float away the box of Havana cigars I had stowed under my bunk to take home to my father. The storm passed. *California* suffered no damage beyond a couple of twisted boat davits and a load of salt on sides and stacks. But our near neighbor that afternoon, the Isthmian Line's *William McKenney* from Boston, did not get off so easily. She lost fourteen men and part of her load of lumber in the squall off Point San Lucas.

When I got back to Boston at the end of the summer I found my College Board scores waiting for me at home. They were so low that they finally discouraged my mother, who had so wanted me to go to Harvard so I could be a doctor. But I didn't want to go to Harvard and was glad to settle for Boston College. They didn't mind my low scores so long as I passed their special entrance examination. That gave me no trouble.

BOSTON COLLEGE I

᠔ Over the years I've found that a lazy person like myself, who makes a living by his wits, tends to rely much on memory sharpened and clarified by this necessity. Clues from memory save a lot of work. Not long ago a Columbia student waylaid me at the end of one of my classes. "I get your *'ipso facto,'*" he said, "and I think I dig *'nemo dat quod non habet,'* but would you mind explaining *'mutatis mutandis'* to me?" Flattered, I enlarged on my little pedantry. But I didn't think it necessary to tell the youth that I heard all these expressions in my freshman year at Boston College, and that the tags come in very handy whenever I want to add a flourish to a bit of rhetoric. A few years ago I found myself on a Ph.D. examining committee at a defense of a dissertation on James Joyce. Something came up about *Ulysses* and someone wanted an example of Homer's onomatopoeia. I threw in the line about Polyphemus heaving the mountain peak after Odysseus so that the sea surged beneath the stone as it fell: *Eklusthe de thalassa katerkomenes hupo petres.*

Afterward Gilbert Highet, who was also on the committee, asked me how I happened to remember that particular line. I made a joke of it, but should have told him that the line came out of my Boston College Greek class when we were worrying our way through the ninth book of the *Odyssey.* Not so long ago I was going over a bit of Aristotle's *Nichomachean Ethics* with some Barnard students and (Lord knows how) the question of Greek attitudes toward modesty in dress came up. A suitable illustration struck me and I passed it on to the young women. It was Iphigenia under Agamemnon's sacrificial knife, drawing the folds of her dress decently about her as she fell. The example was not the fruit of my scholarly research. I simply heard once more the voice of Father Stephen Mulcahey (he died years ago in the fire at Shadowbrook Seminary) commenting on Aeschylus's text in my sophomore year.

Boston College was founded in 1863 but did not thrive until the nineties, when it came under the leadership of Father Thomas Gasson, a Jesuit educator later exiled from the Archdiocese of Boston by Cardinal O'Connell, whose displeasure he had incurred. (Father Gasson spent his last days teaching English grammar somewhere in Canada.) Growing up in Roxbury, I knew that for years Boston College had been almost the sole source of higher education open to boys of poor and lower-middle-class Catholic families of Boston and its environs. Irish with a little money and some pretension to tone sent their boys to Holy Cross, the Jesuit boarding college in Worcester, or even to Georgetown, far away in Washington, D.C. In those days Boston College had no boarders, everyone commuted. A very few Irish families (the Kennedys are the best-known example) sent their boys to Harvard. Boston College was rather different from Harvard. In Myles Connolly's little novel *Mr. Blue,* which once had a certain vogue, Blue is tramping with a companion around the reservoir in Newton just over the Boston city line:

> Boston College, with its solid Gothic tower, stood black against the last smoking flame of a November sunset. We were down in the dark. But no one could mind the dark, even of November, with the Gothic that dominated the hill. Blue caught his breath at the magnificent silhouette.
>
> "That gives me courage," he said, with his face up toward the hill

crest. "Of late, I have been melancholy with autumn—sign of adolescence or old age. But I couldn't be melancholy with that above me. Not that I care for the Gothic, but for what it represents. Sunsets may flare, and the blackness of hades eclipse the earth, but that will endure."

"An earthquake could toss it into the lake," I objected.

"And so could the cataclysm at the end of the world. And so could a man with dynamite. But where that stands there will always be something, though no stone is left upon a stone. . . . No battle for a great cause can ever be forgotten. That up there is no mere group of college buildings; that up there is a hearth and home for the Lost Cause that is never lost, the citadel of a strength that shall outlast the hill and rocks it stands upon."

Thomas Wolfe's idea of "that up there" was less exalted. In *Of Time and the River,* the novelist's alter ego, Eugene Gant, has come from Piedmont Carolina to Cambridge to study at Harvard. He lives in a rented room on Trowbridge Street. Eddie Murphy, son of Gant's Irish landlady, goes to Boston College. At the moment Eddie is standing in Gant's room looking at the Harvard student's bookshelves:

"Watcha do wit all dese books? Huh?"

"I read them."

"Guh-*wan!* Watcha tryin' t' hand me? Y'aint read all dem books. Dey ain't no guy dat's read dat much. . . ."

"Well, I have read them all," the other said. "Most of them anyway, and a lot more besides."

"Guh-*wan!* No kiddin!" he said in a dazed tone and with an air of astounded disbelief. "Watcha want to read so much for?"

"I like to read. Don't you?"

"Oh, I don't know. *You* know," he said painfully, with the slightest convulsive movement of his hands and shoulders. ". . . S'all right."

"You have to read for your classes at Boston College, don't you?"

"DO I?" he cried, with a sudden waking to life. "I'll say I do! . . . *Ho*-ly Chee! Duh way dose guys pile it on to you is a crime! . . . Do you know who de greatest prose-writer was?" he burst out. . . ."

"No . . . who was it? Jonathan Swift?"

"Guh-*wan!*"

"Addison? . . . Dryden . . . Matthew Arnold?" the youth asked hopefully.

"Guh-*wan*. Guh-*wan!*" he shouted derisively. "Yuh're way off!"

"Am I? . . . Who was it then?"

"James Henry Cardinal Nooman," he crowed triumphantly. "Dat's who it was! . . . Father Dolan said so . . . Chee! . . . Dey ain't nuttin' dat guy don't know. He's duh greatest English scholeh livin'. . . . Nooman wrote de *Apologia pro Vita Suo*," he said triumphantly. "Dat's Latin."

Myles Connolly's sketch of Boston College is a period piece, sentimental Catholic state-of-siege. Literature circulated in Catholic lending libraries in those days made out the Church as fighting a gallant rearguard action against a world conspiracy of atheistic Evil, just as the Boston Irish fancied themselves holding a citadel against the Protestant Yankee foe. Much admired was the Englishman Father Owen Francis Dudley's novel *The Masterful Monk*, first volume in a theological Rover Boys series, wherein a handsome Benedictine, Father Anthony, singlehandedly thwarts a sinister world organization, a sort of anti-Catholic SMERSH whose members wear a gold medal engraved *Contra Ecclesiam*. Powerful London representatives of this villainous conspiracy include a "rationalist" named Julian Vedder who combined his larger task with attempts to seduce both body and mind of a Catholic debutante so lovely that no other name could be found for her but "Beauty." It was an extremely serious book written in a style that strikingly anticipated that of Leon Uris.

As for Wolfe, his picture of the Boston College boy errs in a different direction. For one thing, he has the accent all wrong. Some of my classmates may have been a little uncultivated, but none of them ever spoke low-class Brooklynese. Thomas "Tip" O'Neill of the class of '36 and straight out of Eddie Murphy's Irish Cambridge spoke eloquently enough to run for the Boston City Council while still a student. (He lost, but that was the last time the present speaker of the House of Representatives was defeated in an election.)

Boston College of those days was neither a community of knightly young Catholic gentlemen nor a nursery of Studs Lonigans or friends of Eddie Coyle. In the early thirties, "B. C." was attended by about a thousand boys, 90 percent of them Boston Irish. (A neighbor, pleased to hear I intended to go to the college, said, "Good. You'll be among your own kind there." I tried to look at him with cold violence, like Stephen Dedalus.) A few Boston College students were very talented. The majority seemed good-natured lively boys, not given overmuch to art or abstract ideas, but with a modicum of practical intelligence and often a certain natural grace. They were out to have a good time, but they wanted to please their instructors and conned their Horace and Thucydides with diligence. Friends were made as easily as air breathed and energy blew off at illegally alcoholic dances held off-campus and at explosive football games. Holy Cross was our archrival. We considered its students effete; some of them, we heard, went so far as to subscribe to the *New York Times.*

Our Jesuit professors did not have the superintellects that legend gave them. ("Thim Jisuits is cliver min!" I heard one old Irish lady say to another on the Beacon Street trolley.) Some were rather limited in their general reading. Humane men, they had much compassion and understanding—not authoritarian, but rather permissive as teachers and counselors. They would try to observe every boy carefully to see what talents he might have. When a bit of capacity was suspected—academic gift, playacting, or writing—the Fathers made it their business to provide a little stage on which that talent could try itself. If some lad on the freshman football squad made a good block on the field, Father Patrick McHugh, our dean, would be in the locker room after the game to take the boy's hand in his dockworker's fist. He would do the same and more for a fledgling who had just made his maiden speech for the Marquette or Fulton debating societies, or scraped through a fiddle solo at the Musical Clubs concert. Theology apart, the Jesuits encouraged individualism and suavely tolerated the personal idiosyncrasies of their students. This pedagogic flexibility stemmed from the tradition of the Society of Jesus. Recently I read of Descartes that when the philosopher was a boy at the Jesuit school of La Flèche and painfully averse to getting up early in the morning, the Fathers let him stay in bed as long as he liked, provided he did his assignments. I was not surprised.

But if the pedagogy was flexible, the curriculum was not. Rigidly classical requirements for the A.B. degree followed a modified version of the Jesuit *Ratio Studiorum.* If you needed three years of Greek, as I did, you could take an elective course only in your junior and senior years. Latin, Greek, and English literature formed the core of freshman year, taught by one and the same instructor, often a "scholastic," that is, a Jesuit not yet ordained. Sophomore year centered on Latin, Greek, and Rhetoric. We learned how to write a speech, something most people don't know how to do. Jesuits conducted classes in English or in a doggish kind of Latin, disturbing Cicero's eternal rest. Philosophy dominated the two upper years. In addition to two years of required laboratory science, two years of history and two of modern language had to be got through. "Apologetics"—the general name for religion courses—met twice a week in a large lecture hall, its classes generally slept through or doodled at. Our sophomore textbook, Chetwood, stated that Hell was probably located in the center of our earth; but the Jesuit Father in charge of the course relied on his own lecture notes, and we paid little attention to the official text.

A livelier adventure in Apologetics included our public Symposium on Evidences of Religion, a one-shot public affair, brainchild of earnest Father Russell Sullivan, nicknamed "The Masterful Monk." A distinguished audience attended that occasion, the guest of honor his Eminence William Cardinal O'Connell, Archbishop of Boston. A quartet of undergraduate defenders of the faith sat on stage and expounded various orthodox theses. Four skeptical "rationalists" (I was one) were planted stooge-fashion in the house to heckle the lads on stage with carefully rehearsed objections. As all answers to our challenges had been prepared in advance, we poor rationalists had our feeble arguments wrung by the neck one after another without mercy.

Our dress presented a problem. In deference to the presence of His Eminence, Father Sullivan had orderd that all the performers, rationalists and defenders of the faith alike, should wear tuxedoes. But since the affair was a Sunday afternoon thing, I protested such gaucherie, arguing for formal morning clothes. Father Sullivan wished to be correct, and in due course, defenders and hecklers appeared at the Symposium in elegant morning coats, striped pants, and ascot ties, the bill for the rental footed by the college. But the effect of our sartorial taste was ruined by a large squad of undergraduate ushers stiff as boards in hired tuxes. The solecism did not bother His Eminence who, at the end, rose in his scarlet to manifest his satisfaction by a few gracious words to us and the audience.

William O'Connell, who appeared in Henry Morton Robinson's novel *The Cardinal* as legendary overlord of a million Catholic New Englanders, was the son of immigrant parents who settled in the mill town of Lowell, Massachusetts. As prelate, he wielded absolute spiritual authority in his vast Archdiocese and held awesome temporal power in Boston as well. Boston College's most distinguished alumnus, His Eminence resided less than a mile away from the campus in his episcopal palace on Lake Street and Commonwealth Avenue, where he lived and entertained in the style of a Renaissance prince. Any appearance of "Big Bill" on our turf set us to repeating all the stories we had heard about him: his financial genius, his vast real estate holdings, his standing with the Pope, his fabled art collection, the gasoline service stations he allegedly controlled, his Javanese valet, his champion French poodles. Tall, rubicund, of imposing bulk and dimpled chin, he looked in his scarlet robes like an Eastern emperor, a Son of Heaven.

My junior year coincided with the fiftieth anniversary of His Eminence's graduation from Boston College, and we saw rather more of him on campus than usual. For his jubilee, the college dramatic society put on a masque, Elizabethan-style, in his honor. Titled *The White King's Son,* the masque was a transparent and laudatory allegory written especially for the occasion by Father Bonn, a Jesuit of literary bent. The White King's son did good, conquered evil, routed his enemies, achieved a radiant apotheosis. His Eminence had no trouble recognizing himself, and when the curtain fell he advanced with measured tread to the front of the auditorium crowded with expectant students and faculty. Members of the cast (I was an ancient shepherd, with beard and crook) scrounged down on the stage floor behind the curtain within touching distance of His Eminence's august rear and peeked out. The Cardinal descanted on his early triumphs as an undergraduate. "When as a freshman boy I arrived at Boston College," he said, "the dean of studies took me around to my classes to introduce me to my fellow students with these words, 'Boys, here's William O'Connell. Watch out for your honors!' " He went on to tell how he worked zealously at his studies until, he said, "To my utter amazement, I won highest honors in my first year class." He tried for the debating team and there too met success. *"To my utter amazement,"* he boomed, "I won the gold medal." Thereupon he entered the annual oratorical contest and to his utter amazement won that too. Finally his commencement day arrived, and he graduated. "TO MY UTTER AMAZEMENT," he roared, "I won not one, not two, but *every* highest honor given that day."

At the end of my junior year, Boston College conferred an honorary degree on Cardinal O'Connell to commemorate the fiftieth anniversary of his graduation from alma mater. Much head-scratching in St. Mary's Hall preceded the award, for the Jesuits had to think up something extraordinary to give him—he *had* everything already, including the Order of the Rising Sun from the Emperor of Japan. So this was no ordinary degree, no mere doctorate of law or letters, but a superdegree, hitherto unknown to man, devised by the college authorities for the occasion, and made to specifications that alone could do justice to the majestic recipient's unique accomplishments. The Cardinal was elevated to the unprecedented degree of

PATRON OF THE LIBERAL ARTS

His citation read in part:

Many Are His Titles and Claims to Fame
Many His Splendid Achievements and Rare Attainments
A Scholar Whose Academic Excellence Has Won Widespread
Renown
An Author Whose Treasured Volumes Are an Ornament to
Literature
An Orator Whose Golden Vein of Eloquence Is an Inspiration
to the Land
A Gifted Master in Music Whose Exquisite Productions Have
Enriched Our Catholic Hymnody
An Educator
Whose Able Administrations of the American College in the
Eternal City
Whose Fostering Care in the Founding of the Great Papal University
in Japan
Whose Rare Excellence in the Personal Direction of Our Superb
Archdiocesan Seminary
Have Chiselled for Him an Enduring Record in the Annals of
Higher Learning
An Ecclesiastical Statesman
Whose Delicacy of Tact, Profound Knowledge of the Human Heart

and Mastery of the Governing Art
Not Portland, Not Boston, Not Rome Alone
But the Far-Distant Empire of Japan Gladly Acclaim
A Munificent Benefactor of Foreign Missions
An Untiring Spiritual Shepherd of a Multitudinous Flock
His Fifty Years Since Graduation
Have Seen Halo on Halo Encircling His Reverend Brow
Priest, Metropolitan, Dean of the American Hierarchy
Cardinal of the Holy Roman Church

If this near-canonization seems excessive, it should be remembered in charity that the Cardinal had the Jesuits over a barrel. Although an independent religious order, the Jesuit presence in the Archdiocese put them under his jurisdiction. There had been differences, and his hand was heavy. Jesuits remembered the fate of Father Gasson, builder of the college on the hill.

Afterward in the office of *The Heights,* the undergraduate newspaper, the editors chortled over valedictorian John Wright's proposed lead for the story on the degree-conferring:

CARDINAL'S BUTTOCKS BANDAGED AFTER
INSPIRING CEREMONY

In due course John Wright became a Cardinal himself, installed in the Vatican as prefect of the Sacred Congregation for the Clergy.

Ed Duff, a classmate of mine at Boston College, transferred at the end of his sophomore year to Holy Cross, and ultimately became a Jesuit priest of some distinction. Ed's father was a contractor of comfortable income who drove a Hudson Super-Six. One day Mr. Duff was escorting some friends to dinner at a hotel on the North Shore noted for its cuisine. As the party mounted the steps of the hotel, they froze when their entrance was blocked by the egress of His Eminence, William Cardinal O'Connell. Massive, ruddy, and benign, he surveyed those members of his multitudinous flock with the air of a man who has dined well. Bending their knees, the faithful kissed the episcopal ring, and Mr. Duff ventured to express the hope that His Eminence had enjoyed his dinner. Delicately wiping his lips with a handkerchief of fine linen woven especially for him by an order of Irish nuns, His Eminence smiled benevolently.

"My tastes are very simple," he said. "Just a crust of bread and a glass of water."

BOSTON COLLEGE II

૎ Philosophy, Queen of the Sciences, formed the core of the upper-class curriculum at Boston College. Juniors studied logic, epistemology, ontology, and cosmology. As seniors, we concentrated on ethics and on rational psychology—the study of the soul and its vital functions, including thinking. The situation in philosophy at Boston College during the thirties was typical of the scandalous way in which the subject was studied and taught in Catholic colleges throughout the country in those days. Just as the Navy expected Annapolis graduates to be able to perform and instruct well in any branch of naval science from seamanship to engineering, so ordained Jesuits assigned to college teaching were presumed competent to teach any basic subject of the curriculum. They could get by with this in classics, but the results were damaging in philosophy—even though older and more experienced Fathers usually taught the subject. For the most part, our textbooks were mimeographed manuals in which "theses" were stated, terms defined, and theses "proved," and the objections of adversaries dealt with. Most of these theses were said to be "certain." Although what we were taught went by the name of Scholastic philosophy, we had no reading in Aquinas, Scotus, or other schoolmen. We never read a treatise of Aristotle or a dialogue of Plato. Even the teachings of Suarez, the Spanish Jesuit who had refreshed a scholastic tradition gone dry, we got third hand. Modern philosophers like Descartes or Hegel were summarily dispatched as "sophists." A more formal method of erasing these sillies exposed their doctrines to particularly lethal syllogisms:

> The opinion of Locke makes substance a collection of qualities or modifications which modify nothing.
> But a collection of qualities which modify nothing is false and contrary to fact.
> Therefore, the opinion of Locke is false and contrary to fact.

Jesuit fathers of that time and place had little special or graduate training in philosophy and no professional contact with work being done by contemporary philosophers in Europe or the United States. Occasionally they showed themselves aware of the inadequacy of the mimeographed manuals. Reflecting upon a stock "refutation" of Kant he was explaining to the class, German-born Father Fritz Boehm had the grace to add, "If Kant were to come in the back door of this lecture room, you'd see me going out the front." Nevertheless this anachronistic method of teaching philosophy, long since replaced, left a small residue of value. In some way, hard to explain, it imparted a certain sense of rigor that transcended the impoverished arguments used to defend it. Perhaps it just got one into the useful habit of defining terms and making schematics of arguments. Perhaps the canned refutations of Hume and Kant awakened a dormant critical sense—surely the arguments of these philosophers couldn't be demolished *that* easily.

Some years later the entire curriculum of the college, including philosophy, was thoroughly shaken up. Priests with doctorates earned in philosophy joined the faculty, and lay professors supplemented, and in some cases, headed up the work done in the philosophy department. Oddly, a couple of those lay professors turned out to be rigorists of a different type. Disciples of the fanatical Jesuit Father Leonard Feeney, they accused the college of "liberalism." At Saint Benedict's Center near Harvard Square, Father Feeney expounded a ferociously literal interpretation of the doctrine that outside the Church there is no salvation. Once out of curiosity I visited the center, but Father Feeney had me thrown out by a couple of his Slaves of the Immaculate Heart of Mary when I gently questioned his anti-Semitism. He explained James Henry Cardinal Nooman's alleged modernism by asserting that the Oxford reformer was really a Jew. His father had been a moneylender, and look at his nose! Feeney himself was kicked out of the Society of Jesus and later excommunicated from the Church. But all that happened long after I had graduated from the college. At that time Feeney's reputation rested on cute little poetry books he had written, like *Fish on Friday*. Recently someone told me that he had been received back into the Church. It appeared that he had no quarrel with the Nicene Creed.

The classical rigor of the early thirties at Boston College was relieved by the most wonderful opportunity for extracurricular activities. The college orchestra (I played cello) and glee club toured Lowell, Fall River, New Bedford, Framingham, Weston, Worcester, and smaller towns. After the last notes of Ketelby's *In a Persian Marketplace* or Oley Speak's *Morning* had their dying fall, there would be a dance in whatever hall the concert was given. Local girls would appear, real girls in evening gowns and *Bourjois* perfume to dance with us. At our concert for Sacred Heart Academy, Gianelli, our xylophonist, soloed with *Kitten on the Keys.* Afterward, over punch and cookies, I asked an elderly nun what had we played that she liked best. With some embarrassment she said she liked the xylophone piece. "But," she said anxiously, "it was so *worldly.*" Very worldly was our concert and dance at the hospital for the aged poor on an island in Boston Harbor. Cooped up there weeks on end, the young nurses expressed warm appreciation for our efforts.

But the *Stylus* was the darling thing, the college literary magazine of which I became editor. We had a wonderful staff. Connie Dalton and Herbert Kenny were to become top Boston newspapermen, Herb retiring as poet laureate of the city. Louis Mercier, later of *Holiday* magazine, wrote short stories. Jim Connolly, advertising-executive-to-be, wrote on the bourgeois novelist Galsworthy, and Charlie Donovan (one day he would be vice-president and provost of the college) did an essay on the prose rhythm of Nooman. Strange, I can't recall that Phil McNiff—years later director of the Boston Public Library—wrote anything for us, though he was a good friend of the *Stylus.* We abounded in poets. Consider Stephen Fleming and Francis Maguire. Steve towered awkwardly at six feet two, huge hands and feet, voice immense. He always feared that something would stop him from writing, maybe insanity, and he could not handle that. He suffered a mental breakdown, fought it, and died not long after graduation:

> *My pen and candle, Lady. Now remark*
> *That one is slender, one exceeding bright;*
> *Keep swift the flame against the rigid dark,*
> *And let the pen write.*

Frank Maguire was small, a gentle, sweet-natured boy with sandy hair, pink cheeks, and a soft, kind voice. Frank's father had been chauffeur to a rich Boston woman, and at her death she left Frank a small income. He later went on to graduate school at Harvard, taught for a while, served as an Army captain in World War II working in intelligence in the Philippines and in Japan. Frank was an only child, and when his parents died, he found himself alone in the world and after that formed no permanent tie. He settled in New York, in the East Village, published a book or two of poetry, acted small parts in Off-Broadway shows, walked his beloved old dog. Occasionally his verse turned up in the *New York Times* in the days when they still had their little poetry corner on the editorial page. Though he lived into his sixties, Frank never seemed made for this world. When I heard of his death I remembered his lines about a dog barking at midnight:

> *I know baby: as you fear*
> *barking brings no one back.*
> *But it's a noise in an empty world*
> *and it helps to fill the dark.*

We hard-core members of *Stylus* 1933 battled Philistia; our mission, to shock whatever bourgeoisie there might be around. We threw away the Gothic decor of the old *Stylus,* substituting a streamlined modernist format with lots of lower-case and sans-serif type. Our hero: T. S. Eliot, who that winter was offering a series of evening lectures over at Harvard. Faithfully I attended them, watching the great Lord Weary come in from the snowy cold, slowly kick off his overshoes, mount to the lectern, and in measured tones deliver his views on Criticism. He came down hard on some poets. "If Shelley had submitted his poems to the *Criterion,*" he said, "we might have printed some of them—heavily blue-penciled."

Duly I reported Eliot's ruminations to my *Stylus* colleagues and we discussed them furiously, and noted them in our column "The Arts." In our magazine's rich cream-colored pages we extolled not only Eliot, but Yeats, Symbolist poetry, Ezra Pound, J-K. Huysmans, Eugene O'Neill, Elinor Wylie, James Joyce, modern jazz, and the Boston Symphony Orchestra. Our faculty moderator, Father Dave Twomey, did not censor a line by any of us, although he often shook his blond, curly head over what some of the *patres graviores* might think of our arty posturings. The Fathers did not seem to mind.

Stylus carried on a fierce running battle with the *Heights,* the college undergraduate newspaper whose editor and staff we regarded as little better than Neanderthals in matters of culture. In turn, the

Heights staff looked down on the *Stylus* editors as a pseudo-sophisticated clique of intellectual snobs. When the Abbey Players from Dublin arrived in Boston with Barry Fitzgerald, T. J. McCormack, and Sara Allgood to play *Juno and the Paycock, Playboy of the Western World,* and other Irish pieces, the *Heights* took it upon itself to condemn plays and players alike. The outcry sounded like the bawls heard by Stephen Dedalus the night Yeats's *Countess Cathleen* opened the national theater in Dublin. "Rotten meat to flies!" thundered the *Heights* in its lead editorial. "We have our own troubles with our own O'Neills and Dreisers. And when we find ourselves paying court to a prominent invader who jeopardizes his position by handing out an Irish version of the same depressing balderdash, it is tantamount to heaping coals." Metaphors blazing, the *Heights* closed in to demolish the Protestants O'Casey, Synge, and Willie Yeats. Like O'Casey's Paycock, Heights believed the world was in a terrible state of chassis. In reply, *Stylus* poured out its scorn on the reactionary rage. This, we said, was worse than ignorance; it was hooliganism! Father Paul de Mangeleere, a bearded Walloon and our professor of French, chuckled at those youthful tussles on matters of art and taste and cheered both sides on—until one day *Heights* gleefully printed a student letter assailing *Stylus* for high-hattishly espousing the cause of what the letter writer contemptuously referred to as "obscure French poetry spoutings." That day in class Père de Mangeleere publicly denounced the *Heights* as a sheet scribbled by barbarians and acclaimed the *Stylus* editors as defenders of civilized and humane values. "Who wrote ziz meeserable letter?" he bellowed to our class in fine Gallic rage, waving a copy of the offending issue of the *Heights*. "I weel tell you. A PEASANT FROM ZE PEAT BOGS OF IRELAND!" Jim Connolly and John Hanrahan led the cheers. I am proud to recall that a number of football varsity supported *Stylus* in this crisis, including stars Pete Chesnulevitch and Phil ("Moose") Couhig.*

The zenith of our sophisticated snobbishness was reached when we staged the great *Stylus* Art Exhibition. We collected about a hundred color prints of paintings of what is now stuffily called the

---

* In the early 1970s, during my term as a member of Boston College's Board of Directors, the *Heights* was disowned by the college for (among other offenses) jeering at the Jesuits in print in words hitherto unprintable. The action was taken by the college administration, not by the board of directors.

School of Paris. Stripping the walls of yellowing photographs of coach Joe McKenney's old football teams, we transformed the *Stylus* office in the Tower Building into an art gallery. When we had the pictures hung, we sent letters to all the Boston newspapers, inviting their art critics to the tea which was to open the exhibition. No critics came, but the Boston *Evening Transcript,* sensitive even to the most remote stirrings of culture, be it among the very Parthians and Scythians, ran a small story with the condescending heading:

ART MAKES ITS DEBUT AT BOSTON COLLEGE

Nearly all the Jesuit fathers turned out to sip our tea, made from water boiled with agonizing slowness on top of a Sterno can, and they gravely appreciated our Van Goghs, Picassos, Matisses, and Braques. Only Father Terence Connolly had doubts about a rather *louche* Modigliani. "It is not a nude woman, Father," I insisted in my best art-for-art's-sake manner. "It's a *picture.*" Father Connolly remained unconvinced.

The old Boston College pedagogy, holding an easy equilibrium between orthodoxy as to doctrine and flexibility as to people, suited me very well. It "prepared" me for no career at all other than the lazy profession I found my way into: reading books, talking to students, enjoying the sound of my own voice. They were just four good years of life.

As an undergraduate I worked up a fine fury against the ultramontane and doctrinaire aspects of the Church that all the geniality of the Jesuits could not conceal. Now, long a skeptical worldling, I'm sorry that the Church has eased off on so many of the dear old reactionary doctrines and disciplines that made liberals shudder and gave the young something to rebel against. I miss clerical authoritarianism, the ferocious syllabi of errors, anathemas, the Holy Office, the Index of Forbidden Books. With those gone, it's no fun any more. The Church stood for centuries as the great conservative institution of the Western world. A liberal Catholic Church, like a humane penitentiary, seems a contradiction in terms. I can't think of any argument against married priests, at least in the Church as it is today, but I am not edified by the sleeping arrangements of certain radical nuns, Roman clerics proclaiming the Meaningfulness of their Relationships, demicelibate priests confessing to national maga-

zines about their erections or lack of them in the name of sincerity.
They're all so Open and Honest about it. I prefer the ancient bigots
who wrote tracts like "Why I Left the Church of Rome." The bad
old things in the Church are like those villains of Dickens Chesterton
remembered nostalgically—just as they are being dragged off to
prison or to the gallows, we wish they would stick their heads out
through the curtains and make just one more atrocious remark.

L STREET: PIANO PLAYING

ੋੴ Our college diplomas bore the date June 7, 1933. This lay near
the absolute zero of the great Depression. Jobs were nonexistent and
the summer yawned emptily before us. My classmates qualifying
themselves to teach in the Boston public schools met persistent ru-
mors of under-the-counter fees of five hundred dollars to be paid to
a middleman in order to get even a look-in at a teaching job. I
wanted to go to Harvard graduate school to study philosophy and
I needed money for tuition. The heat that summer was murderous,
and it gathered to an ovenlike greatness in our top floor of the Roxbury three-decker. On those stifling nights I would sit out on the
piazza (we never said porch) hoping the lovely girl who had just
moved in next door would come out to talk for a little. Days I took
refuge with the idle at the L Street Baths. There were no jobs that
summer. Experienced businessmen out of work ran errands in the
city for eleven dollars a week.

The L Street Bathhouse was (maybe it still is) one of the oddest
bathing places in the world. A city-operated beach in South Boston,
the authorities set the larger part of it aside for nude bathing for
men. A section for women adjoined separated from the men's part
by a high fence, but that area was smaller and the women had to
wear bathing suits. Not quite accurate to say that men bathed at
L Street in utter nakedness. They had to wear fig leaves. The official
L Street fig leaf consisted of a brief triangle of white cloth held in
place by string, price ten cents. One usually removed one's fig leaf
before taking a dip or while drying off after a swim. But this prac-

tice violated the rules of the beach, and periodically the front office ordered fig leaf patrols into action. These patrols consisted of one or more grim-faced bathhouse employees who marched among the bathers checking to see if all fig leaves were where Adam wore his. On hot weekends, the beach crowded by a couple of thousand men, the patrol had to be augmented by extra personnel. Since the G-string spotters could themselves be spotted far off by reason of the lifeguard trunks they wore, it was easy for bathers who preferred to sun themselves without fig leaf to slip on their *cache-sexe* just before the arrival of the spotter, quietly doffing it after he had passed. To combat such flouting of the law, the L Street authorities would put on spotters who themselves wore fig leaves rather than the conspicuous trunks of lifeguards. Those unmarked spotters—plainclothesmen, as it were—infiltrated the ranks of sun worshipers and bagged numerous offenders. Penalty for a first violation was a public (very loud) reprimand. Second offenders had to leave the beach. Expulsion generally drew mild demonstrations from the massed bathers on the sand, encouraging cheers for the victim, ingenious obscenities for the strong-jawed spotters flanking him.

Odd characters frequented L Street: a Harvard professor of oriental languages, an alcoholic priest drying himself out, a punch-drunk boxer called Pugger Mahoney (an impolite Gaelic pun there), a Symphony clarinetist, a judge of the Massachusetts Supreme Court, a discreet knot of homosexuals, as well as the usual scores of Boston municipal employees indulging their Hibernian laziness. A sickly-looking youngish man used to bring a music box that he made tinkle for him as he lay in the sand; he reminded me of the dying Rimbaud idly turning the crank of his little Abyssinian harp. I belonged to a group of young men who sat with Captain Alwes, a marvelously self-educated retired Army captain (he rose from the ranks) who enchanted us with tales of Malay brothels and head-hunting Moros of the Philippines, then discussed Hemingway novels with us as well as local politics. A pleasant way to pass the time.

My idleness ended in midsummer by virtue of the Beer-Wine Revenue Act of 1933. Beer was back, then hard liquor, and all at once piano players were in demand. (The soulless jukebox still lay in the womb of the electronic future.) I had been cellist for the Boston College Orchestra, and for the Provincetown boat *Dorothy Bradford,* but could also play simple tunes by ear on the old upright piano in our parlor at home. So on the day I heard that the proprietors of the venerable Langham Hotel in Boston's seedy South End had opened up a beer room and were looking for a piano player, I left L Street early to apply for the post.

The night Messrs. Abe and Jack Moscow, the proprietors, pushed me through a hot, jammed barroom, air .thick with smoke and beer fumes, to an ancient yellow-keyed piano that resembled a late Roman sarcophagus. Someone set a white dish on top of the piano for tips (my base pay: twelve dollars a week for six nights' work), and I drove spiritedly into "It's Only a Shanty in Old Shanty Town" in the key of C. A large blonde young woman, called Leila, ordered me to play the song over again in A-flat so she could sing it at the piano. I slyly transposed it to the adjacent but easier key of G. Leila did not appear to notice the half-tone difference and screamed the song through to a sock finish:

> *There's a ka-ween waiting theyuhhh,*
> *With a silvarry KA-ROWNNNN!*
> *In that shantee*
> *In owowowold Shantee Tow-wown!*

I swung into "Frivolous Sal," and voices mellowed by 3.2, plus whatever they used to spike it, took up the ancient air. Somebody put a beer on the piano but, as I did not (then) drink, I shook my head. This was taken as a hint that I preferred cash tribute, and a dime tinkled obligingly into the dish on top of the piano. A big sweating man with wet hair bounded up urgently. Did I know "Southie Is My Home Town"? Because whether I knew it or not, he intended to sing it publicly. His tablemates clapped to encourage him. I was aware that that tune had status in nearby South Boston—undreamed of, the forced busing and ethnic outrage of the seventies—second only to our national anthem, but for the life of me I could not recall it. So I got him to sing the tune in my ear while I fumbled for the proper chord sequences. They were primitive enough. Now the audience became impatient and bellowed, " 'Southie'! Doncha know *'Southie'?* What kinda piano player *are* ya?" At last we had it and burst splendidly into words and music:

> *I was born down in A Street,*
> *Dragged up in B Street,*
> *Southie is my home town!*

> *I may be flip in the mouthie,*
> *But over in Southie,*
> *I'm the nuts for miles around.*
>
> *You'll meet Jimmy Maloney*
> *Pugger Mahoney,*
> *   Clowns that know how to clown.*
> *They may make you or break you*
> *But they'll never forsake you,*
> *Southie is my home town*
> *(I really mean it)*
> *SOUTHIE IS* MY *HOME TOWN!*

Apotheosis! Nickels and dimes rattled joyously into my dish. Someone howled for "Honeysuckle Rose," and I tried to oblige in the original key of F. By this time the interior of the Langham resembled a witches' sabbath. A fight broke out in one corner, and a glass of beer sailed through the air, smashing on the wet floor. A woman screamed. Leila insisted hotly that I kiss her. When I declined, she grabbed me by my tie (it was the last I wore that summer) and tightened the knot. While I was still in the initial stages of strangulation, a bouncer pulled her off. Sympathetic bystanders dropped dimes into my dish.

In contrast to the sweltering summer that preceded, the winter of 1933–34 brought the deepest cold ever recorded in Boston. On December 28, the temperature dropped to 17° below zero; on February 9, to 18° below. That winter I played piano at the Regent, a dreary South End bar stuck on a windy corner of Columbus Avenue know as Heroin Square. Addicts hung around the doorways, but only a few came into the bar. Most of the Regent's customers were on WPA or unemployed. They could afford a couple of beers an evening or one shot of cheap whisky. Business slowed that winter, and from my spot at the piano I could see Mr. and Mrs. Porter, the proprietors, anxiously counting the house from the kitchen. For about four hours during the evening I would play on and off. Sometimes I played accompaniments for a pockmarked woman singer named Dale. On special occasions my younger brother Jack would join me with his clarinet and saxophone, but he caught scarlet fever that winter and nearly died. The pay was two dollars a night. At midnight I would shut the piano and sit up at the bar to have hot tea and bread before setting out into the cold. Often a gentle addict named Fred would sit beside me and quietly plead for the loan (strictly understood, a loan) of a couple of dollars "to pay the landlady." Actually he wanted the money to buy one of those cigarette papers folded over a bit of white powder. When Fred died he owed me eleven dollars. He left me a letter instructing his beneficiaries to pay me. They were nonexistent. I still have the letter.

It was not unusual for poor old derelicts to freeze to death in that area. I remember one February night hiking the frigid mile and a half between the Regent and the Northhampton Street Station of the Boston Elevated Railway, the nearest point of public transportation to my house in Roxbury. It was a half hour after midnight and cruelly cold. A thin hard snow covered the streets, the kind that made a screeching sound when the metal tires of a wagon wheel ground over it. As I passed a flight of brownstone steps about a block from the El on Washington Street, I heard what at first I thought was a cat mewing. It was not a cat, but an old woman huddled up there outside the door of a lodging house. The door must have been locked—otherwise she could have gotten into the vestibule and out of the wind. She was rubbing her bare hands together, crying over and over again, "I'm froze!"

I ducked my head in my coat collar and hurried along to get out of the range of her voice. I hear that cry yet. Why didn't I stop and go up to her? No need to play St. Martin and strip myself of my overcoat. But at least I could have given her my gloves. They were common woolen ones, and I had another pair at home.

In his lachrymose book *The Night Is Dark and I Am Far from Home,* Jonathan Kozol writes about the South End from the vantage point of someone (himself) living there in 1975. Reading his mournful prose about the derelicts, the alcoholics, the heroin addicts, "the poor, the black, the undefended," you might forget how ancient it all is. Incidentally, the affluent are today beginning to buy into the South End, doing expensive remodeling jobs on those fine rundown old brownstones with vestibules to keep out the cold wind.

But it was warm in Harvard's Widener Library where I read and studied during the daytime. (Full-time tuition at the graduate school was only four hundred dollars in 1933–34, but my piano money allowed me only half-time study.) I read Plato with J. H. Woods, one of the last of the old Bostonians to whom teaching at Harvard constituted one of six possible careers open to a gentleman.

Philosophy 12b was the elderly scholar's last course. At its end he retired, journeyed to Japan with his young wife from Radcliffe, and while there (so the story went), died happily in her arms. C. I. Lewis taught us Kant. Myopic and friendly in a dry Yankee way, he looked like a character from a Dr. Seuss book. We went through the entire *Critique of Pure Reason*, section by section, each week handing in to Professor Lewis a full précis promptly returned to us mercilessly annotated in red ink.

Then there was Harry Austryn Wolfson, Nathan Littauer Professor of Jewish Philosophy and Literature. Wolfson looked like a little Russian-Jewish tailor—the shrug, the hunched shoulders, thick round glasses, the ingratiating grin. "So I esk you," he said on first meeting the twenty of us who took his Spinoza course, "you dun't know Meester Tott in Setterday Ivning Post?" He gave a little explanation of the methods of Arthur Train's wily old lawyer who kept "malt extract" in his desk to refresh him. "So ve procid in somethink of de same vay to unreedle de minink of Spinozeh." And the meaning of Spinoza was unriddled in Wolfson's incomparable fashion. With his mighty tools of scholarship, his mastery of Greek, Latin, Arabic, and Hebrew, he pyramided before us at each class great slabs of the history of philosophical theology. From the Greek philosophers and Church Fathers to the medieval Jews and Arabs, from Plato to Aquinas, from Philo to the Kalam, from Aristotle to Crescas, we followed with him the ponderings of the metaphysicians on the divine nature until we came at last to the philosophy of that God-intoxicated man (Novalis called him that, he said) Baruch Spinoza, the Amsterdam lens-grinder and correspondent of the Royal Academy. After the first class with Wolfson, there was no more immigrant's accent; the Jewish tailor's shrug fell away. There remained only an illuminated mind at work, a mental dynamism well deserving Aristotle's name for the highest exercise of the powers of the soul, *intellectus agens,* "the active intellect."

The venerable Alfred North Whitehead taught in my second year of graduate study, still half-time with piano playing. That fall he offered a course called Cosmologies Ancient and Modern. When he began those lectures, Whitehead was seventy-three years old. He had been rather seriously ill the previous spring and did not come to class until the third week of the term; the opening lectures of the course were given by his assistant, Dr. Kaiser. When he finally appeared in the lecture room in Emerson Hall, Whitehead seemed frail, even a little older than his years. His high collar of clerical style (that year he favored a cravat of rich blue) and his gentle way of speaking conveyed the air of a benevolent vicar. Despite his recent illness and delayed start, Whitehead taught the course with confidence and good humor. So far as I recall, he did not miss a class after taking over the desk where William James and Santayana had sat as his predecessors. There were about forty or maybe fifty Harvard young men in Philosophy 3b, most of them graduate students. On Saturday mornings, three or four young women from Radcliffe might come to visit. Whitehead disapproved of that practice (not, I suppose, for antifeminist reasons, but because the young women were not duly registered members of the course).

I took down Whitehead's lectures verbatim in a kind of amateur speedwriting I had developed in my first year of graduate study. It went with the old metaphysician's leisurely pace. His style of classroom delivery differed from that of the formal lectures from which he constructed his philosophical books. Whitehead dispensed his wisdom to us in the form of intelligent and amiable chats. He talked slowly, pausing occasionally to gaze out the window. A diagram on the board would take up a little time: "I do not understand why they should devise chalk the lecturer cannot see!" There were moments, too, for stories like that of the tipsy Cambridge don trying to unlock his door with a matchbox, muttering, "Damn the nature of things!" To his summaries of particular philosophical doctrines, Whitehead would append, "That's Epicurus!" or "That's Hume!" or, in the case of his onetime friend and colleague Russell, "That's Bertie!"— as well as passionate little interjections like "Read the *Symposium!*" or "For God's sake, be clear-headed!"

Whitehead spoke to me once toward the end of his course when I went up to his desk after class to retrieve my corrected term paper, a wildly romantic interpretation of Plato's *Timaeus*. On the cover sheet he had inscribed a grade of *A* and had added in his small neat handwriting, "Very interesting—A. N. W."

Whitehead stopped me as I was ducking away, and asked me where I had done my undergraduate work. On hearing that I had studied at Boston College with the Jesuits, a benign smile lighted up his gentle vicar's face, "Ah, yes. All the world knows and admires the Jesuits. But oh dear me! You must have been frightfully shocked at my muddled philosophy. Your teachers were such *clear-headed* men, and I am in perpetual *terror* of clear-headed men."

That fall and winter I was playing piano at Bob Berger's. My musical skill had improved. No longer confined to the keys of C, G, and F, I could now manage a passable cocktail style, and if it were not too complex, I could even *read* piano music. At that time Berger's was a well-known restaurant on Tremont Street in the heart of Boston's small theatrical district. Show people dropped in late at night for cheese blintzes and steaks. Instead of a beer-soaked upright piano, I now played a well-tuned baby grand. No longer a sweaty shirt with sleeves rolled up—now I wore a dinner jacket with a clean starched shirt and black tie. I played from six to eight for supper, then from ten until three in the morning. After work I would go across the street to the all-night delicatessen to wait for the night-owl trolley to pick me up. The lonely vehicle wandered over half the sleeping city of Boston until at last it groaned into Dudley Street Station, Roxbury, from which point I had to walk the last mile home. In bed at five, I got up again at nine, and ran over to Harvard by subway for my morning philosophy class. Tuesdays and Thursdays I audited Paul Sachs's course in French painting at Fogg. Returning home in late afternoon, I would nap a couple of hours, then get up to read philosophy until time came round to put on my black tie and report to Berger's.

No dish rested on the piano at Berger's. Some people would hand me a dollar, if I played a request for them. Milton Berle gave me two dollars for playing a song for his mother, who stood beside him. One night I was softly playing "Stardust" when I felt two hands on my shoulders and heard the accent of southern Indiana. Hoagy Carmichael then gave me a long story about his ten years' wait to have that particular song published. Hume Cronyn—from *Three Men and a Horse* across the street at the Schubert—frequently visited and stayed to chat. Accordionist Gipsy Markoff (beautiful, with dead-white skin and dead-black hair) always demanded "Begin the Beguine" from Cole Porter's *Jubilee,* which was trying out in Boston before opening in New York. She gave me a ticket so I could see the handsome show. Who could forget June Knight in white and silver, holding a blue scarf as she danced the beguine with infinite grace against a background of shadowy figures bearing palm fronds?

Gershwin's *Porgy and Bess* opened in Boston for a pre-Broadway fortnight that fall. A Gershwin fan since I heard Paul Whiteman's band play *Rhapsody in Blue* at the old Hippodrome on my first visit to New York when I was thirteen, I nearly burst when George Gershwin came into Berger's one night accompanied by his brother Ira and a party of eight. A table had been set up for them on the mezzanine floor. What should I play? I managed "Embraceable You," then switched to "I Got Rhythm"—the wrong notes didn't stick out so much in the livelier tune. Then I tried "Summertime" from the new show I had already seen down the street.

"That was George *Gershwin* that just came in," I said to Bob Berger as he passed by the piano. I was very excited.

"So it's Gershwin, so what?" Bob said. He tried to make out that it was routine. "George is an old friend of mine. Just go on up there and introduce yourself."

I went on up there and introduced myself. The women of his party lowered their eyes as I approached Gershwin as if they were trying by force of thought to close a protective net around him. But he glanced up with a smile when I spoke to him, and murmured thanks for the things I said about his music, and for my playing it when he came in. Then his brother Ira cheerfully broke in with, "Say, Mr. Piano Player, can you play 'The Music Goes Round and Round'?" Ira was more bouncy than George.

Berger's steady clientele included the psychiatrist-poet Merrill Moore. They called him in to treat Eugene O'Neill in his last years, to no avail. Moore had been a member of the Nashville "Fugitive" group, the Vanderbilt University literary circle that included John Crowe Ransom, Allan Tate, and Robert Penn Warren. Moore had supplemented his sonnet writing (he had written more than four thousand of them by the age of twenty-five) with psychiatric medicine and had gone to Vienna to study with Freud. Our acquaintance began one night at Berger's when he sent a note up to the piano to ask if I knew a song called "Baby's Boat." Oddly enough I did. I thought it surprising that a man who was both a fashionable psychiatrist and a practicing poet should be so fond of a sentimental lullaby about baby's boat, a silver moon:

> *Sail baby sail, out upon the sea*
> *Only don't forget to sail*
> *Back again to me.*

Recently I noticed "Baby's Boat" turned up in psychologist B. F. Skinner's memoir of his boyhood in Susquehanna, Pa.

One night I felt queer and faint at Berger's and convinced myself that I had developed a fatal neurological disease. I mentioned it to Moore, and he took me next day to his Commonwealth Avenue office and gave me a going-over without charge. He showed me the photograph that Freud had autographed for him, but to my disappointment he did not ask me to lie down on his analytical couch. All I needed, it seemed, was a little rest and some exercise. He took me next door to the Harvard Club so I could use the gym facilities as his guest. Later he introduced me to Louis Untermeyer, gave me letters to Ransom, Tate, and other ex-Fugitives. Like his own poetic creation, Jim Lane, Merrill Moore died at the full tide of life:

> *I never thought Jim Lane would fall like that*
> *He'd sworn that bullets must be gold to find him;*
> *That when they came toward him he made them mind him*
> *By means he knew,*
> > *just as a barn-yard cat*
> *Can keep a pack of leaping dogs at bay*
> *By concentrating and looking a certain way.*

COLLEGE OF NEW ROCHELLE

ટ⁀ Even today on a September evening, if you lurk in the shadows of the tall elms outside Maura Hall, you can still hear the hum of young women's voices, pitched high by the excitement of reunion after summer vacation and the prospect of first classes. Maura Hall is a Tudor Gothic residence building of the College of New Rochelle, a Catholic school run by the nuns of the order of St. Ursula. My particular September came in the late 1930s, and in the morning I would begin instructing these students. A letter in my pocket set out the terms of the job:

> I am writing at this time to offer you a position in the Department of Philosophy for September. The maximum teaching load would

be fifteen hours a week. Compensation for the work would be $2400
for the year.

Mother M. Xavier

Not a bad break for an ex-piano player with only a master's degree
from Harvard—for a Catholic college, the salary was generous. Depression still lay over the land, and college teaching jobs were rarer
than rabies. I got the job through a tip from a Worcester girl named
Ginny Shanahan who attended the college and whom I had met on
the Provincetown *Dorothy Bradford*. Just before she graduated she
wrote me that a philosophy instructor was planning to resign from
the faculty to return to law practice. She said he had had some trouble with his four classes of required logic. I wrote to the college, sent
references, and in due course received Mother Xavier's reply. So it
was goodbye to dear dirty Roxbury (mothers really do twist their
aprons when their sons leave) and a cheer for the New Haven train
to Stamford, Connecticut, and from there the local stops so hard to
forget: Old Greenwich, Riverside, Cos Cob, Greenwich, Portches-
ter (N.Y.), Rye, Harrison, Mamaroneck, Larchmont, and New Rochelle.

People have written about the nervousness of a new teacher before that first class. Now a born teacher, male—that is, someone who
loves to hear himself talk—may be, as I was, pleasurably excited—
but he won't be the least bit anxious or fearful. He can hardly wait
to sound off. I wasn't even bothered by the rumor that my predecessor, far from practicing law once again in Rochester, was in reality
bedded down in an upstate sanatorium picking feebly at the coverlet
—victim of all those years of four sections of formal logic. My first
class contained fifty young women, all sophomores, a surprising number with red hair. They were at once mannerly and amused. I
checked the roll, then gravely announced a formidable seven-part
distinction of the elements of human knowledge. Fifty heads bowed
over fifty notebooks; pens and pencils scratched. Transfiguration!
For the first time in my life my spoken words were being copied
down by strangers. My career as a college teacher had begun.

Unlike their male counterparts, Catholic women's colleges of
the 1930s were not dominated by the ancient classical curriculum.
They developed from academies for girls of high school age, and
their course of studies lacked the rigidity of the older Jesuit schools.

Having the advantage of flexibility, they adapted themselves more quickly than the men's Catholic colleges to the conventional subject organization of the secular colleges as well as to the employment of lay professors. An English major at New Rochelle would be put through much the same course sequence as her counterpart at Smith or Goucher. Whether her English faculty would have been comparably strong may be debated—I'd say ours was comparable to Goucher's. Decades later, in the 1970s, due to inflation and the trend away from single-sex schools, many of these Catholic colleges for women collapsed or were absorbed by nearby men's institutions—St. Mary's by Notre Dame, Newton (once Sacred Heart Academy) by Boston College, for example. But the College of New Rochelle has survived.

Philosophy—it was compulsory—bulked large in the New Rochelle curriculum, and in this the college differed from its secular counterparts. The *Rules* of the Ursulines, first published in Paris in 1652, had been inspired by the *Ratio Studiorum* of the Society of Jesus and reflected the Jesuit emphasis on philosophy. New Rochelle required three years of philosophy, with sophomores taking a full year of formal logic. Apparently logic was close to the heart of Mother Marie de St. Jean Martin, Prioress General of the Ursuline order, who made a formal visitation to the college during my tenure there. That distinguished Frenchwoman had composed *The Ursuline Manual of Education,* in which she insists that the pleasures of formal logic should be among the happiest memories of any young woman trained by the Order of St. Ursula:

> In reminiscing about the happy past, does she not relive the intellectual joy which she experienced with her schoolmates when under the direction of their teachers they completed a syllogism or succeeded in constructing a dilemma?

Since we had an entire academic year to devote to syllogistic pleasure, I learned to construct, to test, and to dismantle every conceivable kind of syllogism from the simple categorical variety to the multipremised chimeras of the fourteenth century, formal monsters such as William of Ockham used to strike terror into the hearts of his bibulous students as they gathered their sweaty gowns about them to keep out the cold. To supplement the classical material, I used Lewis Carroll's little logic book with its amusing examples of sorites, the syllogistic device Carroll loved best. After making all possible syllogistic arguments jump through nearly all possible hoops, we did a little of the (then) daringly modern symbolic logic. The girls took to it all beautifully. Indeed, my logic classes at New Rochelle taught me (and it was later confirmed at Barnard) that women students can do formal logic at least as well as men, and that the lines—quoted to me at that time almost daily by my colleague, old Professor Otto Schmitz—from Friedrich Bodenstedt's *Aus Mirza Schafi,*

> *Logik gibt's für keine Frau,*
> *Sie kennt nicht andere Schlüsse*
> *Als Kämpfe, Tränen, und Küsse.**

contain no truth at all. Or hardly any.

We had fun in those logic classes; little things made us laugh until we were complained about by instructors in neighboring classrooms. One day I asked Terry Shea to explain the meaning of *connotation,* a logical term we had not yet discussed in class. Terry gave a trite English-studies definition of it and several of her classmates nodded in confirmation. I struck an attitude:

"What fiend in human form told you that?"

"Mother Margaret!"

The class yelled happily, for that particular handmaiden of God had an unusually conservative reputation, and the story spread over campus within an hour after class ended. Of Mother Margaret (no it was Mother Ignatius.) they told the story of how one day in Assembly when the students were a little unruly, she rose to declare with firm dignity:

"Girls, I must remind you that the Ursulines are not only mothers, they are mistresses as well!"

Another day my logic students discussed the formal causes of error, and for the sake of sharpening a distinction, I asked them to volunteer a few deep-rooted causes of human error. One student said prejudice. Another said jumping to conclusions. Then Rita Sullivan half-raised her hand. Remarkable, for Rita, a quiet maid with pink frizzy hair and mucilage-colored eyes, had not spoken a word aloud

* Logic is not for women
They know no other conclusions
Than fighting, tears, and kisses.

in class all term. Softly but distinctly she uttered the word *concupiscence.*

The room hushed, and the girls' faces were beautifully expectant. Even Peggy Smith, habitual latecomer and lotus eater, woke up from her morning nap. I fell back on the philosopher's cowardly dodge:

"Miss Sullivan, what does concupiscence *mean?*"

Shyly she confessed, "I don't know."

Somebody at the back of the classroom said, "You'll find out!" and the class broke up screaming.

In those days the College of New Rochelle student body numbered a little over seven hundred, of whom 95 percent were Roman Catholics. The 5 percent included some interesting ones: Gertrude Cooke, a brilliant and handsome McGill transfer who was radicalized in later life; Kathy Stahl, transfer from Mills College who had a real chauffeur drive her to school; Ursula Leden from Breslau, destined for a distinguished medical career; Elsieliese Schweisheimer, whose father, also a refugee from Hitler's Germany, wrote medical biographies of the great composers. As for the majority, so many are hard to forget: Louise Fox and Rita Callan, red and black hair bent over the piano playing four-hand Bach and Ravel; Louise's younger sister Ruth, future biographer of scientists and wife of music critic Paul Hume (by chance recently I saw their son on television as Celebrant in the Vienna production of Bernstein's Mass); Araceli Riera, the Cuban dancer; mathematician Bernice MacNeill; Elsie DeWolfe's niece, Marie; Ursula Marks, poet, artist, and one of the first WAVE officers of the coming war (in 1944 I would run into her French admirer, Commandant Pierre Sizaire on the beach at St. Maxime); Jeanne Welcher, expert-to-be on Swift and the text of *Gulliver's Travels;* June Tague singing at the Junior Show, "Won't You Come Over to My House?"—so many others!

They were taught by a faculty of fifty or so, of whom roughly a third were Ursuline nuns, the rest laymen and laywomen—not counting the three or four priests who did chaplain duty and taught the religion courses. The faculty included three or four Protestants, one or two Jews, and a Greek Orthodox zoologist, Mary Rogick, after whom one of the recent college buildings is named. Administration rested firmly in the hands of a small executive board of Ursuline nuns. The president of the college, Monsignor Francis W. Walsh, was male, but Monsignor's status (saving his reverence) resembled that of those ancient Egyptian eunuch-nobles assigned to royal princesses as husbands. His role was purely formal.

I spent much of my time in the convivial company of a group of young men who joined the faculty about the same time as myself. They were instructors who had just got their Ph.D.'s or were finishing them. The most original of them, Tom Carroll, later carried out wartime research on wave propagation at M.I.T.'s Lincoln Laboratory; his theories attracted the attention of Louis de Broglie, who welcomed Tom to Paris after the war. Like many physicists, Tom fancied chamber music, and on Saturday mornings he and I would go to the house of Mrs. Courant, wife of the Göttingen mathematician then living as an émigré in New Rochelle. Tom played piano, and I my cello. Mrs. Courant could play practically any stringed instrument, ancient or modern; her favorite was the viola da gamba. For us, she took up her violin and guided us through Beethoven trios. The *Archduke* was my favorite, though there's a passage in the last movement I could never finger successfully.

Courant was not the only German émigré in New Rochelle in those days. Heinrich Zimmer, the great Indologist from Heidelberg, moved into a house on Woodland Avenue just up the road from where we lived near the college. Genial, logorrheic, incredibly knowledgeable in lore and language, West or East, Zimmer was as Aryan as Baldur von Schirach, but his wife Christiane (named for Christiane Vulpius, Goethe's mistress whom he eventually married) was the daughter of the Austrian dramatist Hugo von Hofmannsthal, thus of part-Jewish ancestry. So the Zimmers emigrated to America and settled in New Rochelle. Zimmer gave lectures at Columbia. The two small Zimmer boys did well in New Rochelle grade school, though one of them threw a teacher into shock when he embellished his show-and-tell contribution with a detailed account of certain bizarre sexual practices of ancient India he had heard about from his father, for whom such matters were for any ear that happened to be listening.

Christiane Zimmer's uncle and aunt, Arnold and Mimi (Schereschewsky), lived with them. Old Arnold had once been a fur trader who made journeys to Nizhni Novgorod in the grand days, but now he had little to do but play the piano and read while his wife Mimi baked Sachertorte in the Zimmer kitchen. I played trios with him and our neighbor Jim Cherry, lawyer and flutist, who had moved into the big house next to us on Circuit Road vacated shortly before by the irascible literary critic Ludwig Lewisohn. (Us? Yes, I was married now to Mary, the lovely girl next door in Roxbury.)

Lewisohn used to stand in front of the house watching his four-year-old son Jimmy play on the sidewalk. I liked Lewisohn's book *Expression in America,* though he said some funny things in it, for example: "Whitman must have been a very dreadful person indeed." But I did no more than nod to him in passing, for rumor had it that he was very upset because of his break-up with Thelma Spear, Jimmy's mother, with whom old Lewisohn had been living for sixteen years. Little Jimmy used to spread his dirt-digging apparatus all over the narrow sidewalk, a practice which irked my colleague Tom McManus, an economics professor, when he had to step into the street to get by him. Mary sometimes stopped to talk to the pale, serious child, thereby winning a smile from his supervising father. Poor Jimmy. After Lewisohn moved away, Thelma won custody of Jimmy but put him in a school for unwanted children. He survived to go on to college at Brandeis University where his father had taught. After washing out as a rabbinical student, Jimmy worked at odd jobs for some years until he got a teaching post at the University of Maine, where he eventually became an associate professor. In 1974 in a vinous gun-brandishing muddle, he fatally shot his wife and barely missed killing himself. Sent to Maine State Prison for murder, he wrote two books of poetry there, one of which the governor of the state so admired that he kept it on his night table. While in jail, Jimmy converted to Catholicism. But old Lewisohn, who had turned Methodist for a while, reverted to Judaism.

In my first year at New Rochelle, one of my colleagues was Henri Martin Barzun, professor of French and father of Jacques, later ornament of Columbia University. In France Barzun *père* had founded *Le Simultanisme,* a sort of poetic polyphony recited by chorus. At that time in the college an Irishman named O'Callahan taught mathematics and smoked in his ancient pipe a mixture more deadly than Old Capstan. M. Barzun took exception to O'Callahan's pipe, and properly too, since the men's faculty room (soon to be replaced by an attractive larger one) amounted to no more than a small, ill-ventilated cubbyhole in Chidwick Hall. One morning

M. Barzun entered the faculty room, sniffed disapprovingly, and walked over to the table on which rested Professor O'Callahan's malodorous pipe. "One day," said M. Barzun, "I shall throw that pipe out of the window." "You do that," O'Callahan growled, "and by God and His Blessed Mother, I'll throw you out after it."

Father Joe Moody taught religion at the college, although his field of scholarship was history. Father Moody's saintliness and simplicity exceeded even his astonishing good looks. His influential pamphlet *Why Are the Jews Persecuted?* put the Nazi program into clear historical perspective, placing a good part of the blame on Catholic Christianity. I took comfort in the thought of Joe Moody when for the first time I came in contact with that unpleasant social phenomenon, Catholic middle-class anti-Semitism. Back in Roxbury there had always been a certain amount of good-natured joshing of the Jews who lived packed in flats on Blue Hill Avenue in Roxbury and North Dorchester, but that was innocent compared to the dull malice in the mouths of bored Westchester matrons who called themselves Catholic. At one evening's entertainment I got so annoyed by a particular display of this vulgarity on the part of two women that I invented a dear old Jewish grandmother on the spot and claimed her as my own. Fortunately there seemed to be little or none of that particular stupidity among the young women of the College of New Rochelle. Although many came from bourgeois Westchester families, they were still too full of life and fun to have been soured yet by the suburban anti-Semitism that seemed, in those days at least, a middle-aged phenomenon. They were good girls with warm hearts.* Or so they appeared to me.

So the years passed pleasantly. I now had a dear wife, and a brand new baby, and we all lived happily together in a small apartment near New Rochelle's harbor, from which an electric ferry used to run to Port Washington, Long Island. From our windows in spring and summer we could watch the redstarts in the morning and the bats in the evening flying about the heavy green trees. Warm nights we'd walk over to nearby Glen Island to listen to the music of Glenn Miller's dance band floating out of the Casino. They still played tunes already aging gracefully like "The Dipsy Doodle" and

---

* I can't get along entirely without the word *girl* in contexts where it is now discouraged, though I use "young woman" where I can. Later I'll try to balance "girls" with "boys," not just with "men."

You're just too marvelous
Too marvelous for words
Like glorious, glamorous
And that good old standby amorous.

Classes were fun and the teaching not too hard. But a day came when it seemed clear to me that I must leave the college. First, there was a war on and I felt able-bodied (I heard the news of Pearl Harbor while I was out wheeling little Peter in his carriage), and besides, I had become aware that I was turning into an embarrassment to the college administration.

In the early days of my tenure at New Rochelle, the Ursulines had been careful not to interfere with the teaching of the lay faculty, philosophy included. Since most of my teaching concerned formal logic, there seemed little danger of that. The nuns knew my taste for General Franco was less than enthusiastic. They paid no attention to the complaint of an odious little instructor who tried in vain to get me and others of the junior faculty to sign a petition supporting the disgraceful blocking of Bertrand Russell's appointment to City College in 1940. They avoided any show of concern in the personal affairs and private devotions (or lack of them) of their young faculty.

Late in my stay at the college a change occurred. There came a definite shift in the winds of orthodoxy—why, I don't know. Perhaps the visitation of the Prioress General from France had something to do with it. During her stay at New Rochelle she had conducted a conference on education for the nuns of the Ursuline community. Her published remarks interested me, particularly when she turned her attention to the subject of philosophy and the teaching of it:

> Obviously Christianity must perfect wisdom; and for this reason the philosophy professor has the duty of giving his teaching a religious trend. . . philosophy is a particular as well as a general science. As a particular science it has a side which is difficult of access, curious and dangerous. By this is meant those daring researches into all the recesses of thought and being, into certain questions of ideology, ontology, and similar subjects. This complicated field of philosophy should be left to carefully selected faculties and to solid and trustworthy professors.

I positively did not feel myself to be either solid or trustworthy in this curious and dangerous science and begged the U.S. Marines to take me out of New Rochelle. They said they couldn't use me, but try the Navy. I tried the Navy but was turned down—the first time, anyway. At the college, the situation deteriorated. Some time after Mother General had returned to France, a communication from the dean, Mother Thomas Aquinas, appeared in faculty letter boxes:

> It seems that in an institution that numbers only 40 non-Catholic students in the full attendance of 742 that we owe a duty to our Catholic students. In analyzing our faculty set-up, I realize that we have come from large colleges and universities with very materialistic backgrounds. A great deal of this background we have unconsciously absorbed and just as unconsciously transmit. Do we ever think to give a Catholic point of view in dealing with the non-Catholic texts which we so often use, or do we try definitely to give a Catholic interpretation to the various Protestant theories in literature or in other fields?

That was bad, but worse followed:

> While it is not for me to regulate the devotional life of anyone it seems that a great deal of edification would be given to our students to see our faculty make visits to the Blessed Sacrament in our Chapel. The sight of a big strong man in prayer before the Blessed Sacrament would mean a great deal to our girls.

When I read that, I knew that my days in this grove of *les jeunes filles en fleur* were numbered.

When at last I got my Navy commission and applied for immediate military leave, the Reverend Mother Dean gave me an official letter to read. Written in the warmest terms, it praised my merits as a teacher and expressed the hope that I would return to the college at war's end in my present rank of associate professor. Reverend Mother made a small adjustment to her veil and snowy wimple (alas, the picturesque old habits have long since given way to sensible contemporary dress*) and supplemented the letter with a gentle admonition. It seemed that for a long time the Ursuline community had entertained certain misgivings about my teaching. No criticism of my pedagogical methods; these were above reproach, even out-

---

* Classical Boston story: an old Irishwoman, asked what religious order her newly ordained grandson belonged to, replied proudly, "He's wan of thim Passionate fathers with the loose habits."

standing. No, it was my *philosophy* that bothered them. For some time now complaints had been coming in from students whom I taught in junior philosophy. As seniors those students had to go on to required classes in Mr. Scully's Rational Psychology and found themselves at sea with his vocabulary. What I taught in my junior sections was interesting and no doubt important, but it just did not seem to be *Scholastic philosophy*. I should not think that Mr. Scully, chairman of the philosophy department, made any complaint; his motto was teach and let teach. But the girls, who had come up through my classes, *were* having difficulty in Rational Psychology.

Moreover, certain alumnae had written to the college administration in the same vein: while I was a good teacher of philosophy, what I taught seemed a very peculiar kind of Scholastic philosophy, if indeed it was Scholastic philosophy at all. Even my logic, which still formed the major part of my teaching assignment, had something not quite right about it. Perhaps I had been overinfluenced by "the English school" of logicians. In any case, Reverend Mother concluded with a positive suggestion. Why not plan to take a refresher course in Scholastic philosophy when I came back from the war? For I would come back; every nun was already praying for my safety. I had my Ph.D. now from Columbia, and that was fine. But surely I could afford a little course at Fordham just to brush up a bit on my return. With all my interest in modern thinkers, Reverend Mother was sure that my deepest loyalty was for St. Thomas (it wasn't). And by the way, the Sisters would welcome our little Peter to the new college nursery school free of charge whenever he was ready (they did). We parted with warmest expressions of mutual esteem.

Before leaving for Fort Schuyler to report for Navy indoctrination, I stopped for a moment one afternoon beside the elms shading Maura Hall near the spot where I had listened to the girls talking and laughing on the first evening years before. A bright October day, and the leaves were gold and vermilion. From where I stood, I could see the tower of Leland Castle where the nuns lived, the garden where they put out the statue of St. Joseph on commencement eve to discourage rain, and the lovely chapel where they sang in choir. By pairs, threes, and fours, the college girls were strolling down the walk from Maura Hall on their way to downtown New Rochelle, to the "Ville" as they called it. All wore hats, as the rule required when walking to town. A little shopping, tea at the Boston Spa or Schrafft's perhaps, then back to an hour's studying before supper in the dining hall. Some of the girls noticed me leaning against a tree and waved casually. I waved back. I had not told my classes I was leaving next day. The Irish have a weakness for sentimental farewells.

PART

II

WAR: ARZEW, NORTH AFRICA

§ Commander Amphibious Force Eighth Fleet had his headquarters at Arzew, on the coast road to Algiers, about twenty miles
east of Oran. Arzew was a lovely place in those days. One got there
by motor transport from Oran, driving through St. Cloud with its
storks atop chimneys and high walls dotted with bullet holes from
the American landing now long past. There was yellow dust and
vineyards, a solitary Arab or two with a few goats, and the small
village screened by hills from the sea.

After twenty-three days on the Atlantic worrying an LST (Landing Ship Tank) in convoy from Little Creek, Virginia, to Oran,
Arzew came as a glad relief to our small naval advance base communications unit. By itself, an LST rolls badly enough, but ours was
carrying an LCT (Landing Craft Tank) topside, and with each swell
of the sea the weight of the smaller landing craft made the LST roll
nearly over but not quite. The young skipper had been so seasick
during the first days of the voyage that he had to stay below in his
bunk. Transient officers helped out. I was a little squeamish myself,
but managed to be on deck every day to take my turn with the
stadimeter, the only navigational instrument I was trusted with. You
use a stadimeter to measure the distance between your ship and the
one ahead in convoy. Sometimes I would fail to notice the distance
closing, and that would provoke irritated signals by flashing light
from the convoy commodore.

LST 995 X ARE YOU TRYING TO TAKE IN SHIP AHEAD
BY YOUR BOW DOORS X ACKNOWLEDGE

At Arzew we lived in small beige villas stuffed with GI bunk
beds draped with mosquito netting. There was some malaria about
and we had to take atabrine tablets. We kept our jealously guarded
candy rations tied up in handkerchiefs suspended from the ceiling by

71

a piece of string so the voracious North African ants couldn't get at them. The Navy officers' mess was housed in a seaside restaurant, La Fontaine des Gazelles, where cheerful Italian POWs served us meals. Screened windows looked out northward over the Mediterranean through the blue cut-glass outlines of the headlands. Below, the water was emerald as it swirled over the chocolate-colored rocks, but farther out it looked amethyst with streaks of ultramarine. Toward evening the sky changed to mauve and the warm breeze from the direction of Mostaganem carried a stale musky scent.

Arzew is very different now. After Algerian independence the port turned into a crowded terminal for the Saharan oil pipelines. Today a monster gas liquefaction plant rears itself Oz-like, built with funds from the Chemical Construction Corporation of New York. Giant tankers, carrying liquefied natural gas to America, load in the harbor, now greatly enlarged, that once sheltered Com Eighth Fleet's Amphibious Boat Pool.

Commander of our advanced base support force was Commodore Doughty, a fine-looking man partial to good wines and handsome Frenchwomen from Algiers. He set store by his flag status (the Navy temporarily revived the one-star rank of commodore during World War II) and insisted on privileges due him on its account. The delayed arrival of his flag china irritated him. He also missed the music and dancing he had enjoyed at Algiers and wanted something done about it. He noted that a piano and a few other instruments had been left behind at the Fontaine des Gazelles, but whoever played them had long since gone. Learning that I was a piano player of sorts, the commodore asked me to form a dance band. Surely, he said, there must be *some* talent among all these enlisted men roaming the base with nothing to do. I agreed to work on the project forthwith. The commodore was known to reward small services by authorizing jeep trips to Sidi-bel-Abbès, the French Foreign Legion post at the edge of the Sahara. Near there one could see all kinds of interesting things, including Arab camel drivers preparing for long trips across the desert, sometimes inserting stones in the genital tracts of female camels to prevent pregnancy en route.

After some looking around the base, I scraped together a small group of enlisted men and armed them with the Fontaine's abandoned instruments. Rehearsals were discouraging. The string bass player, a mineman third class, did not know a note of music, but just slapped out on his instrument whatever he happened to hit. Nevertheless, for a while we played nearly every evening at the Fontaine, while the commodore danced with his French ladies and his officers entertained their dates from Mostaganem. Occasionally the RAF band from Algiers would visit, and *they* were good. Everybody jumped to their version of "In the Mood"; for a show piece they'd play their own arrangement of *Warsaw Concerto.*

But the enlisted men had no one to dance with. Ensign Alan Trueblood and I undertook to remedy this lack, for the Navy had taught us that division officers had responsibility for the welfare and morale of enlisted men in their charge. So we checked out a jeep from the command pool, drove to the tiny Arzew church, and put our proposal before the curé, a small bearded Frenchman in a soup-stained cassock. We put on our best manners: Ensign Trueblood's French was perfect, mine much less so. Perhaps, we said, there were some young ladies in the curé's parish who would like to attend our little *réunions* at the naval base, dances held under circumstances of strictest propriety. Everything would be *très correct,* transportation would be furnished by the base, and we ventured to hope . . .

"*C'est impossible!*" He was furious. Were we aware of what we were asking? That he, the curé, should be required to collect for a *dancing* respectable young Frenchwomen of his parish, *jeunes filles* of tender age, some of whose brothers, fiancés, fathers indeed, had been wounded or killed by *ces messieurs* or their predecessors—*incroyable!* To dance with common sailors—Americans! *Ça, c'est un peu trop!* He begged to be excused. M. le curé politely escorted us to the church entrance. Outside in the heat, exotic drums were banging and nasal flutes whined. A small parade of Arzew's Arabs marched down the road, carrying banners in celebration of some Moslem feast. The curé looked at them grimly, muttering, "*Sauvages!*"

Every afternoon a Free French armored group drove their tanks out for firing practice. The tanks had the Cross of Lorraine painted on their sides. Their guns went thump, thump, thump behind the sandy hills, as they waited out the time for their return to sweet France, backed by African Ghoums. Evenings they sometimes harmonized sentimental tunes, many rather old-fashioned. Ensign Trueblood taught me the words of one they sang—something by Chateaubriand about an exile remembering the scenes of his childhood, longing for France, his only love:

Combien j'ai douce souvenance
Du joli lieu de ma naissance!
O ma soeur, qu'ils étaient beaux, les jours de France!
O mon pays, sois mes amours—toujours!

Alan Trueblood was a handsome young officer, tall, high-colored, full-lipped, with curly dark hair, and large brown-green eyes that protruded ever so slightly when he warmed to his subject. He had graduated from Harvard, where he had studied Romance languages (he spoke them all beautifully) and had spent a year in Chile on a fellowship. Western Algeria lies close to Spain, and Alan would point out marks of Spanish influence on those occasions when we had to drive into Oran: the architecture, the facial structures, the place names, the language heard in the streets of the Algerian city which turns its back, as Camus says, on the sea. As we dried off on the chocolate-colored rocks after our swim before evening chow (sorry, that was the word for it), Alan would recite in various languages, even in Brazilian Portuguese, of which I remembered only the word *saudades,* the longing to be where one isn't.

Thirty years after wartime Arzew, I read Alan's magnum opus, just published, an immense book about Lope de Vega. By this time Alan had been for years a distinguished professor of Romance languages at Brown University. His eight-hundred-page volume centers on a single play, *La Dorotea,* that Lope in his old age composed from the memories of an ancient love. Elena Osorio had cherished the poet in his youth, hurt him, and left him for another, richer man. Young Lope could not bear his dismissal and made life miserable for Elena. He hung around, confronted her, insulted her, slapped her face, forged letters, and made evil reports of her and of her friends and family. Elena's father brought suit for libel, and Lope was banished from Madrid. Near the end of his stormy life as artist, lover, exile, veteran of the Armada, man of learning and religion, Lope left that poetic reconstruction of his never-forgotten youthful love affair as a final testament. In the play, Fernando and Dorotea move through a complex version of the steps once danced by Lope and Elena, while Gerard, a bibulous go-between, tries to pair off Elena with Don Bela, a wealthy colonial, just back from the New World. To transform his youthful experience into timeless poetry, Lope used every resource of language, every rich device of baroque rhetoric to construct the strange and difficult drama, meant not for the stage, but for the theater of mind and heart. "Having abandoned the stage to increase his hold on the inner world of the imagination," Alan says in his gentle farewell to Lope and his play, "he now releases this world too, wholly poetry at last into the hands of posterity and tranquilly awaits the hour when life will be relinquished."

At Arzew, and later in France, I liked to watch Alan with Father Stockman, the Catholic chaplain of the naval unit. He sometimes asked Alan to interpret for him when he had a little business deal going, and although Alan was reluctant to engage himself in these affairs (Father was the first Catholic priest he had seen close-up) he found it hard to refuse. The clever Father was as skilled an operator as either of us had seen in the Navy. Shrewd of eye and foxy of face, the Boston Jesuit's inquisitiveness became legend; nobody's business was alien to him. When Father Stockman was not talking (a rare state for him) he emitted from pursed lips a constant, almost soundless, whistle. At Arzew and Oran he made it his duty to accompany the shore patrol on its rounds of whorehouses—a good indication of his curiosity, for an Algerian whorehouse in wartime required a nerveless stomach to enter. (I had to go into one once to retrieve somebody.) Father Stockman took his spiritual obligations seriously indeed. His talks on sex interested the enlisted men far more than the dreary VD films they were sometimes shown:

> Now let me speak frankly to you boys. The married men among you probably realize the truth in what I am going to say. You know that a prostitute, compared to the average decent wife, is rather skilled in the art of sexual love. By knowledge of her trade, she knows how to titillate, to carry sexual stimulation to a high degree of intensity. Now boys, if you patronize prostitutes, and plan to go home to the States after the war to marry some decent girl, and you have made a habit of consorting with prostitutes, you will very possibly find sexual relations with this decent wife unsatisfying. In other words, if you're used to caviar, you're going to get tired of Spam!

Father Stockman was ultramontane, suspicious of French Catholicism, Jews, women, and interfaith services. Once, later on in Naples, where I avoided his spiritual counsel though not his dinner-table conversation, he had a run-in with Fleet Headquarters for denouncing interdenominational services for base personnel. Both the Protestant chaplain and Rear Admiral Spencer Lewis, chief of staff to Admiral Kent Hewitt, favored interfaith services. But Stockman opposed those devotions on the ground that they constituted a violation of canon law as well as an implicit claim that one religion was as good as another, which it wasn't. When the chaplain forbade his Catholic enlisted men to attend an interdenominational Memorial Day divine service laid on by Admiral Lewis, he was summoned to the office of the chief of staff:

"Chaplain Stockman, I just don't understand this. Now, take Commander Duffy. He rides on the same train as you, doesn't he?" (Father Duffy, the area Catholic chaplain, dropped into Naples from time to time to keep an eye on things.)

"He does indeed, admiral."

"But *he* attended one of our interdenominational services."

"Yes, admiral, but Commander Duffy rides in the observation car." And Father Stockman emitted his soundless whistle.

WAR: SOUTHERN FRANCE

&ẹ Most British military historians, including A. J. P. Taylor, believe that the Allied landing in the South of France, in August 1944, was unnecessary. They may be right. All the same, late that month I had to inch myself down a cargo net hung over the side of a Liberty ship serving as transport and get into an LCVP bobbing in the oil-and-blue waters of the Gulf of St. Tropez. In the boat were twenty U.S. sailors in my temporary charge. We all wore helmets, though most of the shooting was over. I had a carbine strapped to my back, a Colt .45 automatic at my middle, and two musette bags dangling from my neck. The bags were filled with $25,000 in francs, neatly printed little notes with the tricolor on the backs. The "invasion money" had been printed stateside and we were to pay all hands with it until things had settled down. (French shopkeepers accepted them with resigned shrugs.) As the LCVP chugged past the *Catoctin,* Admiral Hewitt's flagship, we could see the lovely beach at St. Maxime. Naval gunfire had stopped. Only in Toulon and Marseilles were the Germans still holding out.

Allied shipping jammed the gulf, mostly transports and landing craft. The French cruiser *Gloire* stood by, striped as a zebra for camouflage. Just astern, the old battleship *Texas* swung around her hook. An occasional "Tonk!" came from the beach as mines were detonated by disposal squads ashore. The British destroyer *Kimberley*, Winston Churchill aboard, had long since turned around and departed. With the success of the landing assured, the prime minister whiled away the tedium of the return trip by reading Vicki Baum's novel *Grand Hotel* in his cabin. He had done the civil by an operation he had stubbornly opposed.

The British had never liked the idea of Anvil (later Dragoon), as the southern France landing was called. Originally planned at Teheran to erupt simultaneously with Overlord, the June Normandy invasion, the operation had to be put off until August due to lack of shipping, particularly landing craft. General Alexander, British commander in Italy, was trying to crack Kesselring's lines in the north and fumed at having to strip himself of seven divisions to strengthen the Riviera landing. Churchill wanted to land a force at the head of the Adriatic and drive up through the Ljubljana gap to Vienna before the Russians got there. But American strategy required the capture of Marseilles. A major port other than Cherbourg was badly needed for Allied shipping and supplies, and the Rhone Valley would provide an expressway for General Alexander Patch's Seventh Army to join Patton in the north. Besides, General Juin's Free French divisions, whose tanks rehearsed at Arzew, were eager to fight their way back into their homeland. In the end Roosevelt (with Stalin's approval) told Churchill he must do what had been planned, and the southern France operation was on. It came off as the smoothest amphibious landing of the war. The German commander, General Blascowitz, pulled back most of his forces and ordered only the garrisons of Toulon and Marseilles to hold out. They surrendered on August 28 to French troops under General de Lattre de Tassigny, whom the Allied command had tactfully assigned the specific job of liberating the port cities.

Naturally we knew nothing of all this. We piled out on the wet sand and got lost. A bored beachmaster waved us toward a golf course by the hotel marked Beauvallon. There under the shelter of sweet-smelling pines, the advance guard of our small party was lying comfortably in the shade of the radio truck assigned to us. We ran a mobile communications unit, and our job was to set up temporary radio stations at Toulon and Marseilles as soon as the troops had secured those cities. For the moment there was nothing to do but sit on the grass and eat K rations. K rations came in waxed packages like Cracker Jack, three kinds—breakfast, dinner, and supper—and no prize in any one of them. Breakfasts had rather sorry fig bars wrapped in sticky paper, and suppers featured a peculiarly repellent cheese with hard crackers that had absolutely no taste. Dinners were a little better, for they had tiny meat tins and candy bars, so I ate three dinners one right after the other. An Army unit bivouacked on the golf course gave us coffee. A jeep drove up with three French naval officers, among them Commandant Sizaire, friend of Ursula Marks from New Rochelle. He told me the German naval garrison at St. Mandrier off Toulon had surrendered and showed me a black and gold dagger he had gotten from one of the German officers.

The Beauvallon golf course, a fashionable place in peacetime, looked like a giant pincushion—the Germans had stuck tall sharpened stakes all over it to discourage glider landings. The hotel itself had been turned into a field hospital. I watched the medics helping a few German walking wounded. One man had his face half-covered by a bloody bandage. He was trying very hard to walk, but couldn't make it, and sank down very slowly on the gravel while they went to get a stretcher for him. Beyond the golf course on the road to St. Maxime were burned-out German tanks. Here and there along the ditches, sticks cut from pine branches had been planted with little strips of white cloth tied around their tops. Later the graves registration units would dig up the bodies beneath them and bury them in the military cemeteries already being bulldozed out.

That night I slept in a beautiful house on a hill overlooking the Gulf of St. Tropez. The south wall of the living room was a big rectangle of glass looking down on the bay. A Chinese rug of blue and gold ran the length of the floor up to where a Bechstein piano stood. They said that the house had belonged to a rich Jewish woman who was shot by the Germans in her own garden outside when they caught her trying to transmit information to the Allies a few days before the landing. Later I heard that she was not Jewish, but the rest of the story had been correct. I lifted a copy of Roland-Manuel's

Maurice Ravel from her bookshelves and stowed it away in my duffel bag. Technically we weren't supposed to do that, but I meant it as a gesture of respect.

In the morning the Navy communications unit was ordered to Marseilles. The Germans had finally thrown in the towel there and in Toulon. Six jeeps and our radio truck made up a small convoy that bumped westward along the coast road. We passed through Toulon, badly damaged by naval gunfire. Knots of children gathered at the roadside and threw ragged flowers at us. At a shelled-out bridge, our driver cut off a truck driven by a young French Army woman. She leaned from the cab and shrieked her opinion of our rudeness with a *"Merde!"* or two. Our driver yelled back the only French phrase he knew: *"C'est la guerre!"*

In Marseilles we drove downtown and stopped on the Cannebière, where a crowd of French citizens surrounded us, congratulating and complaining of what they had undergone. A gaunt Frenchwoman in a man's jacket kept repeating, *"Pendu, messieurs, pendu!"* Ensign Trueblood explained to his men that the Germans had hanged her uncle. Already collaborators were being dealt with. Across the Cannebière a gang of young men dragged a woman to the street and started to shave her head. I wasn't much interested in watching that and felt relieved when ordered back to Toulon with a unit of two jeeps and our radio truck. Communications personnel were badly needed in Toulon; at the moment the U.S. naval radio organization ashore there consisted of one Lieutenant (j.g.) Walsh and a radioman third class. So we drove back along the road we had just traveled through the gorge of Ollioule to Toulon. The harbor there was an utter mess, choked with old, scuttled French warships and massive débris from the recent naval bombardment. In the port building, half of it rubble, Admiral Davidson, commander of the fire support groups, talked sternly to the French commandant: "When are you going to get this port cleaned up?" The shabby French naval captain glanced up at the handsome American flag officer towering over him, and shrugged. It was a primordial shrug that started somewhere down near his toes, slowly wound round his torso, then slipped off his shoulders into space. Somehow he seemed to come off better in the exchange.

Behind Toulon rises a low mountain called the Faron and halfway up runs a corniche road that goes to Fréjus. Near the top of the

Faron we found Lieutenant (j.g.) Walsh knee-deep in discarded German ammunition cases and gas-mask canisters. With his radioman third, he was working a TBS, a small transmitter-receiver, powered by a German gasoline generator they had found up there.

"God copulate it," roared Walsh, evidently a man of some education. "Relieve me quick! I've got just five minutes to make town before the bars close." He jumped on the back seat of a motorcycle driven by his radioman third, and rocketed down the hill. In later years, Walsh became dean of faculty of a Connecticut university. He was the liveliest dean they ever had.

At midnight I began the midwatch out on the hill with Lambert, a young radioman from Louisiana. Radio traffic subsided at three in the morning. Only one of our ships had to be moved, the fleet tug *Hopi* needed in Marseilles. We put on our fuzzy-lined cold-weather jackets, for the temperature had dropped sharply during the night. The mistral was blowing, one of the three plagues of Provence, as the old saying goes, the other two being talking and the floody river Durance. The quiet of the dark early morning hours, threaded with the plaintive dit-dahing of the TBS, broke at intervals with the *"Tonk!"* of a detonated mine. Cap Brun, off to the left, was full of them. From the smashed port below, an odor of corruption rose; the sewers would not be repaired for weeks. Offshore in the Grande Rade, the *Gloire* was talking by flashing light to the destroyer *Fantasque,* using the assault code, which had not yet been superseded. At quiet moments, Lambert pushed back one earpiece and chatted softly. A tall, quiet boy just out of high school, he was pleased at having made radioman third after just three months in the service. He talked a bit about the river country near his home, his family, and his schoolwork. Then a German reconnaissance plane flew over the harbor, and the army antiaircraft unit down the hill opened up on it. There was no peace until we were relieved by the morning watch.

Next day Navy communications moved into the apartment house vacated by the German Kommandatura. Here in the yard we ate hot meals of C rations out of tin mess kits, while small French children stood at the fence by the garbage cans, holding out bits of folded newspaper for the scrapings. Alan Trueblood and I were billeted in an empty stucco house on the rue Daniel Melchior. Off watch, miserable with dysentery, I lay on my bunk, keeping an eye on an industrious mouse trying to get into my duffel bag—perhaps he smelled the cheese and crackers in the K rations. There was no water, except what could be drawn from the well in the French-woman's yard across the way. She scolded GIs who helped themselves to her water without asking permission; her accent was Provençal, "vang" for *vin,* "mateng" for *matin.* A young French couple next door brought me hot soup, though they had little for themselves. Another couple, an elderly farmer and his wife, showed Alan their brook; under its bed they had buried two Germans they had killed. Noncombatants are often more violent and vindictive than soldiers.

Radio traffic now speeded up. Ships were unloading at Toulon, Marseilles, and Port de Bouc. The electronic gear from our radio truck had been installed in the former Kommandatura, where the radiomen worked around the clock on a tight three-watch schedule. Coding officers labored in the code room, hunched over registered publications, electric cipher machines, strip ciphers, and British book codes. The communication watch officer, or CWO, flipped us dispatches to be encoded or decoded, their priority indicated by "P," "OP," "O," or whatever. We sweated under the kindly, worried eyes of Mr. Whittaker, the harassed communications officer in charge.

One noisy afternoon full of tonks and bangs from the *déminage* operations nearby (the explosions threw our radio transmitters off frequency) an off-duty radioman ran into the radio shack shouting for Mr. Whittaker. "Lambert's booby-trapped!"

All who could be spared jumped to follow Lieutenant Whittaker outside and down the street to an empty house a block away. Lambert and Silver, both off watch, had gone there to look for Luger pistols. They had heard that the Germans had left some around, and Lugers were the most highly prized trophies in the area, selling for as much as a hundred dollars apiece. Now Lambert lay on the bare hardwood floor of an empty room, his hands blown off and a black, reddening hole in his midriff. Silver stood by shivering; his back had just been lightly peppered by bits from the exploding grenade. Jack Wolfe, the chief radioman, bent over Lambert to cover him with a gray Navy blanket. Lambert managed a half-smile.

"Pretty tough, eh, Wolfe?"

Lieutenant (j.g.) Delbert Lewis from Odebolt, Iowa, died more quickly. In his early twenties, he was tall and skinny, with a gentle manner and wit that drew many of us more talkative types to sit with him in the newly opened Navy officers' mess, a requisitioned restaurant on Toulon's main street. I liked to watch Lewis at breakfast eating his pancakes and Klim. Klim was milk spelled backward, and it looked like white powder stirred up in a glass of water. I couldn't abide the stuff, but Lewis drank it down as if it were fresh milk from the cows on an Iowa farm. Lewis was mine disposal officer of the Toulon naval detachment and spent his time at one waterfront or another getting rid of mines in the dock areas. He had a chief, some minemen, and two German POWs to help him. At Toulon all the German POWs were caged in a stockade near the harbor and formed a labor pool on which the military could draw. Those Germans were grudgingly admired because of their discipline and capacity for long, hard work. I never heard them sing "Lili Marlene"—in fact, I never heard them sing at all. Most were older men and all quite harmless. The bad Germans, Nazis, SS types and such, had been sent away, we knew not where. One day a gang of FFI, the French armed resistance irregulars, showed up at the stockade gate—tough-looking types hung about with tommy guns, machine pistols, knives, and grenades. Their leader flashed a bit of paper and demanded that some Germans be turned over to them. Since their intent appeared homicidal to the young ensign on guard duty, he called for advice over the field telephone. Almost at once the gateway swarmed with junior naval officers confronting the Resistance: "You're not going to take any of *our* Germans."

Lieutenant Lewis's Germans liked getting into diving gear and working down below. They got cigarettes for it and did a little business with them in the POW stockade. Lewis wouldn't let them do dangerous work, for he said that was against the Geneva Convention. He did it himself. The minemen called the two German POWs Hans and Fritz. Fritz was devoted to Lewis. He would carefully help him with his diving gear, step back, knock his heels together, and say, *"Zu Befehl, Herr Offizier!"*

One morning in September at the harbor of La Ciotat down the road toward Marseilles, Lewis and his crew were working on mines off the docks. Afterward a mineman told me what happened. Lewis put on his diving gear and went down into the water to disarm a particularly stubborn mine. Fritz had helped him over the side with his usual *"Zu Befehl"* routine. The explosion came in three stages. First everybody felt the pier move, then the water went all white in a big circle, and then the sound came like somebody hitting a big pillow with a baseball bat. A French destroyer signaled with its flashing light. Out in the roads a Navy crashboat turned on its siren and moved in toward the pier.

Delbert Lewis was a Protestant, so the service for him was held in Toulon's small Huguenot church. I played the organ, managing "Abide with Me," "Rock of Ages," and the Navy hymn, "Eternal Father, Strong to Save." The *pasteur* spoke in French about courage and glory. He said the brave young officer had died for his country, but that we must remember he had died for France too. Burial service took place in the Toulon town cemetery. None of our sailors had experience in firing volleys over a grave before. Just before the second volley one of the men dropped his carbine and the squad had to wait until he picked it up, red-faced. For obvious reasons the coffin was pretty light and they lowered it quickly. Fritz, the German POW, wanted to attend, but that was not allowed. We were sorry. What harm could it have done? He would only have stood there stiffly, heels together, just as he did when he said, *"Zu Befehl, Herr Offizier!"*

I remembered that one morning at breakfast Del Lewis had told me how pretty Cannes and Nice were and that I ought to get myself temporary orders to go down that way. He had just come back from Golfe Juan, where the Germans had built gun emplacements near the beach to look like ice cream stands. Two months after he died I went to Cannes with Lieutenant Adam Knurek. We had orders to temporary duty at Nice and Golfe Juan before being transferred from Toulon to Marseilles for a final month in France. Things had quieted down, bakeries were selling whole loaves of bread again, and the French military were making it rather clear that American naval assistance had delighted them long enough. General de Gaulle had stopped in Toulon for a little victory parade up the main street; a few of us managed to get into the act, trotting behind the French sailors in their white pancake hats with red pompoms just to say we had been in it.

At Cannes, the dining room of the Hotel Martinez was lighted with candles, not for beauty but to save electricity. It was beautiful, all the same. Kindly waiters served hot Army C rations on the hotel's best china (*un petit supplément, m'sieu?*) and some good wines had been fetched up from the cellar. We sat with writer John Marquand's son, an Army lieutenant. As the orchestra played *Tango Chinois,* paratroop officers with soft leather boots danced with pretty French girls from Nice and Grasse. Through the open windows of the dining room the mild breeze came in soft and flower-scented with just a hint of mountain snow. At Antibes, just beyond Cannes, you could see the Alpes Maritimes from the coast. The day before I had caught my first sight of them—near St. Luc at the right turn where the corniche road from Toulon begins to descend to the coast at Fréjus. The jeep had just cleared a long rise in the climbing road shouldered by red earth, fragrant with pines. Far away above the eastern horizon I saw a long frieze of white clouds. But they were not clouds— they were snow-covered mountain peaks. Then I think I understood why old people for whom the future has ceased to exist look so intently at the flowers and trees and hills beyond. They are fixing on them that comprehensive gaze, Proust says somewhere, with which on the day of his departure a traveler tries to carry away with him in memory the view of a country to which he may never return. But Lambert and Lewis were so young. And they both died in such a hurry.

ITALY: NAPLES I

ৡ► In Naples I shared an apartment on the Via Caracciolo with a lieutenant who wore the croix de guerre ribbon with a silver star on it. He told me he had been awarded it for drinking two officers of the French cruiser *Georges Leygues* under the table, after the southern France operation. He spent most of his off-duty time at parties at Caserta, where he said he and his friends all got stinking drunk and sang dirty songs. Unasked, he wrote out for me the words to "The Ball of Killiemuir." After a while he went away and a supply officer moved in. From time to time he gave shelter to pretty refugee women from Eastern Europe, providing them with food and lodging until they felt refreshed enough to be on their way again. One night just before the devout Avery Dulles came to see me with the manuscript of his *Testament of Grace,* I had to shoo to her room the supply officer's current protégée, a blonde Yugoslav given to parading around the apartment at all hours singing songs of love and death.

Avery Dulles, an assistant operations officer on the Eighth Fleet's staff, did not at all resemble his father, John Foster. He was tall, pale, and shy, had dark, curly hair, and stammered a little. While still an undergraduate at Harvard he had published a small book on Pico della Mirandola. He told me a long troubled story about an incident in Boston that seemed to me no more than the usual undergraduate prank. But the Harvard authorities had taken a dim view of it and had threatened him with expulsion. Shortly afterward Avery had experienced a spiritual rebirth, converted to Catholicism, and would have begun study for the priesthood had not the war intervened. Now he wanted me to look over his mansucript and to tell him what I thought about it. Given Avery's grave friendship, I had no trouble controlling my native irreverence. I read the manuscript and told him that it struck me as the story of St. Augustine's youth all over again. As for the writing itself, there was not a comma out of place. That seemed to please him. Toward the end of his duty in Naples, Avery flew to London to visit his father, who was on a State Department mission. On the way Avery fell sick with polio and had to be shipped back to the States to recover. After the war he entered a Jesuit house of studies. He had some trouble deciding between his duty to the order and his debt to Father Leonard Feeney, who had played an important part in his conversion and later defied his Jesuit superiors to become fanatic leader of his Slaves of the Immaculate Heart of Mary. In 1956 Avery wrote to me asking me to come to his First Mass at Fordham chapel. I did not see his father there.

See Naples and die? On the bulkhead of our radio shack in Navy House, the waterfront building we shared with the British, someone had tacked up a poem in purple ditto copy written by an anonymous GI:

> *If I was an artist, with nothing to do,*
> *I'd paint a picture, a composite view*
> *Of historical Naples, in which I'd show*
> *Visions of contrasts, the high and the low.*
> *High-plumed horses and colorful carts*
> *Two-toned dresses on hustling tarts*

There'd be towering mountains, a deeply blue sea,
Filthy brats yelling "Caramella" at me.

And so on for twenty stanzas or more. At first I felt sorry for the filthy brats. They had no shoes on their feet even in cold weather, and in winter Naples can be surprisingly cold. Later I got used to it and no longer minded the little *scugnizzi* pimping for their alleged sisters: "Hey Joe, wanna peesa ass?"

The name "Joe" in wartime Naples was so closely associated with the GIs Bill Mauldin drew in his cartoons that my bourgeois Italian friends up on the Vomero were a little uncomfortable when I asked them to call me that. Once when they brought me to tea with the Duchessa de Caianello, a Swedish-born relic of the Neapolitan nobility, they gently suggested that I not ask her to call me Joe. ("Hey Joe, wanna eat?")

There's a great book about the Naples of 1944 by John Horne Burns, a novel called *The Gallery.* Hemingway said it was the best novel to come out of World War II. Burns, a young Army captain, taught private school in Connecticut in civilian life. After the southern France landing, Burns lingered on in Rome writing, his diversions feverish and irregular. Surprisingly, the local Army authorities let him be. At war's end, he returned to teach at his prep school, but never recovered from his displacement. Like many other talented souls lifted out of home and routine by the war, Burns experienced a deep shift in his moral center of gravity. Algeria started it. Italy finished the job. "The African air, the Ayrabs, the odd behavior of Americans," he wrote, "all worked on me strangely overseas. My laughter shifted to the other side of my face and finally died away altogether."

The Gallery is Burns's souvenir album, its portraits drawn from life in Naples 1944, where the troops of a dozen nations staging for the landing in southern France passed through the Galleria Umberto Primo, the great arcade in downtown Naples that lost all its lofty glass in the bombardments. There's Louella, the dipso Red Cross lady who can't stand the "wops"; two chaplains, one Protestant, one Catholic, who have stumbled by mistake into the Arizona Club and flee the awful place with lethal results. There's Moe, the Jewish combat infantryman; Giulia, the lovely Italian PX clerk; a nameless GI sweating out the tough sixty-shot penicillin syphilis cure at the VD stockade in Bagnoli; two spinsterish males, British sergeants from Caserta, eating their hearts out at Mama's bar in the Galleria, where the homosexual military gather:

> I'm asking you, Esther, to take a good look at all these mad people. For they are mad. And consider the subtle threat that brings them all here together. . . .
>
> Does either of us know what these people are looking for, Magda?
>
> Don't be dull, Esther. They're all looking for perfection . . . and perfection is love of death, if you face the issue squarely. That's the reason why these people live so hysterically. . . .
>
> What does God think of all this, Magda? . . .
>
> Thank Him, if he exists, that we don't know. . . . A new morality may come into existence in our time, Esther. That's one of the few facts that thrills me, old bitch that I am.

After the war, Burns wrote me that he truly believed in the coming of a new morality: it would be carried on the wings of the enlightened young, even though

> Lamentably in the United States there are millions who not only are lashing themselves into another war, but are asphyxiated with phony fiction constructed by formula. In opposition to these dead-heads I've been heartened to discover thousands of our generation who are tired of the old shit and equivocation and going to the parting of the ways with the ancient crud and cant.

Burns could not find his native land again. A displaced romantic, he went back to teaching prep school, but soon quit. His art failed him. He was a one-book man; the next flopped. He went back to Italy, suffered a cerebral hemorrhage, and died miserably in Leghorn. He had seen Naples.

During off-duty hours, I wandered on foot up the stone steps and down the alleys of the unbelievable city. You could reach old churches in the heart of town by walking through the Galleria. Santo Domenico Maggiore still kept its sacristy adjoining, festooned with ancient coffins holding the dust of Aragonese kings who once lorded it over the kingdom of Naples and the Two Sicilies. If you picked your way carefully through the rubble in the nearby Dominican monastery, you could stick your head into the cell said once to have

been Thomas Aquinas's—one of its walls had been sheared off by
an air bomb. In the next street stood all that was left of fourteenth-
century Santa Chiara. The frescoed walls had survived, and the rustic
gardens, too. Then you could walk to the cathedral, where they have
the blood of St. Gennaro (Januarius). He was beheaded near Pozzuoli, they say, under Diocletian in the third century. The material
alleged to be his blood is in a glass vial fixed in a metal reliquary.
At certain times during the year the blood liquefies and the church
is jammed with devout Neapolitans. The dark brown mass bubbles
in the vial and turns bright red. Sometimes the change does not take
place,* or is delayed, in which case the more impatient of the assembled faithful rudely cry out (I can't reproduce the Neapolitan
dialect), "Liquefy, damn ya, liquefy!" Father Stockman believed the
liquefaction a genuine miracle, but added his belief that it is a
rather silly thing of God to do.

The naval officers had their mess up on the Via Francesco Crispi,
where a string trio furnished music for meals, even for breakfast.
The trio shrank to a duo when the cellist was fired for trying to
smuggle out food in his cello bag for his hungry family. As a cello
player and fellow human, I tried to intercede on his behalf with
the mess officer, a tough Supply Corps lieutenant, but to no avail.
While the musicians played "Cuor 'ngrato" or "Appassionata-
mente," Father Stockman talked at table about modernist heresies,
angelic knowledge (it's intuitive; they don't use syllogisms), or the
iniquities of an army supply officer down at the Peninsular Base
Section who did him out of a little perfume deal. The chaplain's
curiosity was boundless, and, since he had entrée everywhere, he
could satisfy it. The Arizona Club did not shock him. He never
missed a hanging at the Aversa stockade. ("Joe, all you could hear
was this gurgling sound!") Military justice in the European theater
fell quick and harsh upon American soldiers who had raped or
murdered.

Shortly before V-E Day, Father Stockman discovered that Martin
Niemöller was being kept under wraps at Capri and brought him to
our table one day at Crispi House. An Allied unit, overrunning a

---

* During the vigil of the first week of May 1976, when the blood failed to liquefy,
thousands raged and lamented outside the cathedral doors. Corrado Cardinal Ursi,
Archbishop of Naples, declared the next day that increased "neo-paganism" was
responsible.

German-held area in the south Tyrol, had picked up the pastor in a village where the Gestapo, equipped with death orders, had taken him together with certain other prominent prisoners from Dachau. Pastor Niemöller was a spare and fine-boned man. I won't forget his lovely smile as he looked intently at me with his sea-blue eyes and took my hand in his firm, warm grip. Someone has said that the reason for the pastor's lonely resistance to the Nazis lay in his simultaneous belief in the truth of the Christian religion and the categorical imperative, Kant's rule that the right is its own justification. Niemöller had refused to join in the Nazi "Germanizing" of the Protestant Church and spoke out (a little late) against Hitler's persecution of the Jews. He was tried by one of Hitler's "People's Tribunals," but some vestigial spark of decency compelled them to acquit him, and he was released from custody. At the back door of the courthouse he was arrested again on the personal order of the Führer, thrown into Sachsenhausen, then into Dachau. I often wondered why Niemöller sided with the Nazis at first, scorned the tottering Weimar Republic, and welcomed Hitler's accession to power in 1933.

Mingled impulses toward order and freedom deep in human nature (if there is such a thing as human nature) take a peculiarly dialectical form in German culture. What seem to be contradictions hang out quite visibly. In World War I, poet Gottfried Benn attended the execution of nurse Edith Cavell—he had the duty as medical officer. After the volley she fell, but her body moved as if struggling to rise from the ground. Dr. Benn assured a horrified witness that this was merely a reflex action. Death must have been instantaneous, he said, pointing to her forehead which one of the bullets had smashed through. That was 1915, the year he wrote "Icarus," the long poem that ends:

> O sun, you rustle forth from out your folds
> each night new universes into space—
> Oh, one of these, obliviously scattered here
> with its young glow is melting down my temples,
> drinks my deforeheaded blood.

Benn accepted the Nazis in 1933, in one breath comparing "those two great minds, Hitler and Napoleon." But in 1941 at the height of the German triumph he denounced them as "hoplites with a machine gun attacking a boy they had promised not to harm."

You don't have to be German to live with contraditions. The

Swiss theologian Karl Barth, professor at the German universities of Göttingen, Münster, and Bonn, found himself kicked out of his post by Hitler. At the end of World War II he wrote that the only way to cure the Germans would be to give them political freedom and to make them responsible for their own thinking and acting. "The Allies," he added, "should impose this task upon the Germans as soon as possible"—a line reminiscent of Rousseau's dictum that Society should loose every man who hugs his chains and "force him to be free." Or Colonel Purdy's in *The Teahouse of the August Moon*—"My job is to teach these natives the meaning of democracy, and they're going to learn democracy if I have to shoot every one of them."

With Kesselring's surrender in the north of Italy in April 1945, military operational radio traffic subsided somewhat. The Navy had hoped for one more landing, a little operation at La Spezia while that port was still in German hands, but that was now judged superfluous. Most radio traffic concerned logistic matters. Sometimes I had to take classified dispatches by air to Palermo in Sicily, an alarming experience for a nervous soul, for at the time the airstrip at Palermo could be reached only by sudden descent between mountains so close one could reach out, it seemed, and touch them on the glide path. The Army Air Force pilots all looked about seventeen years old. One day in mid-flight one of them strolled into the cabin where I was the sole passenger and announced that his magneto had conked out. The end at last, I thought, but it turned out that, while a magneto is an awfully nice thing to have, a plane can fly without it, and we bumped cheerfully into Cappodochino in one piece.

Weary from the grind at Navy House (I was now officer-in-charge of NXG, Radio Naples), I'd clear my head after supper at Crispi House by climbing the three hundred steps of the Calada di San Francesco to the Vomero, then go over by way of the Via Belvedere to the Posillipo and back down the winding funicular road that looked over the bay of Naples, unbelievable at that twilight hour. Vesuvio, dull-blue, slept over the city with only a smudge of smoke at the crater. Directly below me, a boat with red sail would be working its way out from the Mergellina, soon to pass the sumptuous villa of CINCMED, Admiral Sir John Cunningham, who had his headquarters over us in Navy House. Far down the curve of the Via Caracciolo by the Castel del Ovo you could see the lights of

Santa Lucia, the old fishing boat area the song is about. Zi Teresa's was a good restaurant there, specializing in fish. My first time there I ordered *zuppa di peche,* thinking it would be no more than a simple fish chowder. I was mistaken. When the waiter brought the enormous dish, my hair rose a little, for there was a red octopus with staring eyes looking at me, suckered tentacles draped over the sides of a little hill of mussels and other sea life piled in the bowl.

If there was nothing urgent Sunday mornings, I would take the little train that clacked out in the direction of the ancient Phlegrian fields. If you were Allied military you really didn't have to pay, but you got a smile and a *"Grazie infinite!"* from the old trainman, if you did. You could get off at Pozzuoli to visit the Roman ampitheater, its ancient brick walls splashed in big white letters:

VIVA FIORELLO LAGUARDIA!

Or you could stay on until the train came to the fishing village at the end of the line, then hike to Baia, old Horace's favorite resort, and sit at Cape Miseno to look over to Procida, where Lamartine's lovely Graziella once fashioned her ornaments of coral. Or to Ischia, the honeymoon isle, where the philosopher Berkeley dallied so long before returning to Dublin to take his D.D. at Trinity College. From Baia it was not a long walk to Cumae, where Aeneas came to consult the Sybil in her many-tunneled grotto. I climbed down one day to seek the Sybil in her cave, but found only haunted shadows and an abandoned German machine gun already rusting on its tripod.

A pretty reliable jeep went with my job, and I needed it to run official errands outside the city. Once I had to drive down to Potenza beyond Eboli (where Christ stopped) to deliver a package sent by Secretary of the Navy Forrestal to his friend Aileen Branca, an American society woman who had married an Italian noble. Her servants said she was at Ravello, so I drove there all the way back from Lucania. She was away from there too, visiting a dentist in Naples, but her friends the Pansas asked me to stay overnight in a house perched high over Amalfi, right by the spot where Richard Wagner found inspiration for the magic garden scene in *Parsifal.* Mario Pansa was a handsome man in the style of the actor Alfred Lunt. His father had been an Italian senator and ambassador to Britain, and Mario himself had been long in the diplomatic service, and adviser on foreign affairs to Mussolini. His wife, Sarah Jane, was the sister of Stephen (Laddie) Sanford, the Long Island polo player and race-horse owner. At dinner she said little but "Terrible! Terrible!" as we talked about Italy and the war. She looked tired and went to her room as the servants poured out tiny cognacs after dinner, leaving Pansa and me to sit up talking until long after midnight, looking down over the cliff at the fishermen's lights in the gulf of Amalfi a thousand feet below. Pansa talked of Mussolini's various attempts to secure peace and defended his chief to me—"Ethiopia? A colonial adventure?" Although a Fascist, Pansa had turned pro-Ally before Italy surrendered and had helped the Italian underground. For himself and his future career he had no hope. Shortly after the war in Europe ended, he swam out to sea at Torre Astura, near Rome, and never turned back.

Liliana Mormile was the artist who drew portraits of Allied personnel at the Red Cross foyer in the Piazza Carita. Sometimes I would clean up my jeep and ask her to go to the opera with me or even to drive down to Sorrento or Positano. Liliana, whose head might have been painted by Bronzino, took a dim view of jeeps and young Italian women who visibly rode in them. But on occasion she would gently yield and put aside her charcoal pencils. Then we might sit out on the terrace of Sorrento's Hotel Vittoria to look across the four-mile channel to Capri and at all the surrounding *bellezza* while the orchestra played "Sentimental Journey." Liliana courteously affected not to notice the officers from the Peninsular Base Section drinking noisily and making clumsy passes at the Army nurses they had brought with them.

"My God," said a red-faced lieutenant colonel staring at Capri, "this beats anything we've got in southern California!"

For a war, all this sounds very leisurely, cultured, and out of harm's way. Too true. Naples was strictly rear-echelon. My job was exacting, hard on the nerves, its hours long and dull, with serious responsibilities that required answering for the mistakes of others as well as my own. But the work was not dangerous. I knew from talking to them what the combat infantrymen in the north had to go through. I saw them when I visited the base hopitals. Every day at my desk I checked through dispatches about the bodies of GIs being shipped back to the States via Naples with the statement, "Remains not viewable." But I never experienced anything like what Mark Clark's GIs endured up north or what a generation later one of my own sons, twice wounded, would know in Vietnam.

ITALY: NAPLES II

஀ Opera flourished in Naples at the old royal theater of San Carlo under the tight control of a British commission headed by the area commander Brigadier B. U. S. Cripps. The ancient house, all red velvet and faded gilt, was packed every night with troops, most of them British transported from Caserta by truckfuls. A bewigged attendant in threadbare satin would show you to your seat while you waited for the curtain to go up, sending a puff of cold stale air rolling into the stalls from Rodolfo's garret: *"Talor dal mio forziere/ ruban tutti i gioelli."*

Gigli sang in the season of 1944–45 and his *Bohème* was particularly memorable. Though the aging tenor's voice by now lacked the freshness of Tagliavini—also at the San Carlo, with his wife Pia Tassinari—Gigli had a tenderness and musicianship the younger man could not match. There was *Tosca* with Tito Gobbi as Scarpia, *Traviata* with Rena Gigli as Violetta, and the sublime vulgarities of *Turandot*. A disastrous performance of what the Italians called *La Walkiria* came to an end when Brünnhilde, worn out by her exertions, lost her voice and collapsed against Wotan amid the whistles and boos of the Italians in the audience. They would not tolerate shortcomings in opera, even a Wagnerian one. Rows of British military turned indignantly on the Italians to protest the unsporting behavior, and gave the weeping Brünnhilde a standing ovation.

The Royal Opera in Rome had a large stable of top singers, and Victor de Sabata as principal conductor. My favorite walk in Rome took me first to the church of Sant' Andrea della Valle, then to the Farnese palace, and wound up at the Castle of Sant' Angelo—the settings of the three acts of *Tosca*. One night at a performance of *Samson and Delilah* in Rome, a young woman with very white skin and very dark red hair sat next to me. At certain parts of the opera, particularly when Francesco Battaglia sang the aria "My heart at thy sweet voice," she wept audibly. During intermission, she apologized to me, explaining that her tears had something to do with Budapest memories. Alice Fáy was a displaced Hungarian under the protection of the British government, waiting in Rome for transportation to London, there to be married to a fellow countryman, a young engineer in exile doing war work in England. She spoke excellent English, and French too, with many attractive and unusual phrases. A man who knows Magyar once said that Hungarians have a good many odd and often highly trenchant expressions, and for that and other reasons one is seduced into liking them. But I was really surprised to learn that Alice Fäy had been secretary to Frigyes Karinthy, the Hungarian writer.

If you have never read Karinthy's book *A Journey Round My Skull*, please try to find a copy. It's as if Victor Borge had written *Death Be Not Proud*. One day in a Budapest café Karinthy heard trains starting up in the street outside. Only there were no trains, not even tracks. Next day, as the writer was having his tea in the same Café Central, the trains started up again at exactly the same time as they had the day before. But there were no trains. Their noise came from inside Karinthy's head, the first sign of a brain tumor. Other bizarre symptoms followed. Karinthy's macabre humor in describing them resembles nothing else in print, unless you're thinking of a work on the grand scale like Thomas Mann's *The Magic Mountain*. They hustled Karinthy off to Sweden, where his tumor was removed by Dr. Herbert Olivecrona, who had learned his art from Harvey Cushing, the Boston brain surgeon. Karinthy thought they would put him to sleep for the operation, but instead got only local anesthesia. "I don't administer a general anesthetic to Europeans," said Dr. Olivecrona, "for the risk is 25 percent less if the patient remains conscious." Karinthy heard them bore open his skull, saw his blood drip into a pail, smelled burning bone, heard crackings and grindings as the surgeon worked around the malignant tumor, courteously asking at intervals, "How do you feel now?" Karinthy recovered from the operation and returned to Hungary, where a year of happiness was left to him. One of his stories is about a man who refuses to buy new shoelaces, patching up his old ones in successively complicated ways so that in the end one day they trip him up and he breaks his neck. A year after his operation, Karinthy bent over to tie his own shoelaces and died instantly.

Karinthy loved women and they loved him, though he had what we would today call strong sexist convictions. "What a good thing it is that there are women!" he wrote. "No, I'm not thinking of the obvious—just that they are completely different from men and an everlasting promise that one day we may achieve some sort of goal. If God ever pardons the human race, it will be on account of them." (Ah, Kate Millett, my future friend and colleague, I know what unprintable things you'd say to that!) In his Gulliver-tale "Capillaria," he writes, "Men and women—how can they ever understand each other? Both want something so utterly different—the men, women; and the women, men."

Karinthy was immensely popular in Hungary. At the height of his career, he could be found at the Café Hadik in Budapest surrounded by a group of admiring ladies, including his wife. One day a friend, Paul Tabori, tried to push across the café table to him an envelope containing money he had received as Karinthy's share of a story translated and published in a German magazine. Tabori says he felt a swift kick on his shin, as Karinthy hissed, "Not in front of my wife, you fool!" Later in the men's room he apologized, "I'm sorry if I was rude, but a man needn't tell his wife about *all* the money he makes."

Poor Karinthy! And that red-haired girl with the high cheekbones had worked with him, sat with him in cafés, talked with him, and for all I know, made love with him. At midnight we found ourselves standing on the high steps of the church of St. John Lateran singing together very loud a Magyar theme from Kodaly's *Hary Janos:*

Ti-szán in-nen Du-nán túl túl   a Ti szán van egy csi-kós nyá jas túl

I didn't get to Milan until after the German surrender. No opera there, for La Scala had been badly damaged. The stalls were

white with plaster and there was blue sky instead of ceiling. Three
air bombs had gone through the roof, and more than a year would
pass before the noble old house where Toscanini had reigned was
fully repaired and operating once more.*

My journey to Milan at war's end for a brief trip to Switzerland
took twenty-eight hours by train from Rome, a ride that in normal
times takes five or six. Italy has many small rivers, all the old bridges
had been bombed out, and the train had to inch its way cautiously
over the temporary replacements. On the return train from Milan,
equally deadly, I made friends with my compartment mates, two
army sergeants, one of whom was small enough to sleep comfortably
in the baggage rack. I had to sleep on the floor. The sergeants were
getting off at Pisa, where they were stationed as guards at the prison
stockade. They told me about a crazy old man they had to look after,
an American who had assed around with the Fascists, broadcasting
propaganda and such. Everybody at the stockade called him Ezra,
but the sergeants didn't know his last name. After hours, they said,
he was allowed the run of the camp commandant's office, where they
let him use one of the typewriters. He was typing Chinese poems,
the sergeants said, real nut stuff. Since I seemed interested, they invited me to break my journey at Pisa to come have a look at Ezra.
They were sure their captain would let me see him; he was a good
Joe. Reluctantly I declined. I was overdue at Naples. Besides, I didn't
feel much like gawking at the man as he sat there grizzled and wild
like his mad Pierre Vidal, tapping out his Chinese poems from
which, the sergeants said, he rarely looked up at anybody, not even
the captain. What could I have said to him? Only that there were
certain lines of his hard to forget:

> *I am thy soul, Nikoptis. I have watched*
> *These five millennia, and thy dead eyes*
> *Moved not, nor ever answer my desire . . .*

I turned down another invitation on that long haul back from
Milan. On the last leg, I had to take the ride on an Army truck
driven by a German POW from Rome (still the end of the train line)
to Naples. Three Army reporters for the *Stars and Stripes,* all ser-

---

* Years later on a tour of Europe, Yogi Berra, then manager of the New York
Yankees, heard his first opera, *Tosca,* at La Scala. Afterward, an American reporter
asked him how he had liked it. "Okay," Yogi said. "Even the music was good!"

geants, packed in beside me and we chatted the hours away, sitting quietly only when the truck ground slowly past the great shattered hill of Monte Cassino, where the Allied advance to Rome had been held up for so long, and at what cost! The reporters told me they were hopping off the truck at Aversa to cover the execution of German General Anton Dostler, who was to be shot that very day. Back in March 1944, an American reconnaissance unit had been put ashore from a small boat to blow up a tunnel between Genoa and La Spezia. They were caught by the Germans and, although in uniform when captured, had been shot out of hand by order of General Dostler under the Hitler commando directive. Dostler had been tried by an American military tribunal in Rome, and now he was going to be shot himself at the Aversa stockade. Wouldn't I like to come and see the show? They'd take me in with them. I said I'd take a rain check. Later in Naples I ran into one of the men from the *Stars and Stripes* up at the Camaldoli monastery enjoying the view. He told me the whole thing had gone off without a hitch. What seemed to stick in his mind was the way bits of gray fluff from the general's tunic flew out from his back when the rounds hit him.

My Stateside orders had come in at last, and a few friends sent parting gifts. George Weiss, an Air Force pilot from Foggia, brought over a watercolor he had painted, a North African landscape he knew I liked. Mario Cassadi of the Italian Navy (he worked at Navy House in liaison with Dick Dale, my Royal Navy opposite number) got his comrade Lieutenant Siro, submariner and war artist, to make me a picture of the LST 995. Liliana Mormile did a portrait of me at her house up on the Vomero. She later exhibited it at a show in the Bottega d'Arte on the Via Dei Mille, but it didn't win a prize. In parting she gave me an Italian translation of *Tonio Kröger* and a black-and-gold shoulderboard from her old Fascist uniform.

Finally one morning the great slow transport, loaded with returning troops, backed away from a gray dock into a gray harbor. The voyage was without incident save at the beginning. There was a stowaway on the ship, a pinch-faced little Italian girl who looked about eight years old, maybe nine. They found her aboard just five minutes after the Italian pilot dropped away. Thin and cold in her rusty black dress, she was sitting behind a life raft on the port side of the boat deck when they discovered her. How she sneaked by the ordinarily sharp Marine guards on the gangways will remain a minor puzzle of demobilization history. Of course, it was only a matter of minutes to recall the pilot boat by radio. The transport's skipper ordered the waif hauled up before him and dismissed her briefly, for he was preoccupied with the safety of his ship in the local waters where mines still turned up. She was sent down from the bridge under escort of the junior officer of the deck, a red-headed mustang ensign, to the main deck. GIs and ship's company crowded around the mite as she stood woefully by the rail with her embarrassed officer escort. They tried to get her to talk, but she stood mute, hanging her head and pulling at a fold in her dress. She did accept a candy bar, however.

"Come on, sister, what's your name?" a soldier in dungarees said, squatting beside her.

"She don't capeesh," a sergeant said. "Speak Eyetalian to her, Mike." He nudged Mike.

"Hey kid, *vieni qua!*" Mike said. *"Come si chiama?"*

She shook her head. Somebody hooted *"Prego dago!"* and got the standard echo *"Grazie Nazi!"* The soldiers meant it kindly; they were just nervous and excited.

"Whaddaya wanna go to the States for anyway? See the high buildings?"

"Nah," said the sergeant. "She wants to be a GI war bride!"

That got a laugh all around. She sniffed and rubbed at her dirt-stained cheek, but no tears came.

"Leave the kid alone!" the mustang ensign said to the sergeant. The GIs, silent now, shifted uneasily while the ensign looked anxiously over the side for the pilot boat.

"Poor little bastard," someone muttered. "Look at her arms." They were thin, and the dark patches under her eyes did not go well with the pallor of her pinched face.

"So why *couldn't* we take her along?" The sergeant who had made the crack about the GI brides got to his feet. "What the hell, we could feed . . ." The mustang ensign shook his head. The ship had hove to now and rolled easily in the swell. Someone yelled "Pilot!" and we all crowded the rail to watch the boat make fast.

The mustang ensign picked her up in his arms and moved toward the rail. The child peered fearfully down toward the gray water below, then stiffened in fright.

"Don't be scared," the ensign said. "We've got a special bosun's chair for you. You'll like that. Nice ride." He turned his head. "Hey Boats, let's go!"

A heavy-set chief pushed through the crowd, carrying a short board with lines attached.

"Christ, are you gonna put the kid over the side in *that?*" the first sergeant asked.

"Safe as a church," said the J.O.O.D. "Okay, chief?" Together they lashed her securely to the board in a sitting position. She was white and scared, but not crying. She was clutching the candy bar in her right hand.

The chief and two seamen heaved up the bosun's chair with the little girl made fast to it. As they swung her around, she faced inboard for a moment, with the wind blowing her matted black hair away from her face. She didn't say anything, but gave a little goodbye wave with her right hand, the one holding the candy bar. It was a Baby Ruth.

There was a ragged chorus of goodbyes, take it easys, and arrivedercis that quickly fell dead. The quiet was broken by the J.O.O.D.'s "Lower away," needlessly sharp. A couple of seamen paid out the line slowly, taking care not to bang the rig against the side. On the forward deck of the pilot boat, the Italian boatman caught her gracefully.

The crowd at the rail didn't break up until some time after the transport had got under way again and the pilot boat was nearly out of sight. Word was passed to secure the special sea detail, and the ship pointed its lead-colored nose toward Gibraltar, to the western sea beyond, to an America that would never be the same again.

PART

III

BARNARD: MONTY & HELEN

ᢒᢇ Someone told me that Yale was looking for instructors for their expanding postwar philosophy department, so I went up to New Haven, where the annual meeting of the American Philosophical Association was being held. The place crawled with philosophy teachers and graduate students listening to papers being read or fraternizing with colleagues and friends. Younger scholars, many of them war veterans, queued up for interviews with department heads of colleges and universities that had teaching jobs to offer.

Taken individually, philosophy teachers and graduate students seem just as nice as anyone else. God loves them, and they have immortal souls, as have members of other professional associations. But to behold them in the mass is another matter. To this day the sight of thousands of them at a meeting of the American Philosophical Association plunges me into a state of agitated depression. Instantly I am back at those early meetings where people avoided you if they thought you were unimportant or couldn't do anything for them, or if you were looking for a job. You talked with them, they smiled cordially at you, but all the time their eyes were shifting away to look across the hall to see if they could spy someone of more substance to whom they had to say a few words, leaving you with their unspoken, "You do not interest me."

On that day I stood respectfully before the chairman of Yale's philosophy department, an older man, precise, judicious, rimless glasses. He had the measured dignity of a man who knows his worth, moves deliberately, and makes no unnecessary gestures. At the end of each interview he carefully wrote down something about the candidate in a little black notebook he held in his hand. Now he looked at me.

"Your name suggests that you may be a Roman Catholic."

When they say "Roman" that way, I thought, you may as well pick up your marbles and go home. I was tempted to ask what difference it made. Instead I suggested that I was a Catholic by upbringing and tradition, but that I did not go to Mass every Sunday nor did I take orders from the Pope. He glanced at my *vita* on a piece of typed paper. It appeared that I had taught at a Catholic college for some years. In view of the liberal views I claimed, would I comment on that? I didn't think it useful to discuss the Ursuline doubts as to the orthodoxy of my teaching, so I just said what I had taught there mostly was formal logic. Was I a Thomist? No. What *was* I then? Not anything, really, I said; I had no particular philosophical point of view I could identify. I just liked philosophy and enjoyed teaching it. The chairman of department thought for a moment. Would I consider myself bound by Catholic doctrine in any way that would affect my teaching of philosophy? I said that I did not consider myself so bound. He asked a few perfunctory questions about my graduate work, intimated that there was something to be desired in my training in the history of philosophy, then closed the interview by making a neat glyph in his little black notebook.

The Yale trip came awhile after that day I had thrown my duffel bag down on the walk in front of our house in New Rochelle and run up the steps to Mary waiting there on the porch, four-year-old Peter beside her solemnly holding a little American flag in his hand. Once inside the door we hugged one another for a while. Then Mary fetched from his crib in the next room a large, smiling infant I had never seen. In Naples I had learned of his arrival in this world when a communication watch officer handed me a Red Cross dispatch that had just come in to the radio shack. Now, fourteen months later, I was meeting Colin for the first time. After a bit the four of us made a tour of the house and garden. It was a lovely place we rented cheaply from an elderly New York businessman whose wife had died there. Sunday mornings he used to come out from the city to walk silently in the garden his wife had tended. But now he had sold it to a woman who asked us to leave because she wanted the house for her son and his new wife. The postwar housing push was on.

The fact of two children, the need to find other living quarters, the restlessness after a long tour overseas where the Navy provided for everything, all added up to the need to find a new job. Though I had received a cordial letter of welcome back to the College of New Rochelle, I did not want to stay there. I had to get out of the Catholic college business. For a while I thought of abandoning teaching. Maybe the Foreign Service, advertising copywriting, a job on *Time,* even free-lance work for magazines like Bill Nichols's *This Week,* which had bought a couple of my stories. I went into New York to see Bill at his office on Lexington Avenue, but he advised me to get back to the classroom—teachers were going to be needed in the postwar world. In the end I agreed with him, and that's why I went up to Yale to see the chairman of department, but my name suggested that I might be a Roman Catholic. So much for that.

Next day I went down to Columbia to see Irwin Edman, who had been on my committee when I defended my dissertation for the Ph.D., a project supervised by that gentle scholar, Horace Friess. Edman patted my knee and sent me across Broadway to Barnard, the women's undergraduate college of the university. He had recently talked with Monty and Helen, who had told him they were looking for an instructor. I already knew Monty rather well, for I had taken a course with him before entering military service and had from time to time been invited to his house in the Village. Monty was William Pepperell Montague, Johnsonian Professor of Philosophy at Columbia, and for many years head of the Barnard philosophy department. Helen was Helen Huss Parkhurst, his friend and colleague, who had recently taken over the Barnard chairmanship from him. Monty had been one of the New Realists in the old days and had known William James, Royce, Santayana, Palmer, and Munsterberg at Harvard.

Monty's book *Ways of Knowing* had a certain reputation in the late 1920s and early 1930s. The poet Yeats had been impressed by a 1926 review of it in the *Times Literary Supplement,* in which the reviewer reproduced Monty's summary of three possible beliefs about the nature of the world outside us: (1) Everything perceived, even so-called illusions, exists in the external world. (2) Nothing exists except in the mind as elements of experience. (3) The physical world, existing independently of our thinking, can be known through more or less unlike "representations." Against Bertrand Russell who, Yeats said, mixed (1) and (3), the poet defended the philosopher Berkeley's position that for something to exist, it must be in some mind—there is no material world existing independently of us:

> *And God-appointed Berkeley that proved all things a dream,*
> *That this pragmatical, preposterous pig of a world, its farrow*
> *   that so solid seem,*
> *Must vanish on the instant if the mind but change its theme.*

Yeats wrote to T. Sturge Moore, philosopher G. E. Moore's brother, that his own personal belief about the reality of the external world conformed to the position listed as (2) by Montague.

Monty was a character. With his rubicund nose and his air of insouciant dignity, he bore a remarkable resemblance to the comedian W. C. Fields—a likeness brought out by the art historian Julius Held, who drew a nearly full-length cartoon of Monty, wreathed and in Greek dress, for a retirement party we gave him at Barnard. Monty drove an old Lincoln Zephyr every day from his house near the Village to Morningside Heights and back again, simply by aiming it in the general direction of his destination, never looking where he was going save for an occasional glance out the window to correct the drift of the car. I was riding with him one day in midtown when a traffic cop stopped him for wavering over to the wrong side of the street in rush-hour traffic; the puzzled policeman let him go with a warning. Monty lived in a brownstone house on West Eleventh Street with his wife, a physician, and his colleague Helen Parkhurst. Each member of the *ménage à trois* occupied a separate floor, the three levels connected by an inside staircase. Dr. Montague worked at a municipal clinic for wayward girls with venereal infections. Monty liked to remark that the admission requirements of his wife's clinic resembled those of the old colleges that asked for competence in Latin and Greek; the young women were expected to offer gonorrhea or syphilis, preferably both.

Once Monty invited Mary and me as his guests to a Columbia dinner to honor a distinguished historian of philosophy from Cornell. Montague fascinated Mary by his way of letting his cigarette burn away neglected in his mouth, the ash drifting down over his front. From time to time Monty would reach in his pocket for his whisky, which he kept in a Listerine bottle. Mary dates her lifelong discomfort with academic types from that dinner. Everyone at our table talked loudly about everything he or she knew, but nobody listened to anyone else. One professor's wife arranged peas and carrots in a pattern on her plate, shouting for all to look, for this was the way atoms were put together to form a certain molecule. Well do I know these table conversations in academe. Spaniards of the Golden Age called such displays *bachilliera* after the habit of those with a new bachelor's degree from Salamanca of displaying their learning unasked. A wise fellow of those days, Juan Covarrubias, hit it off in his manual of morals in words that *nudniks* in philosophy departments should commit to memory:

> How great a discourtesy it is for someone who prides himself on his learning, when he finds himself in the company of serious persons, to try to push everything that is said too far merely to show off, and to turn a quiet conversation or a gathering that has other purposes into a formal disputation.

Mary was impressed by the man on her left, a strong-featured scholar with a German accent who said disrespectful things about people present. While the guest of honor was addressing us from the podium, the man nudged Mary, nodded toward the speaker's wife nearby, and whispered, "Isn't she ugly? Just imagine being married to that old bag!"

He told Mary his name was Paul Tillich and that he lectured at Union Theological seminary. Mary thought him very interesting.

Montague was an evolutionary theist. He believed that God did not fully exist yet, but was working in the world like a yeast. Most members of the Columbia department found any form of theism incompatible with their radical secularism. They preferred something called "Naturalism," a term used by Santayana and popularized at Columbia by Frederick Woodbridge and his junior John Herman Randall. Naturalists held that all events in this world or out of it had a natural explanation, not a supernatural one. Beyond Nature, there was simply more Nature. One might, in a pinch, talk about God as an ideal, but not as an actual being. Old John Dewey had allowed that the word *God* could be used to name the unity of our aspirations for human betterment. Others, like Ernest Nagel, held that the idea of God had become so thoroughly soaked with supernaturalism that it would be better to discard it, as a philosophical concept, altogether. Younger positivist philosophers thought it idle to dispute about the matter since the proposition "God exists" is neither true nor false, but meaningless.

Monty's Columbia colleagues regarded his quirky metaphysics with respectful amusement and named him Johnsonian Professor, an honor that carried with it no extra money. They used to send him all the philosophy buffs Irwin Edman couldn't handle—the amateur metaphysicians that walked in off the street—insurance salesmen, fur manufacturers, wholesale fish dealers, and the like, all of whom had thought up elaborate world-schemes the understanding of which they firmly believed would unriddle the mystery of the universe. Monty used to tell a story about pragmatist William James who was visited at Harvard by a Bostonian who had invented one of those weird cosmological schemes. All Being, she declared, was divided into two great principles, the Thick and the Thin. James told her that if only she had lived long ago in pre-Socratic Greece, her theory would have earned her an immortal place in the history of philosophy.

Monty was irritated by the philosophical errors of that terrible trio—Idealists, Pragmatists, and Positivists—but came down hardest on those who defended the Authoritarian Way of Knowledge, the characteristic epistemological method, he believed, of those loyal to the Vatican and the Kremlin. To Monty, as to Waymarsh of *The Ambassadors,* the Roman Catholic Church appeared as the octopus, the monster with bulging eyes. Although he liked me personally and supported me to the limit of his conscience for the Barnard instructorship, Monty could not get over his intense suspicion of anyone who had been brought up a Catholic and wished to move in the intellectual world. After indoctrination in that dangerous faith, how could one possibly escape a permanent, even if unconscious, *Catholic twist* of the mind? To Monty, being born a Catholic was rather like having a kind of congenital defect which, if not carefully watched, could rapidly deteriorate into intellectual malignancy. That I had gone to a Jesuit school, had actually taught at a Catholic college, fascinated him. He asked me confidentially (voice lowered, meaningful glances in the direction of the kitchen where the Montagues' Irish cook grimly presided), whether I really thought the majority of Roman priests were celibate. How did they *manage?* he wanted to know. At the time of my candidacy for the Barnard opening, he wrote me:

> I hope you understand that the fears which I express about Catholicism do not in any way represent the attitude of our college, which makes no discrimination toward prospective members of its faculty, but only our department opinion as to the need of the philosophy we teach being free from authoritarian bias of any kind, whether from Rome, Moscow, or Geneva. Monotheism, polytheism, or atheism are equally permissible attitudes for a teacher of philoso-

phy, so long as their respective hypotheses are not defended on authoritarian grounds.

At first, Monty's friend and colleague Helen Huss Parkhurst gave me a hard time too. Helen inhabited the third floor of the establishment on West Eleventh Street. Sixtyish, she looked like an amiable little witch, her gray hair combed in bangs yellowed by the Camels she chain-smoked. Helen came from that fine old Bryn Mawr tradition of feminism and scholarship associated with the leadership of M. Carey Thomas. "When I want an intelligent conversation," she once confided to me, "I go to a woman, not to a man." A sound scholar, Helen had written a solid if rather old-fashioned book on aesthetics, *Beauty and Other Forms of Value.* She was often mistaken for Helen Parkhurst, the progressive educator who founded (and was later fired from) New York's Dalton School. That confusion annoyed Barnard's Helen Parkhurst, who considered the Dalton Helen an awful person and made no secret of the fact that she had blackballed the latter for membership in the Cosmopolitan Club.

Barnard's Helen Parkhurst overflowed with energy, despite a diabetes so severe that she had to carry around with her little cans of orange juice in case of insulin shock. She had decorated the ceiling of the Barnard philosophy seminar room in blue and gold, embossed the ceiling with signs of the zodiac, covered benches with what appeared to be black samite. When, after some delay, I joined the Barnard faculty as instructor, she gave me books I could not afford to buy and sent little gifts to my children. She readied funds to lend John E. Smith—he taught philosophy and religion at Barnard before going on to a successful career at Yale—to help pay for the publication of his dissertation on Royce. At that time Columbia had a stupid rule, since rescinded, that no Ph.D. could be granted before the dissertation had been published or contracted for publication. Mary sold her engagement ring to help pay for mine.

Personally generous, Helen Parkhurst was ideologically severe. She had strong views on religion and shared Monty's profound distrust of the Roman Catholic Church. Though influenced by his romantic liberalism, she disassociated herself from his freewheeling metaphysics. "I don't believe there's a God," she told me, "and I *hope* there's no immortality." Despite my suspect background, she offered me a one-year appointment at Barnard provided that I met

Dean Gildersleeve's approval. But only for a year. After that, I'd better plan to move on. She promised to write to certain department heads she knew in other colleges to see if they had a less tenuous position to offer me. She knew of a particularly good opening coming up the following year at a respectable southern college, and she would write a strong letter to its dean on my behalf.

"I shall make no reference in my letter to religious issues," she told me. "However, I think you should know that the likelihood is that you would receive a questionnaire which would require you to commit yourself more fully as to your past and present affiliations. There are two points on which colleges in the South are adamant: divorce and Catholicism. You say you are entirely sincere in describing yourself as uncommitted to Catholic dogma. If this means what it seems to mean, your wisest course would be to join your wife's church. (She is a Presbyterian, is she not?) This would also be desirable in the case of trying for a job in the smaller colleges in the North."

"But I don't *want* to join the Presbyterian Church," I said. "If someone has to become Protestant to get a job teaching philosophy in an American secular college, academic freedom, free inquiry, and all those liberal ideas are a joke. Suppose I felt like walking into a Catholic church to hear Mass or just to sit down out of the heat of the day. I'd like to be able to do this with no questions asked."

"If you actually regard the Catholic Church," Helen replied, "merely as an unusually congenial place of prayer, you would not be cut off from it in that respect by affiliating yourself with a Protestant sect—any more than from a Buddhist temple or a Mohammedan mosque, both of which also offer an opportunity for praying to one's God. Mind you, it isn't particular beliefs about life and death and the universe that are the obstacles in Catholicism for me, but rather the authoritarian basis for them, and frankly, I'm more troubled by your apparent failure to understand this than by anything else. Your promise to treat metaphysical and other issues objectively would not be enough. What philosophy calls for is a whole-hearted preaching of the all-importance of each individual's use of reason and independence of thought. Perhaps the whole issue could be brought to focus in one's attitude to some historical figure in philosophy. Take Giordano Bruno, for example. To see Bruno as anything less than a martyr in the cause of free inquiry would leave me dissatisfied."

She looked at me worriedly from under her yellowed bangs. She was right in sensing a certain lack of sympathy on my part for the heretic gyrovague Bruno, one of those half-mad magic-masters who hung around the skirts of the Scholastic tradition during the Renaissance, their minds inflated with occult and Gnostic visions, and not interested in scientific method at all. Bruno was put to the stake in Rome's Campo de Fiore in 1600, and of course none of us approved of that. So it was not the moment to say that I thought Bruno was a nut. I kept still. Helen thought for a moment while she pressed another stub on the fuming pile of Camel butts in her ash tray.

"I tell you what might help. Before you accepted the appointment here, you might write out a Credo."

"A what?"

"A Credo. A full and frank statement of your basic philosophical and religious beliefs. Your ultimate concerns, as Paul Tillich says. I think it would be a way of clearing up any ambiguities that might remain in your case. But let me make it plain that I am not trying to dictate or to intrude on the privacy of your conscience."

Why did they think people must have "ultimate concerns"? I really didn't *have* any, and very little conscience to intrude in. All this emphasis on subjectivism, inwardness, and soul-searching struck me as having little to do with liberalism, free inquiry, scientific method, and the rest. It struck me as very Protestant. (But I didn't say that.) In any case I did not write my Credo. I declined the appointment under the terms offered to me: a salary of $2,400 with the rank of instructor. At New Rochelle I had been an associate professor, with a Ph.D. and a published book that had nothing to do with religion or theology. It had gotten some good reviews.

When I reminded Helen that I had a wife and two children to support and that we couldn't make ends meet on $2,400, she was sympathetic, but both she and Montague thought I should take the job, even at that low rank and salary, for my own professional good. Helen said that teaching at Barnard carried considerable prestige. She mentioned a novelist of note who had been invited by Dean Gildersleeve to teach a course of her choice at Barnard. Noted novelist wired back: DELIGHTED TO ACCEPT. GREAT HONOR. MONEY NO OBJECT.

Later when I became chairman of the Barnard philosophy department, I gave much attention to salary when interviewing candidates for teaching positions. In no case did I allude to the honor of the thing. I left that to the Irishman of old who, being run along to his testimonial dinner in a sedan chair without a bottom, observed that if it wasn't for the honor of the thing he might as well have come on foot. As for the candidates' religion or lack of it, my philosophy resembled that of another Irishman, Fluther (I saw Barry Fitzgerald do it) in O'Casey's *The Plough and the Stars,* "I think we ought to have as great a regard for religion as we can, so as to keep it out of as many things as possible."

All that worry about Catholics was not peculiar to Barnard College in those days. It was standard in academe, much of it a manifestation of what Peter Viereck called "the anti-Semitism of the liberals." Walter Kaufmann recalls that when the Thomist philosopher Jacques Maritain joined the Princeton faculty in 1948, a senior professor expressed fear that Maritain might try to convert his students to Roman Catholicism and profoundly hoped that the French scholar would not be assigned to undergraduate teaching. But the only recommendation Maritain ever made about the Princeton undergraduate curriculum was that Marxian studies should be taught as they were in Paris.

I leave it to others to tell the story of discrimination against Jews in American higher education. Barriers blocking their entrance into faculties of higher education did not tumble until the end of World War II. Islands of exception existed, like the New York City colleges, where Jews flourished. But even at liberal Columbia, where there was a number of Jews in the philosophy departments before the war, a future president of the American Sociological Society was told frankly by a senior professor who admired her work that she had two strikes against her: she was a woman and she was a Jew. But this obvious point of distinction can be made: many Jews wanted to become professors, but few Catholics did. Most Jews were oriented to higher education from their cradles, trained from childhood in the tradition of analytic and critical scholarship that is part of any good Jewish education. Irish-Catholics of my acquaintance wanted to be city employees, athletic coaches, lawyers (so did Jews), presidents of department stores (the president of Jewish-owned Stern's in New York was named Riordan), police commissioners, domestic prelates, or politicians. Nothing derogatory, as Fluther would say. Other things being equal, a good politician is as valuable as a good professor, if not more so. Nor are the categories exclusive—there's Wil-

son of the old days, Kissinger and Moynihan later. The kind of
teaching that attracted the Irish was the public school sort. In Boston
they quickly achieved virtual monopoly of the public school system,
a control analogous to that held until recently by Jews in New York
City. The respective monopolies stood until lately, when ethnic and
desegregation issues cracked the solid fronts in both cities. Call the
job of schoolteacher a classic means to upward social mobility, if you
like. Or if you wish to be hard on the Boston Irish, a fitting profession for those with small ambition, a municipal-clerk mentality, and
a desire to secure their pensions.

Helen Parkhurst and I ended our discussion on my consenting
to have an interview with Miss Gildersleeve. As head of the college,
Helen thought, the dean might be able to find a little more money
somewhere in the budget. Besides, no one could obtain a Barnard
appointment without the dean's personal scrutiny and approval. To
Helen and to all the older Barnard faculty, Miss Gildersleeve was
Barnard, just as de Gaulle was France.

BARNARD: GILDERSLEEVE &
MRS. MAC

ક્ર≫ "Well, Mr. Brennan, tell me something about yourself. I understand you are awaiting separation from the Navy. I have very warm
feelings for the Navy."

Dean Gildersleeve was trying to put me at my ease, but succeeded only in scaring me nearly to death. She *looked* scary, as Olive
Chancellor in Henry James's *The Bostonians* must have looked—
dark, haunted eyes in a strong, cadaverous face; long upper lip that
closed firmly over a grim mouth. Virginia Gildersleeve became dean
of Barnard in 1911 and remained head of the college for thirty-five
years, retiring in 1946 to make way for Millicent Carey McIntosh.

Barnard College is named after a nineteenth-century president
of Columbia University, Frederick Barnard. He opposed evolution
in the biological sciences, but not in higher education. In 1873 he
declared his belief that if Darwin's theory of evolution were proved,

then it would be impossible to believe in the existence of God. Should science demonstrate evolution to be true, he said, "Give me, then, pray, no more science. I will live on in my simple ignorance as my fathers did before me." Yet in the early controversies over coeducation, he had more progressive views. Beginning with 1879 his reports to the trustees of Columbia College set forth claims not only for the rights of women to higher education, but also for their admission to Columbia College on equal terms with men. President Barnard's trustees at Columbia conceded that arguments in favor of women's higher education had some weight. Bryn Mawr, Vassar, Mount Holyoke, Smith, and Wellesley had already come into existence in response to growing female aspiration to higher education. But Columbia trustees hesitated at the thought of women sitting in the same lecture rooms as Columbia students. Their presence would be distracting. Moreover, for women to take the same strenuous examinations as men might risk undue strain on female mental health. So President Barnard's plea for coeducation at Columbia was set aside in favor of a compromise arrangement: separate but (some day, it was hoped) equal facilities for women after "the plan of the Harvard Annex."

As it turned out, Barnard College followed a branching different from Harvard's Annex. Radcliffe never had a faculty of its own; Harvard instructors could only *repeat* their classes for Radcliffe students. Today, apart from the Radcliffe Institute—a graduate research center for women scholars—Radcliffe has been almost totally absorbed by Harvard. Radcliffe diplomas are no longer awarded; undergraduate men and women alike receive Harvard degrees.

In contrast, Barnard remained independent of Columbia in that up to now the college has retained its own faculty and trustees, as well as endowment. Yet it is the official undergraduate college for women at Columbia University. Columbia College, the university's own undergraduate school, is today still all-male. Young women under twenty-one who wish to take their bachelor's degrees from Columbia must enroll at Barnard. At graduation they receive their degrees from Columbia University. Women over twenty-one may, if qualified, enroll in the university's School of General Studies.

Over the years, Columbia and Barnard have moved closer, with more sharing of faculty and courses. The Barnard-Columbia agreement of 1974 permits almost total course cross-registration of Columbia and Barnard students. Yet under that agreement Barnard still remains independent of the university financially and retains its own trustees, president, and faculty. Many Columbia administrators resent the arrangement, for it means that Columbia College cannot admit women, as Princeton, Yale, and many other hitherto all-male institutions began to do in the early 1970s to their subsequent financial, academic, and social profit.

Traditionally, Barnard trustees, administration, and faculty have fought to preserve Barnard's autonomy, at the same time guarding the school's right, as a university college, to use university resources —Columbia courses and libraries, for example—on payment of an estimated fair share of the costs. The majority of Barnard students are either indifferent to proposals of complete merger with Columbia or actually favor it. To be where the boys are still exerts a strong pull on girls conditioned from childhood to look to college as a mate-finding as well as an educational institution. In the 1970s the women's movement and its effects stiffened the spines of a significant number of those who would otherwise have opted for full merger. But many believe it is only a matter of time before Barnard succumbs to increasing pressures from Columbia and allows itself and its students to be fully absorbed by the university.

Had it not been for the strong leadership of Virginia Gildersleeve in the first half of the century, it is likely that Barnard would have disappeared as an independent college for women long ago. Under her firm hand Barnard grew from a barely tolerated morganatic adjunct of Columbia to a university college, respected and autonomous, within Nicholas Murray Butler's scholarly imperium. Gildersleeve was a particularly able representative of that older generation of American women who made distinguished careers for themselves and did not think it necessary to apologize for their unmarried state. At the time of my interview with her shortly before her retirement in 1946, she was still glowing from her recent apotheosis at San Francisco. President Truman had sent her there as the only woman member of the United States delegation that helped frame the United Nations charter. That experience was followed by a flight to Japan with General MacArthur as companion. France was preparing to award her the cross of the Legion of Honor.

Like many personages who frighten people, Miss Gildersleeve was said to be shy. As a girl she had lost a brother dear to her and never got over it. Later she evaded the loneliness, so often the price talented unmarried women of her generation had to pay for their careers, by living part of every year with her friend Caroline Spurgeon, the English Shakespeare scholar. Miss Spurgeon died in 1942 in the New Mexico desert house the two shared as a vacation retreat, and the now-legendary Barnard dean lived alone once more.

But already she had fallen in love with a much younger woman, Elizabeth Reynard, an assistant professor of American Studies at Barnard. World War II brought them together and soon they were inseparable. When the Navy Department consulted Miss Gildersleeve about the part women's colleges might play in forming a women's reserve, Miss Gildersleeve sent Elizabeth Reynard to Washington as her representative plenipotentiary. Later, Gildersleeve became chairman of the Advisory Council on the Women's Reserve, and Reynard was the second WAVE officer to be commissioned. The first, Mildred McAfee Horton, president of Wellesley, became commandant of the WAVES.

Between the two of them, Gildersleeve and Reynard put Barnard on a war footing, and the college was soon jumping with paramilitary exercises. The curriculum bristled with auxiliary courses so that Barnard's "trained brains" (a favorite Gildersleeve phrase) might better serve a nation at war. When Miss Gildersleeve went to San Francisco for the ceremonies attending the signing of the United Nations charter, the Navy tactfully assigned Lieutenant Reynard as her personal aide. A photograph of the woman Virginia Gildersleeve describes as "this soft-voiced, small, feminine person . . . a uniformed officer of our senior military service" is set with poignant effect in the closing pages of Miss Gildersleeve's autobiography, *Many a Good Crusade.*

The Gildersleeve–Reynard relationship represented an interesting case of a social arrangement common among unmarried professional women, dating from those years of the nineteenth century when women began to enter professional life in small but significant numbers. That unmarried women should live together in affectionate friendship was widely accepted in the American past. Few seemed to worry about it or call it "lesbian." In recent years such relationships have excited scholarly interest. Anna Wells's biography of Mary Emma Woolley, president of Mount Holyoke College from 1900 to 1937, identifies as lesbian the long friendship between feminist Miss

Woolley and Jeanette Marks, professor of English literature, with whom she shared her home until her death in 1947. Nothing startling in this. Most people want to love and be loved, and their sexual lives adapt to the circumstances in which they find themselves—though it's my guess that many, if not most, of the well-known friendships between prominent unmarried women of the Woolley–Gildersleeve era, if erotic at all, were implicitly rather than overtly so.

Professional women of Gildersleeve's time were expected to be single, and the fact that she did not look like the marrying kind probably played a real, though subordinate, part in her selection as dean by the Barnard trustees. Barnard's first dean, Emily Jane Smith, alarmed the trustees by marrying a few years after her appointment. When, after a decent interval, she discovered she was pregnant, she resigned—to the relief of the trustees, who would have had to fire her if she had not.

In our own era of sexual permissiveness, I've noticed that academics are rather quick to apply "lesbian" to an unmarried woman whose closest friends are women, using the word not in the hearty "right-on" way of the militant Sapphists of the feminist Left, but in a pejorative, critical sense. More than one of Miss Gildersleeve's successors as Barnard heads have had to endure talk behind their backs of their alleged lesbian friendships with other women. These gossips were not witless students but mature and privileged types from the urban, academic world.

What made the Gildersleeve–Reynard friendship more noticeable was the way the aging dean wore her heart on her sleeve, giving her beloved friend the privileges and preferences of a court favorite. As the time for her retirement drew near, Miss Gildersleeve became obsessed with the notion that Reynard should be her successor as Barnard head and tried hard to get Nicholas Murray Butler to accept the idea. But the aged Columbia president by that time was in deplorable shape: blind, married to a second wife who (many believed) discouraged him from seeing his daughter by his first marriage, so that the old man had to totter over to the Faculty Club to visit with her. In any case, there was nothing President Butler could do about Miss Reynard. At Barnard, the trustees were unwilling and the faculty did not like her style at all. The end of the story is a little sad. Two years after Dean Gildersleeve's retirement, Elizabeth Reynard resigned from Barnard to live with her ailing chief in a refurbished (old-American) mansion in Bedford, Westchester County. The younger woman died first, after a painful and crippling illness. Virginia Gildersleeve lingered on until 1965.

Miss Gildersleeve concluded the interview with a friendly, "Well, Mr. Brennan, we shall explore the possibilities." (In academe, presidents, deans, department heads, and committees always "explore" things.) The masklike countenance brightened with a smile, and her parting handshake was almost literally upsetting. Developed over years on receiving lines as a technique to discourage guests from holding up the procession, Dean Gildersleeve's grip imparted a spin that turned me through two quadrants of a circle and quite unsettled the grace of my exit from her office in Milbank Hall. As it turned out, I had to decline the instructorship she offered me (at $2,400 per annum, still) and taught at the college during her final year only as part-time lecturer. My full-time Barnard service began with the first year of her successor, Mrs. McIntosh, whose title was soon changed by the trustees from dean to president of Barnard College.

Millicent Carey McIntosh turned out to be a short, sandy-haired woman with an air of earnest determination. She was equipped with small, keen blue eyes especially designed to deter human weakness. At Mrs. McIntosh's inauguration as head of the college, Katharine McBride, president of Bryn Mawr, made this clear:

> Millicent McIntosh unites in her character the highest qualities of firmness and honesty. The soul of integrity herself, she demands integrity in others. To those who need her help, to all who meet her in sincerity, she is kindness and understanding itself. But for the *irresponsible* and the *shifty,* she has neither tolerance nor time.

Since I belong more to the clan of the Shifty than to the tribe of Integrity, I did a little shifting in my seat right there. For the first year or two Mrs. McIntosh and I circled around each other warily. After that we became good friends.

Mrs. Mac firmly believed she was carrying on the great tradition of American feminism, although some militant feminists of Barnard's later years hooted disrespectfully at her high evaluation of domestic and wifely virtues. Mrs. Mac was the niece of M. Carey Thomas, early leader of the fight for quality higher education for women. The first woman to get a degree from Johns Hopkins, Miss Thomas had to sit behind a screen while attending classes. She became the most renowned of Bryn Mawr presidents and her ashes lie buried in the court near the college library. Mrs. Mac reminded us that her aunt did *not* say of Bryn Mawr women, "Only our failures marry," nor even "Only our failures *only* marry."

When Miss Thomas learned of her niece's near-simultaneous decisions to marry and to accept the headship of New York's fashionable Brearley School for girls (background of the film *The World of Henry Orient*), she thought about the job for a moment, then said, "Very well, Millicent, go ahead and take it. You can have your babies in the summer." With her husband, Dr. Rustin "Rusty" McIntosh, head of pediatrics at New York Babies' Hospital, Mrs. Mac had five of them. She never wearied of giving undergraduates, alumnae, and junior faculty of Barnard the benefit of advice based on her experience of marriage, family, and career.

Millicent McIntosh had unflagging energy and burned up a lot of it tidying Barnard, whose finances had fallen into disarray in the last years of the Gildersleeve era, as the old dean, bemused with her international role, paid diminishing attention to the college's fiscal state. When Mrs. Mac took office, the Barnard faculty was a little top-heavy with superannuated professors. She did her best to sweep them out, but faculty autonomy often blocked her broom. "Do you mean to say I can't *fire* him?" she asked plaintively while trying to get rid of some old coot with tenure. Grimly to a group of alumnae, "I was happy enough to come to the college at a moment when it could use my housewifely talents. . . . I can tell you that there is not one of them that has not been used." She was harder on women than men. She believed that the fatigue she heard middle-class women complain of stemmed from moral weakness. "Let's admit it," she'd say. "We women *enjoy* suffering. If you have good health, you have no *right* to be tired." I heard her tell a group of Barnard undergraduates that her newly married daughter was very happy and well-adjusted except for an unaccountable morning weariness that made it exceedingly difficult to get out of bed and start the day. Mrs. Mac found that matutinal lassitude hard to understand, though the young married women in her audience (they kept straight faces) did not.

Occasionally Mrs. McIntosh tried the patience of younger faculty members struggling to make ends meet by her well-meant advice on domestic economy. She infuriated more than one young faculty wife by telling them how to economize by buying cheaper cuts of meat. Advising those with lean purses, she seemed sometimes to forget that her success in combining marriage and career owed more than a little to the fact that, because of the high income she and Rusty enjoyed, she could afford to hire adequate domestic help. I remember soothing one instructor after he had heard Mrs. Mac entertaining a faculty group in the Deanery by accounts of her own children at Putney, a Vermont progressive school for the well-heeled, where one of the McIntosh offspring was pleased to find he could keep his pony at school. In reprisal some Barnard faculty members circulated unkind fables about the McIntosh family. One concerned the McIntosh daughter, a student at Radcliffe, who had to write a theme on some memorable personal experience for her writing course. Other young women handed in scorching papers with titles like "My First Time with a Harvard Boy" and "Pot and Mad Love in the East Village." But Mrs. Mac's daughter knew what she owed to herself and her family; her topic was "The Rainy Sunday We Stayed Home and Made Penuchi."

As part of her charge to graduating seniors, Mrs. Mac urged that they always keep one *difficult* book going in their personal reading. Was there a trace of Puritan heritage here—a conviction that if something is worthwhile it cannot be enjoyable? (Mrs. Mac's background was Quaker.) Years later I was reminded of that when John A. Hannah, appointed head of the U.S. Agency for International Development (AID) in 1969, reminisced about his accession to the presidency of Michigan State University. "It was too late for me to become academically respectable," he said, "but I did make a point of reading at least one book a week that I didn't want to read." To such souls, salt of the earth, virtue cannot be pleasant nor the good easy. For Mrs. Mac, life was earnest, and she was not amused to learn that Nietzsche took earnestness as an infallible sign of low metabolism. Hers, she assured me, was perfectly normal.

When the Kinsey Report on *Sexual Behavior in the Human Male* came out, some publisher hastily commissioned essays from prominent personages to include in a paperbound book about the Report. Mrs. Mac's piece bore the title "I Am Concerned." She was *always* concerned. Once she stopped me on Broadway between Bar-

nard and the main Columbia campus to tell me that the night before
she had finished reading Francis Steegmuller's new translation of
Madame Bovary and had been impressed by its moral implications.
To her, Flaubert's novel was a story of irresponsibility sternly dealt
with, of romantic silliness punished.

"Joe, do you have your students read *Madame Bovary* in your
Philosophy and the Novel course?"

I had to confess that they did not.

"You really ought to have it on your list. It might put some
sense into a few of those girls' heads."

In the fifties, the Ford Foundation began a six-year sponsorship
of a project called the Barnard Education Program to train a small
number of Barnard seniors for elementary and secondary school
teaching without having to major in Education (a discipline thought
unsuitable as a Barnard major) or having to fulfill the many inane
requirements for certification and teaching licenses laid down by the
State Education Department in Albany. My job was to organize and
chair a weekly meeting called the Education Colloquium, as well as
to devise and teach a course in Philosophy of Education. I decided
that guests would be offered twenty-five dollars expense money if they
came from off campus, nothing if they were Columbia people.

William Heard Kilpatrick, then in his nineties, spoke three
times. So did his fellow emeritus, George S. Counts, survivor of the
radical wing of the now defunct Progressive Education Association.
Lawrence Cremin, later president of Teachers College, came and
Harold Taylor, past president of Sarah Lawrence. Gilbert Highet
told our young aspirants how he almost became a pop musician,
modestly smiling at our expressions of relief that the threatened loss
to classical scholarship had been averted. Old-line liberals like Horace Kallen and Sidney Hook reminded us of what we owed to John
Dewey. B. F. Skinner came down from Harvard (for twenty-five
dollars) to tell us what his pigeons could do when positively reinforced. Marya Mannes swept in trailed by NBC sound men, and
diminutive journalist Harriet Van Horne made us think for a moment we were listening to Katherine Mansfield. (Harriet wore much
jewelry, and around her neck a small dead animal with glass eyes.)
George Sokolsky, the syndicated columnist, warned us of sinister
world events to come; the United States was fighting the Korean war,
and he correctly prophesied our future intervention in Indochina.

Nobel Prize winner physicist Polykarp Kusch followed Father Ludwig Räber, rector of the one-thousand-year-old school of the Benedictine monastery at Einsiedeln, Switzerland, model of "Mariafels" of Hermann Hesse's novel *The Glass Bead Game*.* When the Soviet cultural attaché came up from Washington to show us a film on education in the U.S.S.R., the film projector broke down. The Russian diplomat looked around the room, smiled nervously, used his best Soviet tact to bridge the pause:

"Is not technical institute. Is woman's college!"

One day, President McIntosh approached me on campus and asked, "Joe, when are you going to invite me to speak at your Education Colloquium?"

"Why, Mrs. McIntosh, this is so sudden!" I said, and invited her on the spot.

After she made her excellent talk, discussion ensued, and Mrs. Mac worked her way around, as was her wont, to matters domestic. She expressed her belief to the undergraduates present that it was a husband's *duty* to help his wife with housework. Suddenly she swung round to the chairman's table where I was daydreaming a little: "Don't you agree, Joe?"

I had better, since Mrs. Mac knew that I had small children. Of course I agreed, but ventured to ask if she cared to make any distinction between those responsibilities that might normally fall to the wife and those that should be dutifully assumed by the husband. Certainly there was a distinction, she said. For example, a husband could very well do the dishes, or even some laundry, but she did not think it was quite his job to put diapers on the baby. Would I accept that as a sample distinction? I, who fancied myself a diaperer of some skill, could not resist.

"That, Mrs. McIntosh, is what we philosophers call a distinction *a posteriori!*"

Always good to take a joke at her expense, she seemed sometimes ill at ease with the arty or overintense. One day she heard that Harold Taylor and I were having lunch at Barnard and asked if she could join us. Harold had brought along an unexpected guest, friendly Erick Hawkins, the well-known dancer and choreographer.

---

* Some years later, Rev. Dr. Räber reciprocated by inviting me to address his seminar in philosophy of education at the University of Fribourg (Switzerland), and I most enthusiastically did.

At the luncheon table, Hawkins directed his passionate attention to President McIntosh whom he believed to be a wonderful person:

"Ah, Mrs. McIntosh, I have always wanted to meet you. I feel— I feel your power, your vibrancy, your dynamism, your—*beauty!*"

Fixing the enraptured choreographer of "Here or Now with Watchers" with her stern and critical eye, M. Carey Thomas's niece uttered the flat monosyllable she often employed to end a line of conversation she considered had gone far enough:

"Yes."

Later she was pleased to hear of the success of Twyla Tharp who had studied dance with Hawkins, among others. Twyla transferred to Barnard in 1961, the year before Mrs. Mac's retirement, shifting her major from pre-medical studies to art history before graduating to the dance world where her choreography quickly attracted attention. "She is certainly not yet a good choreographer," sniffed Clive Barnes on seeing Twyla's "Re-Moves" in 1966, "yet she is bad in an interesting way." To an interviewer who asked if she had studied her art at Barnard, Twyla replied, "Dance at Barnard? Listen, I was taking three classes a day at different studios in the city. Why the hell would anyone want to flit around the Barnard gym when there were all those dance studios in New York?"

Many feminists rejected Mrs. McIntosh's doctrine of marriage-cum-career because of certain priorities she insisted that a wife yield to her husband. "Once you undertake marriage," she told her undergraduates, "your husband and family come first; whatever is best for them is best for you." Yet to this debatable statement of conjugal obligations of the woman's part, Mrs. Mac always added her conviction that for college graduates marriage is a partnership in which husband and wife plan their lives with awareness of need of the personal fulfillment of each. That a woman makes the most satisfactory wife and mother if she realizes herself intellectually as well as emotionally seemed to Mrs. Mac two perfectly compatible ideas. She was not troubled by the vagueness of notions like "self-fulfillment" and "self-realization" that turned into slogans in feminist discussions of later date. Easy enough now to make fun of Mrs. Mac's ideology of family-cum-career, but some of it stuck with the students and stayed with them after graduation. The president of a small New York advertising firm acknowledged her debt in 1976:

I was certainly one of the many Barnard students to be influenced by Dean McIntosh's philosophy of marriage and Do-Something. She articulated the importance of keeping yourself alive as an individual—whether through a career, volunteer work, or reading a book a week. At our recent twentieth reunion she added that since life is unpredictable, it behooves every woman to have some method of supporting herself, in case it is ever required. That advice is on target today as her basic philosophy was twenty-five years ago.

Later in 1976, this from a professional designer:

It was the president of Barnard, Millicent McIntosh, who was my strongest role model. She was an accomplished woman in a position of authority, the first woman I ever heard speak in a public convocation, openly, generously, about *both* her professional and private choices and experiences . . . a model which has had a most direct impact upon my attitudes and behaviors, as a professional designer and teacher.

Despite her belief in the priorities of husbands' requirements in marriage, Mrs. Mac blew up if a woman on her faculty reneged on what she considered a professional commitment. When an instructor wanted to quit in midsemester because her husband was being transferred to Texas, Mrs. Mac hit the ceiling despite the fact that the woman's department head had no particular objection to letting her go. Mrs. Mac had not yet cooled down when she told me about it: "I didn't know whether I was more furious at her or at the husband who put her up to it. Men simply have *no conscience* where their wives' professional obligations are concerned. I tell you, Joe, I gave her a bad quarter of an hour. If women want to be treated by men as professional equals, they must learn not to jump when their husbands snap their fingers."

Mrs. McIntosh returned to haunt the dreams of radical feminists of the 1970s. Toward the end of Erica Jong's *Fear of Flying*, the heroine, Isadora, experiences a revelation of self-identity, a moment of high resolve to go forth to forge in the smith of her soul the uncreated conscience of the race of women. Just before this epiphany comes a dream sequence in which Mrs. Mac appears. Isadora is back at her college graduation, mounting the steps of Columbia's Low Library to receive her diploma from Mrs. McIntosh. The Barnard president hands her a special scroll of honor, and remarks sternly, "I must tell you that the faculty does not approve of this," adding that only Isadora's high academic standing permits the presentation at all, and that the faculty hopes that she will voluntarily decline the honor. The scroll permits Isadora to have three husbands simultaneously.

My first sight of Erica Jong (Barnard '63) came as the result of a misunderstanding. I read a notice one day stating that Erica Mann would read her poems Thursday afternoon in the College Parlor. I assumed this meant Erika, the daughter of Thomas Mann, and went to the reading with Eugenio Florit, Professor of Spanish and a poet in his own right. Eugenio was under the same mistaken impression. Arriving a little late, we found a handsome undergraduate with shining blonde hair reading to a roomful of Barnard students a poem (as I recall it) about pomegranates and penises. It occurred to Professor Florit that he was having trouble with his hearing aid, and we quietly left. Erica acquired her better-known last name by her marriage, since dissolved, to a Chinese psychiatrist. Her academic record was indeed excellent, and at a talk to Barnard alumnae in the spring of 1976 she acknowledged her debt to the high quality instruction she got from the Barnard English department. She recalled that as an undergraduate she listened at Barnard to a visiting critic from "the rabbinical American literary Establishment," explaining that women can't write because they don't have blood and guts experience. She quoted Doris Lessing to the effect that long ago women learned not to interrupt when men start explaining why and how women can or cannot do this or that. Erica added that women writers find themselves in a dilemma: if they are tender, they are criticized for being soft; if Amazonian, hard. They just can't win.

The period at Barnard known as "early McIntosh" coincided with the reign of fear associated with various congressional committees investigating "un-American" activities. By 1953, Senator McCarthy had turned his attention to American colleges and universities allegedly infiltrated by Communists, fellow-travelers, and other subversives. It is hard to convey to those not around at the time a sense of the atmosphere of fear that pervaded so many levels of American life at the time. Nearly everyone in authority was terrified at the mere thought of McCarthy's baleful glare. Barnard President McIntosh was not frightened, but thought it prudent to draw up a plan just in case some investigating committee in Washington should summon a Barnard faculty member for questioning. One morning she called top administrators and department heads into her office (I had just become chairman of the philosophy department, due to the unexpected death of my predecessor, Gertrude Rich) and, after committing us to confidentiality, told us of her intention to propose to the Barnard trustees the following procedure:

(1) If one of us is called for questioning by a congressional committee, he shall be encouraged to answer questions freely.
(2) If he says that he was formerly a Communist but is no longer, the president's advisory committee shall talk with him to clarify his status.
(3) If he invokes the Fifth Amendment, he will be suspended temporarily, with pay. During the period of his suspension, a joint committee of faculty members and trustees will be appointed to investigate the situation and to make recommendations. It is expected that the committee's recommendations will normally fall into one of the three categories set down in the Harvard procedure: (a) Reinstatement with no penalty. (b) Reinstatement on probation for specified length of time. (c) Dismissal.*

Somebody leaked the news to the *New York Times* and the story came out in the paper next morning, noting Barnard's proposal to suspend any faculty member who invoked the Fifth Amendment. Mrs. McIntosh was wild. Confidence had been breached at that meeting and Barnard trustees wanted to know who was responsible. Despite an investigation laid on to hunt down the source of this un-Barnard activity, the informer was never, so far as I know, identified. In any case, the Barnard trustees refused to accept Mrs. Mac's recommendations. A conservative lawyer on the board stated his belief that no Barnard faculty member should be penalized by suspension, with or without pay, for invoking a constitutional right. What Harvard did or did not do was its own affair.

Some years later Mrs. McIntosh had the courage to appoint

* Use of the pronoun *he* without *she* throughout Mrs. McIntosh's proposal reflects older usage. Up to this time the only sure-fire Communist associated with the name of Barnard College was an alumna, Judith Coplan, a government employee, arrested in March 1949 by the FBI and charged with espionage. Judith Coplan's trial ran about the same time as the first Alger Hiss trial. She was found guilty, but her conviction was later reversed.

Stanley Moore, an admitted former Communist, to the Barnard philosophy department on my recommendation at a time when no college in the country would touch him. (Samuel Milbank, then president of Barnard's board of trustees, backed her up.) Stanley Moore was a handsome, brilliant scholar, a former member of the faculty of Reed College in Oregon where he had quickly risen to the rank of full professor. During World War II he had served as an Army captain in the European theater, where he met his first wife, war correspondent Marguerite Higgins. During postwar congressional investigations it came out that Stanley had at one time belonged to the Communist Party. Subpoenaed by the House Committee on Un-American Activities, Moore admitted his former membership in the Party but refused to give the names of suspect colleagues. He was interrogated at length both in Washington and at Reed College. Despite the opinion of one board member who, after taking Moore to lunch, pronounced him "a real American and a Republican at heart," Moore was fired by the Reed trustees.

For years Stanley Moore was unemployable. But Barnard and Millicent McIntosh took him back from exile into academe, and he taught happily on Morningside Heights until Mrs. McIntosh retired as president. Her successor, Rosemary Park, declined to promote Moore, in effect dropping him from the faculty. His Communist past did not bother her so much as his personal style; nor was she impressed by his book on Marx's critique of capitalist democracy. Moore was an extraordinarily well-read man (less common among college professors than you might think) and the faculty admired him. To make an amusing point at lunch in the Barnard faculty dining room, he could quote Proust or Rilke as easily as he could cite Engels or Plekhanov. Yet despite faculty support and an assortment of Moore fans that included Herbert Marcuse, the Barnard *Bulletin,* and Erica Jong (she pronounced her course with him "the best I ever took at Barnard"), Stanley Moore was let go. He returned to his native state to join the faculty of the University of California (San Diego) where William McGill, at that time president at San Diego, led the subsequent fight for Stanley Moore's retention against Berkeley and the political powers at Sacramento. The fight was won. Stanley was awarded tenure and a full professorship.

Soon after Stanley Moore's departure from Barnard, Rosemary Park resigned from the Barnard presidency (Columbia could not find a place on its faculty for her husband, a Byzantine scholar from California) and followed Moore's track to the University of California, where she became a university vice-chancellor. Tiring of that post ("They sent me all the crud!"), she accepted another with the title Professor of Higher Education. Then William McGill, Moore's defender at San Diego, left the University of California for the East Coast to take on the presidency of Columbia University. As for Erica Jong, the inclusion of "a professor of philosophy (U. Cal.)" as one of Isadora's lovers in *Fear of Flying* has been interpreted as a tip of her hat to Moore, though not necessarily to be taken as an autobiographical reference.

One last incident from Mrs. McIntosh's early days at Barnard in the era of anti-Communist excitement. A young Barnard philosophy instructor, far from home and family, informed me as her department chairman that she planned to marry a man, unemployed and penniless, who was a card-carrying member of the Communist Party, U.S.A. Would it make any difference to her Barnard job? Not to me, I said, but as a matter of prudence she should let Mrs. Mac know about it just in case the newspapers got hold of it first. She left for the president's office, shaking. Mrs. McIntosh heard her through, frowned a bit, then offered her the Barnard Deanery for her wedding reception. The offer was accepted with joyous relief, and on the following Saturday an improbable group of characters of all shades of race and ideology gathered in Dean Gildersleeve's old drawing room for the rite. After the ceremony we toasted the couple in champagne donated by the president of the college.

It was American champagne, sensibly priced.

I saw her last in the fall of 1976 at Jacquelyn Mattfeld's inauguration as Barnard's fourth president. On final sabbatical leave at the time, I had not planned to come in to New York for the ceremony in Morningside Heights' Riverside Church until the secretary of the inaugural committee phoned to say that Mrs. Mac had requested that I be her partner in the academic procession. So there was much hurried demothballing and airing of my cap and gown as well as stitching, for with the years the old gown had acquired as many rents as the robe of some Pharisee outraged by an upstart rabbi millennia ago. Mrs. Mattfeld, who took her doctorate in music at Yale, asked for plenty of it at her inaugural; so organ, brass, and the Barnard-Columbia choir obliged with some of her favorite Renaissance and seventeenth-century bits. The Barnard board of trustees had contrived a large medal, a new insignia of office for this and future Barnard presidents. As the emblem was ceremoniously hung about her neck, choir and brass burst out into a "Hosanna" from some Renaissance Mass. While multiple and reiterated hosannas rang through the packed cathedrallike interior of Riverside, spotlights played on Jackie Mattfeld's thrown-back face, all bones, intense, blond, smiling, saviorlike. For a moment I expected a segue into "Jesus Christ Super Star."

Afterwards, while I was walking Mrs. Mac to her car, I asked how she had liked the music. She said it was very nice, but there was just too much *of* it. I warned her that I planned to put her in some pages of a book and that, while admiration for her was expressed in them, there would also be some teasing things said. She looked at me:

"Well, I should hope so."

LEVITTOWN

༨ Levittown, Long Island, may some day find a Nathanael West to be its Homer. We moved there in 1948 to make do on my Barnard instructor's salary, and stayed until the early 1950s. That period was Levittown's golden age.

William J. Levitt, blasting cap of the postwar Long Island housing boom, began his project in 1947 with a few hundred low-rent houses for World War II veterans. It was built on tracts of potato farmland that had been infested by the golden nematode. Hundreds of houses turned into thousands, and the monster Levitt development thirty miles east on the Island from Manhattan spread quickly across a half-dozen rural school and tax districts. By the early fifties, Levittown's population passed the twenty-five thousand mark, a figure that has now more than tripled. It is hard to give accurate figures on Levittown since it is not a single political entity, but a name applied to a large area of Long Island's central plain where the houses are Levitt-built, but which crosses various township, community, school, and postal-district lines. The first Levittown houses were built

in what used to be called the Jerusalem school district, and that became Levittown proper. But miles of Levitt houses soon spilled across
the borders of School District Number 5 into adjoining communities
with older names like Hicksville, Wantagh, and Island Trees. The
place name Jerusalem has now disappeared, which some antiquarians
regret for they like the old Biblical names of certain Long Island
communities like Jericho and Babylon. Bethpage, where we live
now, gets its name from the place where Jesus paused on his way
from Jericho to Jerusalem.

The original Levitt houses were garageless two-bedroom Cape
Cods with unfinished attics. The houses sat on neat squares of lawn
and lined streets curved to form mazes so complex that many early
Levittowners on their way home from work had to knock on doors
to be steered in the direction of their own. Levitt houses were decent
and comfortable save for the floors on winter mornings when, on the
way to the bathroom, your feet met the heat from copper coils buried
under the floor tiles and you had to dance like St. Sebastian on the
hot coals. Original Levitt Cape Cods rented only to veterans at sixty-
five dollars a month. Ranch houses first built in 1949 sold for five
thousand dollars and could be secured for veterans for a down payment of one hundred dollars. Those who bought them early, before
the community was opened to nonveterans and the rental units
phased out, turned a neat profit when they sold them. In 1976 those
same Levitt houses, whether or not improved by garages or other
additions, were selling for a minimum of thirty thousand dollars.

Levittown rapidly filled up with young couples from all parts
of the country, hard-working, ambitious, and fertile. As the early
inhabitants moved up the economic ladder and out of Levittown to
larger quarters for their growing families, their places were taken by
an older crowd moving out from Brooklyn and Queens. But in the
first years of the expanding community the population was young,
jumping, and miscellaneous. No blacks, though. Original Levittown
leases contained a lily-white clause binding the lessee against renting
to or harboring, except as servants, persons "not of the Causasian
race." I wrote in protest of this clause and so did a number of veterans whose doubts concerning racial matters had been deepened by
visits to certain camps in Germany and Poland at the war's end. The
Caucasian clause quietly dropped from Levitt leases and sales contracts. In any case, blacks showed little inclination to move out to

Levittown, since they lacked the economic basis to sustain themselves in a commuter enclave so far from New York and so deficient in public transportation.

Levittown had no direct rail link to the city, where most original breadwinners of the community worked. One had to go three miles north to Hicksville or three miles south to Wantagh to get a train to New York. Car pools were a near-necessity in the community's first years. We had a small yellow Crosley that made only a few pool trips before its wretched little engine burned out. Car pools helped to form strong social bonds. So did the morning coffee visits of the wives in Levittown kitchens.

Levittown's relative isolation and its large, energetic population brought civic heat quickly to a boil. Scores of community organizations sprang into being. Some coexisted happily, others waged bitter guerrilla war on one another. Ideological lines quickly divided Levittown into two main factions. Catholics tended to be conservative and suspicious of radicalism. Jews, on the whole, were liberal and very active in educational affairs. Protestants divided between the two camps. Soon it became sociological chic to do surveys of Levittown, and the giant community quickly turned into a happy hunting ground for young social scientists doing their Ph.D. dissertations. As public library trustee and chairman of the District 5 education association (a reform group very unpopular with the local school board and administrators), I was frequently interviewed.

When we Levittown pioneers arrived in the new community there was no public library, so a self-appointed library committee visited Bill Levitt to ask his help in establishing one. The busy man referred us to his father, Abraham Levitt, known as Vice-President in Charge of Grass Seed. Old Abraham had strong feelings about watering the greenery that the Levitt builders had neatly planted around each house. "Had I the power," the patriarch growled, "I would send to jail those who water shrubbery with the direct stream of a hose. That is murder!" Father Abraham expressed sympathy for our desire for a public library and drove the committee around to look at possible sites, promising us that he would ask son Bill to donate land, not a building, if we could get tax support from the Levittown citizenry.

That wasn't easy. Reflecting the anxieties of the surviving farmer population of the area, the local school board discouraged our bookish ambitions. Later, when we had succeeded in getting a budget, the school board treasurer brought suit against us in Albany under the state education law on charges that we planned to squander public money on a bookmobile, an unnecessary and dangerous object. The Long Island newspaper *Newsday*, itself growing phenomenally, printed letters to the editor denouncing library partisans as wastrels, pseudointellectuals, pinkos, schoolteachers, and Communists. We even collided with the bloodmobile group, whose zealous partisans wanted to keep all Levittown in a chronic state of civic hemorrhage. To anyone who granted their sanguinary premises, they proved with rigorous logic that a bloodmobile would mean more to the community than a bookmobile. Extremists circulated flyers showing an expiring baby with the legend, "Books Will Not Save This Dying Child." The infant mortality rate in Levittown at this time was just about zero.

A stormy school district meeting in 1950 ended with the taxpayers voting by a narrow margin to establish a public library with an annual budget of fifty thousand dollars. So the library committee became trustees of a storefront library on one of Levittown's "Village Greens," where we hung on by our fingernails in constant fear of reprisals. For no sooner had the library been established than a community move to abolish it was begun. At that time it was still possible to terminate the existence of a public library by taxpayers' vote. To defend ourselves we tried to get one of the community's most distinguished citizens, Judge Norman W. Horowitz, to join the library board of trustees. At first His Honor expressed pleasure at the invitation and prepared to lend the board prestige by contributing his presence. But someone advised him that the library trustees were considered a "controversial" (Levittown euphemism for "Communist") group, and the judge, now justice of a high court of the state of New York, told us of his second thoughts:

> I am more than happy to become a member of any organization which works for the good of the Levittown community. I have dedicated myself to that good. But it would not be to our mutual advantage for me to engage in anything promiscuous. I will support any worthwhile civic enterprise, but nothing promiscuous, you understand. I'm sure, nothing promiscuous!

As library trustee I had occasion to consult with representatives of the local Butterfly and Moth Society concerning a place of meeting. The cocoon hunts had a certain reputation as rather dashing affairs. As a courtesy, I was given a ride in one of their lead cars at a nocturnal moth-and-cocoon stalking. When members spied their prey, they would leap from their cars to snatch specimens of the elusive Hymenoptera like white hunters in Africa of old, jumping from their Land Rovers, Mannlicher 6.5s at full cock. Once, two indignant female members of the society were questioned by police in a patrol car for their loitering at night around street lights in a community adjoining Levittown. Nothing promiscuous—all they were soliciting was moths.

Levittown school board trustees varied in character, some intelligent and competent, others about halfway between *Pithecanthropus erectus* and early Neanderthal. The primitive types often used their position to discharge personal *Angst* in speeches replete with agrammatical appeals to God, patriotism, and moral decency. Since for a long time they were nearly the only outlet for political emotion, taxpayers' meetings resembled Tim Finnegan's wake, and terrifying fights went on sometimes until five in the morning. So fearful did those public displays of civic boneheadedness become that the state legislature had to pass statutes to confine the brawls within the conventions of civilized warfare. Battles for control of school boards swung ding-dong. Neanderthals would hold office for a couple of years until the voters kicked them off the board in sheer disgust. For a time they would be replaced by progressives, referred to contemptuously by their opponents as "People-Lovers," a few of whom *were* a little irritating. People-Lovers included militant humanists, ethical culturalists, radical Unitarians, ADA stalwarts, earnest global-thinkers, natural childbirth enthusiasts, vasectomy advocates, ethnic "understanders" who imported black children by the day to play in puzzled dignity in Levittown back yards with virtuous neighbors invited to look on over the fence. Another two years and bingo! Off the school board would go the People-Lovers with their Democratic Values and Understanding of Others, and back came the Neanderthals with their God, American Flag, and Censorship.

Like the guardians of Plato's Republic, Levittown school board conservatives were much given to censorship of arts and letters.* One

* Censorship became a Levittown tradition. As recently as March 1976, trustees of the Island Trees School District removed from school shelves at night a number of books they considered objectionable. At a news conference held after the raid, a board member read bits from Kurt Vonnegut's *Slaughterhouse-Five*, noting passages in which Jesus Christ was called a bum and a nobody. Conservative parents approved the

school district destroyed a batch of Young People's Records when a local veterans' organization discovered that an American Legion council in California had determined that one of the officers of the company that manufactured the records had at one time been a member of a Communist-front organization. So smash went the records of "The Little Fireman," "The Little Brass Band," and the rest—terrible records, really, but they should have been junked for aesthetic, not for political, reasons. A caboose of censorship followed the cantata "The Lonesome Train" all around Long Island's new suburbia, not on account of its subject—Abe Lincoln's funeral—but because the composer or his Uncle Max had taken the Fifth down in Washington. Our neighbor Westbury's community orchestra could not use the public school of that locale because, for one thing, a singer who had performed at a past concert had publicly defended the Rosenbergs.

Levittown school drama productions were carefully checked for hints of illicit love. An adult amateur group was forbidden use of the public school buildings for their performance of *Come Back, Little Sheba.* "The play has sex in it," said Mrs. Keogh, the assistant principal, "and our children should not have *assess* to it."

She need not have worried. Children and parents alike stayed comfortably at home in their small Levitt living rooms, one and all enjoying assess to that new wonder, television. Every afternoon at five the kids religiously watched Buffalo Bob Smith's "Howdy Doody Show." ("Say, kids, what time is it?") Our own children were proud to be able to tell their schoolmates that Clarabel, the clown who blew his little horn and squirted people with seltzer water, was really Mr. Lew Anderson, who lived down the street from us on the corner of Cord and Homestead Lane. We grownups tried never to miss "Victory at Sea" or "The Show of Shows" with Sid Caesar and Imogene Coca, and those unforgettable dancers, the Hamilton Trio. As a philosophy teacher, I cheered Caesar's portrayal of the German professor interviewed by reporters on his new metaphysical book which, like an important section of Heidegger's *Sein und Zeit,* was about Nothing.

We went on television ourselves at the time, thanks to our oldest

---

removal of the alleged "garbage." Liberals were outraged. The president of the local teachers' association compared the seizure in the Bicentennial year to the action of George III against the American colonies.

child, Peter, then twelve, and his budget-minded mother, who capi-
talized on her son's enterprising spirit. On his own, Peter decided he
wanted to join the Marines when he grew up, and he wrote a letter
to that effect to their recruiting office in Hempstead. The recruiter,
a master sergeant, saw a chance for a little publicity for his service
and arranged a well-photographed ceremony in which Peter was
made an honorary sergeant in the U.S. Marine Corps. They gave
him a small Marine shirt with red sergeant's stripes and a framed
certificate to go with it. Mary sent in one of the pictures to John
Reed King, master of ceremonies of "There's One in Every Family,"
a popular daytime television program that featured families with a
member who did something unusual.

She was promptly notified to appear at CBS with all the family
and the Marine recruiter. On the morning arranged, eight of us
piled into a military station wagon—Mary, the recruiter, and I, plus
five children, the youngest of whom, Nick, was still in his portable
bassinet—and drove to New York. During the program all of us sat
on camera while Peter and his recruiter were presented to the studio
audience. The M.C. then interviewed Mary while the recruiter held
little Nick. The audience was then asked to show by their applause what money (thirty, forty, or fifty dollars) Peter should be
given for each successful answer to the series of questions about to
be put to him. Their enthusiastic response was carefully measured
by an impressive applause meter, and Peter got the maximum. (From
backstage we could see two men behind the applause meter, one
cranking up the red line, the other ringing the bell.) Peter was asked
to complete pairs of names: Hansel–Gretel, Roy Rogers–Dale Evans,
and the like. He correctly answered five hundred dollars' worth of
questions, and in addition we were all given prizes.

We must have made something of a hit, for in a few weeks we
were invited back for a repeat performance, this time with Mike
Wallace as M.C. Peter didn't have quite as much luck this time,
for Mike Wallace pulled a stopper on him by asking him to shut his
eyes and tell him what color tie he (Mike) was wearing—a rather
tough question, since between the studio and the CBS office where
Peter first met him Mike had changed his tie. But Peter got a couple
of hundred dollars more and additional prizes were dragged out for
us. Altogether, besides Peter's cash, we took home a Tappan Gas
range, a red Huffey bicycle, a yellow Irish Mail, a Tiny Tears doll

(for Ainslie), a set of dishes, a wrist watch (for the Marine recruiter), a pedigreed cocker spaniel, and for me—not the handiest man in the world—a huge red metal box of Proto professional tools. To this day I don't know what some of them are *for,* though I still use a surviving adjustable wrench for fixing leaky faucets.

To avoid any possible appearance of public rivalry with Barnard's Millicent McIntosh, the number of whose children we equaled at that point, I asked John King and Mike Wallace to let me keep a low profile during the programs. When they turned to me briefly to ask what my job was I just smiled enthusiastically and said, "Teacher."

Teachers in the Levittown schools of those days were by no means docile. Most were young, inexperienced, and enthusiastic. Some had unusual and stimulating ideas. A young fourth-grade teacher refused to take her class on field trips to such tired old places as the Hempstead town sewage disposal plant, one of the regular stops on the school "enrichment" program. She preferred instead to lead her charges to the more refreshing air of Belmont racetrack, just over the Queens border from Nassau County. A snag developed when the teacher requested her class to ask their parents for two dollars each so she could bet it for them on the ponies. Some puritan spoilsport telephoned the school office and the party was canceled. The children were heartbroken—they did so want to see those ponies.

One bright young teacher constructed a pedagogical device that quickly achieved fame. It was a large assembly of plywood and painted cardboard made to look like the side of a house with twenty-eight windows corresponding to the number of children in that particular class. In each window she pasted a small school photograph of each child with his or her name neatly printed underneath. If a little girl, say, came to school in the morning without her hair brushed, with dirty fingernails, or unscrubbed teeth, a cardboard shutter was closed on that unfortunate's picture so that on that particular day she could not look out of her window and thus would remain unseen by her classmates. The results reported were impressive: no other class had such slick hair, clean and unbitten nails, and gleaming teeth. But I heard, faintly blowing in the wind, the creaking of some psychiatrist's couch of the future.

But it was a rival class that year that produced the boy who won

the district-wide championship for clean, shiny teeth. After he had
accepted his prize, a local representative of a pharmaceutical company asked him what brand of toothpaste he used. The boy said that
every morning he brushed his teeth with the well-known laundry
bleach, Clorox.

Religion flourished in Levittown. Many new householders who
had not hitherto thought of entering a church now solemnly filed off
Sunday mornings to one or another of the prefabricated houses of
worship that had sprung up on all sides of the community. Old-line
agnostics found themselves ushering and eldering, radical anticleri-
cals taught Sunday school, while roaring atheists read the Lesson or
took up the collection. First-home ownership often revives traditional communal behavior. Some of the early Levittown intellectuals, however, sturdily refused to follow the worship-together trend.
Our good neighbor Ward Madden, professor of education at Brooklyn College, reared his children in the strict secularist tradition of
John Dewey. One day at our kitchen door I overheard his small son
Bobby conversing with three playmates. They were talking about
where each went to church. A Catholic lad said he went to St. Bernard's, and the two others declared for the Presbyterian church and
the Jewish Center respectively. But when they asked Bobby where
he went, he replied with dignity, *"Naturalists* don't go to church."

Listening to small Levittowners playing in our yard, one could
enjoy a spectrum of social attitudes that ranged from brotherly concern ("Don't you hit my sister! *I'll* hit her!") to threats of biological
warfare ("I'll spit my germs on you!"). Small politenesses were directed toward adults: "Would you like one of my toads for your
baby?" or "Thank you, but we have better spaghetti at home." Our
own little girl, Ainslie, whose first complete spoken sentence was
"Gimme that whole thing!" soon learned self-control on social occasions. Whenever, walking with me, she might be offered a cookie by
a neighbor, she would say, "I'll have to ax my father." She did come
close to seeing her father's big toe axed off when I took her one day
on a visit to a Hempstead pet shop to see some little monkeys. As we
stood inside the store watching them, a trap door suddenly opened
up directly under my feet. A boy store helper coming up from the
cellar caught sight of me above him and backed down, dropping the
heavy door on my foot so that I was held painfully by my caught
big toe. Three-year-old Ainslie stood by in silent horror while I

howled like an antique hero in his death agony. Instead of getting someone to lift the door off my toe, the distraught pet-shop manager came running up to me with a glass of water. I was freed only when two male customers pooled muscles to lift the trap door off my foot, and then I did sit down and drink that glass of water, wishing it were something stronger. The toe was not broken and I took comfort in a check for $150 plus medical expenses from the pet shop's insurance company. Before the nail dropped off, it turned the color of a Tahitian sunset, a spectacle Ainslie pleaded with me to share with any company that came to the house.

Except in the coldest weather, Ainslie was inseparable from the white sailor hat I brought her from the Brooklyn Navy Yard, where in those days I worked summers writing Navy training manuals for extra income. Strange how children cling to odd bits of clothing gear. Ainslie's older brother Colin made himself a pair of spectacles out of wire used to fasten milk bottle caps. Wearing these on his nose, he would knock on neighbors' doors, announcing that he was "the Meenan Oil man." Most people would let the serious five-year-old inside and pretend to buy his fuel. He lost one of his best customers, Jack Coogan, a Marine reservist down the street, who went off to the Korean war and got himself killed.

Ainslie wore her sailor hat, brim turned down all around so that her solemn little face could hardly be seen as she rode up and down Levittown's sidewalks on her red tricycle with a black rubber horse's head attached to the handlebars. Her pockets were stuffed with carrot sticks, for the tricycle was really a horse named Daisy. Ainslie's basic tricycle route took her as far as the house where Rusty the cat lived. She rarely went beyond, for her brother Mario, her senior by fifteen months, once told her that if she rode further than that she would get lost and then the police would come and take her away in a squad car with flashing red lights and put her up for adoption so she would have to change her name and live with another family far away.

A number of the neighbors were unusual. Down the street lived a kindly housewife who fed curious neighborhood children dog-milk by the silver teaspoonful. Her pet spaniel, mother of numerous small litters, was chronically oversupplied. That woman belonged to the local La Leche organization, a group of mothers dedicated to breast feeding for human babies. Like Alcoholics Anonymous and similar groups, La Leche women of Levittown rallied round warmly to support one another, visiting or telephoning fellow members in crises with words of lactic encouragement. On Petunia Lane (Levittown streets were nearly all "Lanes"), a Navy veteran had his little house and yard rigged up like the LSM he had commanded at Ulithi. From his neat front lawn rose a tall, white mast on which colors were broken out at 0800 each day while his wife and three children stood morning quarters. On our own street, some doors down from us, there lived a jolly family with many "uncles" and cheerfully larcenous children. On Saturday afternoons the oldest daughter, a comely lass of eighteen, would arrive home from a girls' reform school to spend the weekend with her family. For good behavior she was given a pass, off-campus so to speak, and indeed as she stepped from her taxi, smart luggage in hand, she did look like a Vassar girl arriving for a Princeton weekend. But her father kept close watch on his younger daughter in junior high school, no doubt determined that she would not have to go on to an institution like her sister's. As I was scratching my lawn one morning, he told me proudly of her date the night before, "It was the foist time she was ever out wit' a boy of the opposite sex!"

The redundancy reminded me of an old Navy chief in Naples whom I overhead chewing out the midwatch for errors in procedure: "Leave us have no repetition of this reoccurrence!"

A notable Levittown eccentric was Al Coram, who lived in one of the houses back of us on the next street. Thirtyish, balding, and heavily bespectacled, Al was an electronics technician at Republic Aircraft and an early disciple of Ron Hubbard, leader of Scientology, a creed then known as Dianetics. Al blamed the world's troubles on "engrams," psychic markings that cause destructive behavior and prevent most of us from ever reaching that state of creative serenity known to Dianetics people as "the Clear." An occasional visitor to our house, Al liked to inspect electrical appliances in the kitchen and living room. If Mary gently cautioned him on his rough handling of her favorite lamp, Al would shake his head, sighing, "Engrams, engrams!" He was given to scaring his timid wife by such tricks as fastening black rubber spiders to the toilet seat, explaining her terror by engrams that needed to be rooted out. An early high fidelity freak, Al wired his house for sound from rooftop to concrete foundation slab. On his return from work at Republic, he would unload from his car trunk masses of electronic equipment to add to the array already installed. Al believed that all recorded sound should be played back at least at the decible level of the original source. In the case of ordinary recordings such as his favorite, Berlioz's *Requiem* (grand orchestra, monster chorus, and four brass bands), the resulting disturbances on the Richter scale were relatively low, save to poor Mrs. Coram, who had to work in the kitchen with the house shaking. But trouble with the neighbors began when Al began to put on recordings of actual earthquakes and volcanic eruptions. The police were called when he played at top volume his prized new recording of the invasion of Saipan. Al explained his neighbors' disapproval by the concepts of Dianetics. Once when I was talking to him on the sidewalk, a passing housewife looked at him grimly. He turned to me with a knowing smile: "Did you see the rude engramic stare that woman gave me?"

Gentler sounds emanated from the Levittown Chamber Music Group, to which I belonged. As a community enterprise, our prestige was rather low. A sociological survey of Levittown organizations made to determine their standing in community opinion showed that we rated just five-tenths of a point above the Levittown Cardiac Club. The group was composed of piano plus string quartet (I played cello) and we practiced once a week, alternately at pianist Frances Biloon's house, violist Frank Konopasek's, and first violinist Sol Berson's. After rehearsing a Brahms quintet or Beethoven trio, we would relax over refreshments in the kitchen of our hostess of the evening and talk until long after midnight. Miriam Berson's cheese-cake and challah were highly esteemed, Frances Biloon's lox and bagels won murmurs of admiration, while Julia Konopasek contributed the best all-round baking.

Our leader, Sol Berson, was made for the part of Yuri in *Doctor Zhivago*. A young research physician with flaming eyes and flying black hair, Sol scorned the standard Levittown M.D. uniform—neat shirt, bow tie, good tweed jacket—in favor of any old work-pants-and-windbreaker combination he just happened to have. Not just a medical doctor, but physicist, biochemist, mathematician, chess master, lover of world literature, and connoisseur of Italian painting, Sol Berson passionately loved everything human, particularly his family and friends. He burned with fanatical devotion to his medical research and was mad about music as well. Sol bent to his fiddle with the concentration of a shaman, his magic bow invoking the spirit world of the immortals. He was a *Himmelstürmer;* no musical height existed too steep for him to try to scale. Sol had no mercy on the limitations of the rest of us, but dragged us relentlessly through all the standard chamber music literature within or beyond (mostly beyond) our capacities. His tempi forever aspired to the condition of presto. Two measures into the *rondo alla zingarese* of the Brahms Piano Quartet in C, and Sol would already be four bars ahead, leaving stragglers to catch up with him as well as we could.

During the days Sol worked like a man possessed at his laboratory in the Bronx Veterans Hospital. With his colleague, physicist Rosalyn Yalow, he opened up the way to the use of radioisotopes in detecting and measuring hormones in the blood with significant application to glandular disease, and to virus and cancer research. The radio immuno assay (RIA) developed by Berson and Yalow is so sensitive that it can detect an amount of substance measurable only in billionths of grams. In 1975 an adaptation of the RIA test was used to detect minute traces of curare in the exhumed bodies of patients alleged to have been killed nine years before by the New Jersey physician known at first only as "Doctor X." Medical scientists in the know believe that only his premature death in 1972 kept Sol from the Nobel Prize, an award those closest to him knew he ardently aspired to.

In 1976, Roz Yalow, Sol's collaborator, became the first woman to receive the Lasker Award in basic medical research, traditional stepping stone to the Nobel Prize in medicine; she got it for the work she did with Sol on radio immuno assay, and the award cited Dr. Solomon Berson as co-discoverer.

For his friends or for anyone in need, Sol would drop everything and run to them. If he happened upon something wonderful in art or music or mathematics, he would jump into his car, no matter how late the hour, taking the book, problem, reproduction, or music score with him to wake up a friend with the marvel. I remember him driving up to our house to show me a copy of a Dürer engraving he had just discovered, and to take Mary to a meeting or a visit I couldn't make. Once on an hour's notice he carried me off to hear Heifetz play for a few patients at the Bronx Veterans Hospital. (The unsmiling violinist talked to the patients simply without the slightest condescension after each piece he performed.) For a friend suffering from an ordinary hangover Sol would drop his research at a critical point and drive fifty miles to relieve him. *Anyone* could call Sol Berson and he would come—one reason why he slept about four hours a night.

Nearly twenty years after the Levittown Chamber Music Group had been dissolved, Sol heard that our son Mario had just been shipped back wounded from Vietnam, with a kidney complication that puzzled the doctors at Walter Reed Army Hospital in Washington. Sol—at the time professor and chairman of the department of medicine at New York's Mount Sinai Hospital—got on the phone to Washington at once and stayed in touch with the case until Mario was discharged nearly a year later.

The year before Sol's death brought him many honors. He went to Sweden to get the Medal of the Swedish Medical Society and returned to this country to be given the Gairdner Award, the Dickson Prize, the New York Academy of Medicine Award, the Ricketts Memorial Award, the American College of Physicians Award. In April 1972 he went to a medical convention in Atlantic City and lay down exhausted in his hotel room for a nap. While he was asleep his heart, prematurely worn out, stopped beating.

Sol Berson loved Schubert's music. In the old Levittown days he drove us through the Quartet in D (*Death and the Maiden*) until we could play it well enough to give a public performance at Hofstra University's Little Theater. One of his favorite Schubert pieces was the big Quintet in C, the one with the double cello part. Sol told me once that the Adagio seemed to him a beautiful attempt to console someone for an irreparable loss. For lighter moments he fancied certain Hungarian composers (I'm sure Sol had a touch of Russian gypsy blood in him) like Kodály, Dohnányi, the early Bartók. Our very first public concert appearance as the Levittown Chamber Music Group found us at the Jewish Community Center, where we were introduced to a full house by Murray Rudnick. Murray, an experienced M.C. with minor Borscht Belt experience, was much in demand for local affairs. Our program began with Dohnányi's Piano Quintet in C minor, and Murray was equal to the occasion:

"This splendid aggregation"—Murray indicated us as we sat onstage, Sol Berson tapping his bow impatiently—"this splendid *aggregation* who set an example to all culture-loving citizens of this great community of Levittown are going to favor us by performing as their first selection that masterpiece of Russian music, the famous piano quintet by . . ." Here Murray paused for a moment, eyed the printed program uneasily, then bravely took the plunge—

"JOHNNY—in four movements!" *

Shortly before we moved to Bethpage in the early 1950s, Barnard's Thursday Noon Meeting invited me to speak about Levittown. Mark Van Doren's wife was in the audience, listening intently. In my talk, "Suburban Schizophrenia or Misanthropy in the Split Level," I leaned rather heavily on the more grotesque aspects of the new community and played up some oddball characters and practices I had encountered there. Then I made up a pastiche, imagining what Nathanael West might write about Long Island's new mass suburbia. Tongue in cheek, I argued that Levittown was a microcosm of the world, concluding my remarks with Tennessee Williams's quatrain:

> *We are the gooks and the geeks of creation*
> *Believe it or not is the name of our star*
> *Each one of us here thinks the other is queer*
> *And everyone's right, for all of us are.*

Afterwards, Irita Van Doren came up with a worried expression and advised me earnestly to get out of that place before I cracked-up. I assured her that we had passed some of the best years of our lives there and that I had hoked it up a bit in my talk. She went away, unconvinced, shaking her head.

COLUMBIA: IKE AND OTHERS

ᏽᎧ If you enter Columbia University's Butler Library by the big north door and climb the long stairway to your left, you will see up there a portrait of a dignified old gentleman, gowned in Oxford

* The Levittown Chamber Music Group has been forgotten but not Billy Joel, songwriter, pianist, and singer, who grew up in Levittown in the 1950s. Joel, whose recording of "Piano Man" sold a million copies, used to hang out at one of the village green with the Emerald Royals, a school gang who went in for pompadours and black leather jackets.

scarlet, clutching a rare book to his side. That is Nicholas Murray Butler, Columbia's imperial president. At intervals during his long reign he dreamed that he might be nominated by his party (Republican) for the presidency of the United States. He never made it. Butler also appears in a larger painting on the other side of the grand staircase, a panoramic horror commemorating the visit of Their Majesties, King George VI and Queen Elizabeth of Britain, to Columbia in June 1939. The royal couple stand stiffly on a blue-carpeted dais in Low Library, the domed building that provides the backdrop for the annual Columbia commencement as well as broad stone steps on which students sun themselves in springtime and talk of love or political action. In the painting, the Oxford-gowned Butler is reading an address of welcome to the king and queen while below university trustees and faculty look on respectfully. Virginia Gildersleeve is easily recognizable in the right foreground. Two Irish-looking New York cops stand back to back, scanning the robed faculty ranks suspiciously.

Facing Butler's likeness from the corresponding position at the top of the right staircase hangs a portrait of a bald, smiling man in the robes of an honorary doctor of laws. He is not clutching a book but balances one on a small table with a Columbia University catalogue. To make his affiliation beyond doubt, his Columbia hood and mortarboard lie on an adjacent table with two Columbia University commencement programs. He is Dwight David Eisenhower, former supreme commander of Allied forces in Europe, who became Columbia's president in 1948 and held the office until sworn in as president of the United States in January 1953.

Unlike President Butler, Eisenhower had spent little time dreaming of high political office during his professional career. He had belonged to no political party until after the end of World War II, when the possibility of the White House was put to him. The presidency of Columbia would be an interim position, a grooming place of sufficient dignity and visibility. So it was Ike, and not old disconsolate Butler, who was nominated by his party (Republican) and elected to the presidency of the United States.

Shortly after he took office as Columbia's president, Eisenhower crossed Broadway to Barnard, where he talked to students and faculty at an all-college assembly. The occasion was nearly disrupted by a dog belonging to one of my students, a blind Mexican named

González. She attended my ten o'clock philosophy class led by a guide dog of doubtful breed and nasty temper. The evil-looking hound would lead his mistress to her seat in the philosophy room, growl softly, then lie motionless under the seminar table at her feet. At the end of the hour he would rise, growl another warning, and lead Miss González to the door, while we all carefully backed off to give them room.

The assembly for Ike's first visit was held in the gym, with the entire faculty and student body present. In her doctor's robes Mrs. McIntosh introduced the new Columbia president after a little trouble with the microphone had been straightened out. ("Is this thing working?" was Mrs. Mac's usual opening at assemblies.) After the welcoming applause had died away, Eisenhower began to speak, but at his first words a furious clamor rang through the hall. For some reason, Miss González's dog did not like Ike, or at least the sound of his voice. Eisenhower stopped, smiled good-humoredly, then tried again. No use: the frenzied barking began all over again. Once more Ike stopped and grinned while Miss González struggled to persuade her faithful companion to shut up. The gym was so packed, and she and her hound so jammed in the middle, that neither she nor the dog could be gotten out.

Ike began again, and this time managed to get on a bit with his speech, although intermittent outbursts from the dog continued. Ike told us how unqualified he felt himself to be as president of a great university like Columbia (*Rowf!*), what a pleasant thing it was to be welcomed at the university's college for women, and such pretty young women at that (*Rowf! Rowf!*), what an honor it was to be introduced by President McIntosh and what fine things he'd heard of Barnard scholarship (ARGHRRROWF!), and so on. Ike handled the situation well. No scholar, he was nonetheless president of the university, but clearly not the sort of man Gratiano describes to Antonio, the kind who dress themselves in wisdom, gravity, profound conceit, entertaining a willful silence:

> *As who should say, "I am Sir Oracle,*
> *And when I ope my lips, let no dog bark."*

The usual account of Eisenhower's Columbia presidency goes something like this. As a military commander, the general was accustomed to running things through a staff. He brought his own to

Columbia and at first tried to operate the university that way. But Columbia's administration and senior faculty did not take kindly to the military staff system, so a compromise was worked out. Dean Pegram of the graduate faculties would run the academic side of the university without interference from above, while Ike and his staff could sit back and observe how things were done in academe. Ike could best serve the university by his genial presence and immense prestige. But it soon became clear that Ike was chafing under his academic robes. As early as 1950 he began itching to get into politics. Ike did not take kindly to confinement on the Columbia campus and, as the four years of his tenure spun out, it became easier to find Ike in downtown Washington than on Morningside Heights. He preferred the company of Manhattan corporation executives to the more modest contacts available to him at Low Library. Still, the story went, despite widespread faculty hostility, Eisenhower managed to find a few good friends in its ranks, among them my senior colleague at Barnard, Raymond "Steve" Saulnier.

Steve Saulnier, chairman of Barnard's department of economics, later went down to Washington on Ike's invitation to serve on the president's Council of Economic Advisors, a post Steve held for six years, four of them in Eisenhower's second term when he became chairman of the council. Then he returned to the Barnard faculty. Prolix and affable, Saulnier liked to sit at lunch with junior professors and to expatiate on the American fiscal scene. After he retired from his Barnard teaching, he withdrew to his basement in Lehman Hall where, with his wife Estelle as assistant, he carried on various kinds of research and consulting work. While our acquaintance spanned nearly thirty years, for some reason he always addressed me as "John," although the most recent letter I had from him had "John" crossed out and "Joe" substituted.

Saulnier's account of Eisenhower at Columbia differs from the usual story in certain respects. According to Steve, Eisenhower arrived on Morningside Heights with a "staff" of two military men in mufti. One, a colonel, worked in an office close to Ike. The other man, an academic type of lesser rank, soon drifted away to become president of some smaller university. Steve first met Ike in 1940 when his fiscal advice was sought at the Pentagon on some budgetary matter. He saw little of Ike at Columbia. Eisenhower did not sit on boards of corporations, though he had a post on the board of a relatively small New York bank, Central Savings, and he had an office there. Columbia faculty hostility was real and widespread, especially when Ike's presidential candidacy loomed. Steve began acting on Eisenhower's behalf when a big anti-Ike advertisement appeared in the *New York Times,* signed by a regiment of Columbia faculty, including Henry Steele Commager and Allan Nevins, both prominent historians. The ad made much of the danger of military ways of running things. Steve thought the manifesto unfair, got on the phone, and managed to scare up a few Eisenhower supporters on campus, among them the popular Dean Carman and Lou Little, director of athletics.

Like most of the Morningside Heights faculty, I fancied Adlai Stevenson, Ike's Democratic opponent in the presidential battles of 1952 and 1956. But much of the anti-Ike opposition at Columbia was rather mean and some mounted to hysteria. Enchanted by Stevenson's wit and wisdom, Irwin Edman stated that Ike could offer the country only "simple, stupid integrity." That annoyed me. Not an integrity man myself, always more at home with the shifty and equivocal, I believe there are times when simple, stupid integrity comes in handy. The men of Thermopylae stuck to their posts, even though they knew

> *That Ephialtes rises in the end*
> *And at last the Persians will get through.*

Ironic that Eisenhower, man of integrity, should have selected his vice-presidential running mate from the ranks of the shifty. As a young congressman, Richard Nixon had caught public attention in 1948 as a shrewd questioner on the House Committee on Un-American Activities, and Karl Mundt, acting chairman of the committee, appointed him to head a subcommittee to look into Whittaker Chambers's allegation that Alger Hiss was a Communist agent. When Eisenhower selected Nixon as his running mate for the 1952 election, Nixon had been senator from California for two years. Six weeks before the election, the New York *Post* broke the story of a secret Nixon fund gotten up by a group of the young senator's well-heeled constituents to pay some of his political expenses, including travel to and from California. Though Nixon correctly argued that many congressmen and senators enjoyed much cozier arrangements, including battalions of relatives on the federal payroll, the public uproar over "the Fund" made the upright Eisenhower so uneasy that he would have dropped Nixon as his running mate had not Nixon's famous "Checkers" television defense convinced the Republican National Committee that Nixon was an asset rather than a liability to the ticket and satisfied Eisenhower that his young vice-presidential candidate was as "clean as a hound's tooth."

Years later, after Watergate, I asked Steve Saulnier about his impressions of Nixon, knowing that he had much personal contact with the vice-president in his years on the president's Council of Economic Advisors. Steve said that it never occurred to him that Nixon was anything but an able, honest man, but that, unlike Eisenhower, he preferred "to do things alone." Also, he was a much more political man than his boss. As a good Republican, Steve Saulnier was shocked and dismayed by the Watergate burglary and could make no sense of Nixon's behavior in the sequel. He was convinced that Nixon knew nothing about the break in the beginning, but that, when he found out about it, he made the terrible error of trying to cover it up.

Like so many academics, I did not care for Richard Nixon or for his way of doing things. As president, his administration could cite important positive accomplishments. His use of Henry Kissinger as foreign policy adviser and special assistant,* later as secretary of state, was far shrewder than Ike's employment of John Foster Dulles, a permissive relation that formed the weakest side of the Eisenhower administration. Historians will rate Nixon's China détente as an important achievement. But with Nixon there was always a trail of deviousness oozing damply from "the Fund" up through Cambodia and Watergate. The spectacle of the president of the United States caught sweeping a series of illegal acts under the rug and trying to lie his way out of it was not edifying. All the same, the hysterical way so many people behaved while the president was being cornered did not seem edifying either. In the rush of professors to faculty secre-

---

* In his memoir *On Watch* (1976) retired Admiral Elmo Zumwalt, former chief of naval operations, titles his first chapter on his enemy Kissinger, "The Assistant." Did he intend the reference to Malamud's novel of that name? After an interview with Zumwalt as CNO, Kissinger exclaimed, "If there's one thing I can't stand, it's an intellectual admiral." When President Carter made clear long before his election that Kissinger had been around long enough as secretary of state, I thought of Schiller's *Fiesco:* "Der Mohr hat seine Arbeit getan. Der Mohr kann gehen." ("The Moor has done his work. The Moor can go.")

taries to type up their latest letters to editors concerning the immorality of Richard Nixon and his unfitness to remain in office, I found myself hanging back wondering.

The *New York Times* assured its right-thinking readers that the televised procedures of the House Judiciary Committee leading to its recommendation of impeachment represented a successful test of strength of the American constitutional system. So did my politically mature Columbia colleagues. I'm sure they were right. But sometimes it seemed to me that I was watching a public trial, with members of the committee behaving like judge and jury combined. In the court scene in Lewis Carroll's *Alice in Wonderland,* the Queen of Hearts demanded sentence first, verdict afterward. In Nixon's case, it was trial and verdict first, with another trial to come, in the Senate, had matters got that far. Public display of moral virtue became wearisome, as did so much solemn self-righteousness on the part of our representatives to Congress, conscious that millions of eyes were watching them on television. Listening to the committee members individually reciting their bills of particulars against Nixon (Holtzman from Brooklyn: "He has trampled on our liberties!"), one might think they were indicting King George III. But then, I suppose, the Bicentennial was approaching.

If there is such a thing as human nature, there is a spot at the core of it that gets intense pleasure from watching the fall of a man from high place. It is comforting to know that God puts down the mighty from their seat, although He often forgets to exalt the humble. Nixon fell from highest office and place of power amid every manifestation of moral satisfaction from multitude and élite alike. More than a few had fun kicking him when he was down, including those who published or savored personal details of his last miserable days in the White House. Many never pardoned Gerald Ford for pardoning a man already destroyed. Maybe "destroyed" is not quite the right word. Certainly, he was not financially ruined, and the 1977 Frost television interviews showed a surviving remnant of the curious resilience that has marked Nixon's career.

Academics bear some responsibility for what happened to Richard Nixon. It was not only the nation's journalists who built up to the point of obsession public fascination with the office of the presidency and the man who happened to occupy it. For every professor of history or political science who wrote a book or article about

Congress or the Supreme Court, there were a hundred analyzing the presidency and president. I believe such bug-eyed concentration on the executive helped to make the imperial autonomy of the presidency Richard Nixon was condemned for exploiting.

Eisenhower's Columbia tenure spanned the early Cold War years when genuine fear existed that Soviet expansion would lead to atomic devastation of the United States. Ike's genial side did not show when the subject was communism, or Soviet Russia, as he called it. At his farewell address to the Columbia faculty in 1952 I happened to be seated near him and noticed that whenever he touched on Communists or their sympathizers at home and abroad, in government or universities, an angry red flush crept up his neck. That was the Eisenhower who as president would let Julius and Ethel Rosenberg go to the electric chair in Sing Sing, though he could have commuted their sentences to life imprisonment.

I thought that the execution of the Rosenbergs was a mistake. Not that they were innocent. They probably did pass atomic bomb sketches and other classified material to Soviet agents. They may or may not have believed that in so doing they were acting in the interests of world peace. I believe there are times when capital punishment is appropriate. Certain crimes *deserve death*—the torture-murder of children, for example—and if they deserve it, why shouldn't they suffer it, if there are no mitigating circumstances? But that was not such a case. Judge Kaufman based his justification of the Rosenberg death sentence on a faulty argument: if a person convicted of premeditated murder of one human could justly be sentenced to death, how much more so should then sentence be passed on those who transmitted secret information which, if used against this nation, could kill millions of innocent Americans? But there is no evidence that the Rosenbergs intended the death of even one American. True, they were not convicted as ordinary murderers, but as spies under a wartime espionage act still in force in 1953. But Judge Kaufman gave the impression that the act *required* the death penalty. The Cold War was still on. Areas in public buildings had been marked off as bomb shelters and in schools little children crouched under their desks in bomb drills. Such was the fog of fear in those days that even Eisenhower's kindly nature desisted pleas for mercy for the Rosenbergs that poured in from everywhere, including the Vatican.

After Ike left Columbia, I had only fleeting glimpses of United States presidents, ex-presidents, or presidents-to-be. Former President Truman turned up on campus in the spring of 1955. One could attend his Radner lectures as well as those peppery get-togethers with Columbia students politely known as "seminars." Who couldn't help admiring the decisive little man, whether he was relieving General MacArthur of his Pacific command in Korea or writing to Paul Hume, music critic of the *Washington Post,* offering to punch him in the nose for his unsympathetic comments on his daughter Margaret's singing voice? But Truman was not at his best with the Columbia students. He snappishly put down their respectful but penetrating questions, brushing them aside with the air of someone who regarded them as a bunch of young kids who really didn't know what they were talking about. But they did know, and Harry did too, but by that time he was getting on in years.

Lyndon Johnson presided at the French Institute's golden anniversary dinner at the Waldorf-Astoria in May 1962. I went as guest of Leroy Breunig, professor of French at Barnard—later dean of faculty and interim Barnard president between the régimes of Martha Peterson and Jacquelyn Mattfeld. Johnson, then Kennedy's vice-president, had the touchy job of introducing the speaker of the evening, André Malraux, author of *Man's Fate* and, at the time of the dinner, de Gaulle's minister of state in charge of cultural affairs. Throughout the dinner Malraux twitched in his place beside Mrs. Johnson. At intervals Lady Bird gently offered her partner conversation-making questions, but sometimes received in reply only a sample of Malraux's famous facial tic and a colossal shrug. Vice-President Johnson seemed to realize that he had a Temperament on his hands and presented the minister to the guests with a deft little speech gotten up for him by someone who knew a bit about the rare bird he had to introduce. As speaker, Malraux appeared to be still under the spell of his recent art-and-culture superbook *Voices of Silence,* for he managed in one-half of one short paragraph of his allocution to mention Shakespeare, Michelangelo, Piero della Francesca, Velasquez, El Greco, Cézanne, the sculptors of Chartres, the Egyptian and Sumerian masters, Rembrandt, Monteverdi, and Beethoven. But he had a good word for us Yankees too and at the close of his speech, blazing with passionate abstractions, he offered a generous toast to the United States in incandescent French:

I lift my glass to the only nation that has made war without loving it, achieved the greatest power in the world without seeking it, held in its hands the most terrible weapon of death without longing to use it.

Two years after that gala dinner Kennedy would be dead, Lyndon Johnson president, the Tonkin Gulf resolution passed by a myopic Congress, the nation bogged down in a vicious mess we knew nothing about, let alone sought or loved: a war in a distant land abandoned by Malraux's own countrymen after Dienbienphu, war of the zap-death, the smell of which had risen prophetically years before from the pages of *The Royal Way,* Malraux's novel of Indochina's heart of darkness.

Jack Kennedy came by Columbia once in the fall of 1962. I was walking back from lunch in the faculty dining room in Hewitt on the way to my one o'clock logic class in Milbank when I noticed some students lining the sidewalk on Broadway. When I got up to my classroom I asked the logicians if they knew what was going on down there and they said that President Kennedy was due to come by about one-fifteen. I said, "So what are we doing here?" and we all piled down three flights to the street and joined a knot of students at the corner of Broadway and 119th Street. We got there just in time. A big black convertible was passing with Kennedy sitting up in the rear so everyone could see him, waving and smiling. I was struck by the peculiar greenish-bronze cast of his skin and the odd copper-color of his hair. When I mentioned it later, someone told me it was an effect of his Addison's disease, while another said there must be something wrong with my color perception.

Jack Kennedy was the beau ideal of the Columbia faculty, his wife Jacqueline their pin-up girl. "Lifestyle" tripped on everyone's tongue and all admired the Kennedys'. One morning I saw Lionel Trilling standing near the cashier's desk in the crowded Columbia bookstore. I went over to say hello to him but didn't, for, as I peeked over his shoulder, I saw he was inscribing one of his own books to Jackie Kennedy.

One afternoon just about a year later when I had finished teaching that same one o'clock logic class on the third floor of Milbank, I took the subway train downtown from 116th Street, the Columbia station, and got off at Fifty-ninth. It was Friday, I had no afternoon office hours, and the weather was mild for November. On such Fridays I liked to walk along Central Park South as far as the Plaza before heading downtown for Penn Station and the Long Island Railroad train for Bethpage and home. I enjoyed watching the rich people coming out of their hotels and getting into their fine automobiles. They looked so beautiful, both the rich people and their cars. But that day there was something unusual in the air. A big Lincoln Continental had pulled up beside Essex House, and a little crowd of people stood by its open front door on the street side, listening to the car radio the chauffeur had turned up so everybody could hear.

Somebody on the radio was talking excitedly. I asked a woman what was going on and she said that President Kennedy had been shot and seriously wounded in Dallas, Texas. Just then the man on the radio said, "President Kennedy is dead." We all looked at each other for a moment, rich, poor, and middle. Then we began to talk rapidly and even to touch each other on the arm. Soon I left and walked back toward Columbus Circle and down Broadway in the direction of Times Square. It was very strange. A hush had fallen over the city. New York for once was silent.

BARNARD: UNICORNS & DRAGONS, 1950s

ᢄᢣ In the great postwar faculty turnover on Morningside Heights, a few old dragons and unicorns were left behind. Over at Columbia, John Dewey had long since retired, but in my early Barnard years I could take a small Barnard philosophy class across Broadway to Philosophy Hall to hear him talk to the Graduate Students Association. Dewey was in his nineties then, but his harsh voice still firmly grated out his stubborn ruminations. Their recurrent theme was his conviction that the task of philosophy required us to *grapple* with social problems—to make the worse better, to improve the social situation not by contemplation but by action. It was a commonplace that Dewey wrote badly. But he could get off a few good lines like, "While saints are engaged in introspection, burly sinners run the world."

Dewey was a thoughtful and considerate man. He wrote to *everybody*. He knew I was teaching logic at Barnard and from time to time would send me an article of his on the subject. To Dewey, logic was the study of methods of inquiry, not the formal systems of today with their symbolic calculi, truth tables, and quantification runes. One article of his came in a manila envelope on which he had scrawled my name and address, then thriftily added the legend No Writing under the one-cent stamp he had stuck on before mailing. But there *was* writing in it. The old Vermonter had scrawled comments on the margins of the article itself. I have it still, battered envelope, "No Writing," and all.

At Barnard, the formidable Gertrude Hirst, emeritus professor of Latin and Greek, refused to retire but continued into her eighties to offer, unsalaried, her class in Greek to any students who would come to it. Nobody dared ask her to stop. Miss Hirst did not consider herself eccentric but believed others could be. A Barnard biology professor died so soon after his retirement that he did not have time to clean out his office. When a younger colleague opened a cupboard there, out tumbled two thousand shirt cards, the sort laundries used to use for packaging. The scholar had been carefully hoarding them for purposes unknown since he began teaching as an instructor. Miss Hirst told me that once in the Midwest she met an elderly woman and politely asked her where her home was. She received the reply, "My home is in Heaven, but my postal address is Kalamazoo, Michigan."

Miss Hirst's brother was Francis W. Hirst, an old-line English liberal who, as a young man, had assisted John Morley with his life of Gladstone and later became editor of *The Economist*. The Hirsts came from an old Yorkshire family, a remote eighteenth-century branch of which included the renowned eccentric Jemmy Hirst, whose custom was to ride bareback on a bull accompanied by his pet pig. Jemmy's fame reached the ears of King George II, who commanded him to audience in London. The genial fellow made the assembled courtiers crack up when he seized His Majesty's hand with a hearty shake and invited him, as one plain old party to another, to drop in on him at Yorkshire any time His Majesty pleased.

Miss Hirst herself had roots in history. When she was a child, her father took her to see old Mr. Weatherhead who, as a Navy man, had seen Napoleon on the deck of the *Bellerophon* before he was taken to St. Helena. She remembered the election of 1874 when Disraeli overturned the Gladstone government.

As a young woman, Miss Hirst left England after finishing her studies at Newnham College, Cambridge,* to take a teaching position in Louisville, Kentucky. After that, except for summer visits home, her life and career were spent entirely in the United States. Yet she remained the Platonic Ideal of the indomitable Englishwoman. She considered herself part of England itself, much as an embassy in a foreign country is extraterritorial and inviolable within its walls. The law that required her to register annually in New York as an "alien" infuriated her. Italians were aliens, Greeks too, and so were Russian Jews. But in her eyes an Englishwoman could hardly even be properly called a "foreigner" no matter where she lived.

No one affronted Miss Hirst with impunity. When Nicholas Murray Butler, presiding at a Barnard faculty meeting according to the custom of the days before I came to the college, asked Miss Hirst to raise her voice, she replied, "I am speaking quite loudly enough, thank you," and continued in her quiet, even tones. I was at Barnard when a mugger seized her on Claremont Avenue where she lived and tried to snatch her handbag. Miss Hirst fetched the fellow such a buffet with her cane that he fled, leaving her person and handbag intact. She was devoted to her students, but tolerated no shoddy work. On those occasions when her patience had been exhausted, she would write to the dean of studies, "Miss Jones and Miss Smith are illiterate. Please report to the proper authority. Gertrude Hirst."

Miss Hirst had "her" table in the Barnard faculty dining room, and only those she approved of were allowed to sit there. She also had her own chair for tea in the Ella Weed Room, a faculty common room in Milbank Hall that had an enormous fireplace mosaicked in

---

* Nineteenth-century graduates of women's colleges at Cambridge were not awarded degrees, but certificates. Long after Miss Hirst left Newnham, the university changed that discriminating regulation and Miss Hirst's certificate was superseded by a Cambridge baccalaureate. Although women were raised to degree-taking status at Cambridge in 1922, they still were not allowed in a man's room unchaperoned; and if they received men for tea in their own rooms, they had to wheel their iron beds out into the corridors.

Moorish green and gold. Whoever through ignorance sat in Miss Hirst's chair in Ella Weed was soon silently stared out of it. I did not know of her sovereign lunch table and as a new faculty member I one day cheerfully sat down opposite her. Narrowed eyes in a large pale face scrutinized me through rimless glasses. I was asked to identify myself, then silence reigned for the rest of the lunch. Later, my colleagues told me that to sit at Miss Hirst's table without invitation was simply not done. I said that my mother had taught me to be polite to elderly people, particularly to old ladies, and prepared to avoid Miss Hirst's table in the future.

When next I passed Miss Hirst's table at lunchtime, I was stopped by a commanding nod and cordially invited to sit down. I did. She had a way of getting an interesting conversation going at lunch by saying very little. But what she said was definitive and admitted no appeal. Her small group talked of politics and literature, of English pottery and Latin classics, and what we liked best to eat. One day the subject of milk came up (I usually had a glass with my lunch) and Miss Hirst inquired of the people at the table whether they liked to drink milk or not. Three of my colleagues said they liked milk, more or less, and three said they couldn't abide it. Miss Hirst considered a moment, then rendered her verdict: "Anyone who knows anything likes milk."

Miss Hirst had her prejudices, among them that peculiar form of anti-Semitism nineteenth-century English liberals did not seem to find inconsistent with their enlightened views. She always referred to Barnard Jewish students as "Jewesses," and did not conceal her preference, other things being equal, for non-Jewesses. She was deeply disappointed when her star pupil Elspeth Davis, who taught history at Massachusetts Institute of Technology, married Walt Rostow, later foreign policy advisor to President Johnson with unfortunate results. But Bob Lekachman, brilliant young Barnard economist and Jewish, ranked high among her court favorites and was often bidden to sit at her right hand. Miss Hirst's anti-Semitism may have been hardly more than a manifestation of classical English snobbery, for she felt very much the same way toward Armenians, though she thought what the Turks did to them was as bad as what Hitler did to the Jews. She had a particular aversion to Makarios of Cyprus; to her the Cypriot Archbishop was simply a murderer.

She was fond of children and often invited me to bring my

small ones to visit her. They liked her, for she was delightful to them and found them all sorts of curious knickknacks to play with. They loved running up and down the long hall of her apartment at 39 Claremont, sliding wildly along the polished floor. When the noise reached a certain level, Miss Hirst would bring out her stopper, a large Dundee cake served in thick slices with glasses of milk. She poured tea from a lovely old English silver tea set.

One day Miss Hirst took me to lunch at the Park Avenue apartment of her old friend Charles C. Burlingham, the eminent lawyer, then in his one-hundredth year. Mr. Burlingham had become blind and a little deaf. On our way to the dining room, he took my arm in his powerful grip and bellowed confidentially, "How *is* Gertrude? She seems a little feeble. Is she taking care of herself? How courageous of you to take her to see me!" Unsmiling, Nora Brennan, his Irish cook, winked at me almost imperceptibly. As a souvenir of the lunch, Mr. Burlingham gave me from his library a copy of the first edition of Paley's *Natural Theology* and later left some volumes of Taine on his hall table for me to call for. He died soon afterward, having passed his centennial birthday.

When the first signs showed that Miss Hirst would not forever preside over her big round table in the faculty dining room, Tom Peardon, dean of the Barnard faculty, arranged for her faithful to give a small black-tie dinner for her at the Century Club. On that festive rainy evening, we vied with one another thinking up graceful toasts with appropriate classical allusions. I made a crude mistake in citing a Latin tag, saying, *"In medium virtus stat."* After dinner she quietly pointed out the error to me—not *medium,* but *medio.* Before she went to bed that night she wrote each of us a note, thanking us for the dinner and expressing the hope that we did not get our feet wet going home.

Time came when Miss Hirst could no longer do for herself on Claremont Avenue and she moved to a well-appointed nursing home in Croton-on-Hudson. She lingered there until well into her nineties. Before she died I drove over from Bethpage with two of the children to see her for the last time. She lay comatose in a criblike bed, curled up like a sleeping infant. Her English silver tea set now stands on the sideboard of our dining room. But the children who ate her Dundee cake are far away.

Miss Hirst's defense of the study of classical humanities is as good as any I've read and much shorter. She set it out in the fore-word of her *Collected Classical Papers:*

> Teachers of Greek and Latin have an inestimable blessing, not shared by all their colleagues, in that the material they handle is almost all of high quality, some of it transcendently so. My lot at any rate has fallen in a fair ground—every day to read and teach some of the greatest authors, trying to understand their thoughts, and their place in the world they lived in, and not least to study their words and the way they wrote. "Only words are certain good." Happy are those who have this firm refuge amid the changes and chances of this moral life. "If I could have my life over again," said Jane Harrison, "I would devote it not to art or literature, but to language. Life itself may hit one hard, but always, always one can take sanctuary in language. Language is as much an art and as sure a refuge as painting or music or literature. It reflects and interprets and makes bearable life; only it is wider, because more subconscious life." If the votaries of this faith, even though a scanty band of scholars, can keep a tiny candle burning, or, let us say more boldly, can hand on the torch, their lives will not have been useless.

John Day was a member of that scanty band, a mild and gentle unicorn compared to Miss Hirst's dragonhood. Though much younger than Miss Hirst, he died before she. Still vigorously on active duty when I first knew him, his kindly face had as many wrinkles as the bits of ancient parchment he pored over to decipher. John Day was a specialist in Greek epigraphy, easily spotted on campus by the green bookpack slung over his shoulder as he made his daily treks to Butler Library's Papyrus Room. His course in epigraphy did not have a large enrollment, but nearly everyone agreed that John Day was the dearest man on campus. One day he decided to lay on an open lecture on Greek epigraphy, and to this end captured a veritable lion of the subject, Eric Turner, a papyrologist of international repute. John Day announced with a beatific smile that Professor Turner had consented to speak on the topic, The Classical Scholars of Oxyrhynchus.

The Barnard–Columbia community did not seem to want to know about the classical scholars of Oxyrhynchus, for only about a dozen turned up to hear about them. But those happy few had a great time. Professor Turner, an elderly Englishman, observed in a humorous aside to the water pitcher that Oxyrhynchus was not an exotic animal, as some might believe, but a locality five hundred miles up the Nile on a branch of that great river where the dry sands of the area have preserved the papyri buried there. He told of a twenty-four-volume work on the Oxyrhynchus papyri that contained 2,425 texts and that Rudolf Pfeiffer was able to finish his great edition of Callimachus when he came to Oxford as an émigré from Germany and found the Oxyrhynchus papyri. He then explained how papyrus was made by splitting the plant vertically down into long slivers and pounding it. The smooth face of the creamy surface is called the *recto* and the rough side the *verso*. Unlike modern paper, papyrus is not sized; there is no coating.

Professor Turner then drew a sample of papyrus from his pocket, and wrote something on it. "I have written on this papyrus with a fountain *pen*," he said, and peered for some seconds at the pen as if it were an ingenious little gadget from the planet Venus. He went on to point out that professors of papyrology copy and edit Greek classics with the aid of papyrus scraps they find at Oxyrhynchus and other dry, sandy places of Egypt. By scrutinizing surviving bits of old prize essays and poems, they can tell us much about what happened to ancient texts as they passed from hand to hand, edition after edition, down the centuries. We scrutinized with him the sentence, "Cleon is accused of sucking up to the populace." Now take this particular scrap, said Professor Turner, waving another bit of papyrus at us, "If we change the *mu* to a *nu* and the *iota* to a *tau*, the whole thing becomes perfectly clear—the usage is exactly the same as in that well-known work, the thirty-eighth Harangue of Libanius!" He looked round at us triumphantly.

At the end of the lecture, Professor Day, as chairman, called for questions. No one dared say a word except Gilbert Highet, Columbia's Anton Professor of Greek and Latin, the only person in the room who *could* ask a question: "Are there any promising sites left?"

"I'd rather keep that under my hat, Highet, if you don't mind. The British, of course, are now *non grata* in Egypt, and the Italians got cold feet."

"Vogliano?"

"Well, yes. He always said that he had permission to excavate at any time. But there's an awkwardness—he's dead, you know."

Professor Turner ended the question period with a friendly

exhortation to all students present to consider a career in papyrology.

"The field is wide, the material rich! All we need is more workers."

A memorable lecture. I rank it with one I heard Bertrand Russell give on perception at Columbia years earlier. It was brilliant. At the end, the philosopher G. E. Moore, a pink-and-white cherub of a man, walked slowly up to Russell from the back of the room, screaming plaintively, "No, no, no, no! That's *not* what I mean when I say, 'I see this matchbox'!"

John Day's tiny candle was kept burning, the torch handed on. At least one younger scholar used the fire to illuminate connections between classical problems and our contemporary social concerns. In her recent book *Goddesses, Whores, Wives, and Slaves,* Sarah Pomeroy points out that documents written on papyrus form an indispensable source for studying the position of women in society in the Hellenistic and Roman periods. They are the ancient equivalent of the private letters and diaries we use to find out about women of later times.

As a feminist, Professor Pomeroy looks at the long history of classical attitudes toward women—from Hesiod, who attributed the woes of mankind to Pandora, the first woman, to the Stoics, whose syllogisms demonstrated that women's duty in this world is marriage and motherhood. A fully realized woman makes the male insecure, hence the Greek division of goddesses according to separate powers of virginity, eros, and motherhood. The fact that modern women are frustrated by being forced to choose "between being an Athena —an intellectual asexual career woman—or an Aphrodite—a frivolous sex object—or a respectable wife-mother like Hera shows that the Greek goddesses continue to be the archetypes of female existence." Professor Pomeroy concludes that the ancient confinement of women to loom and hearth and the long tradition of antifemale ideas carried on by the poets and philosophers of antiquity are "two of the most devastating creations in the classical legacy."

While I am not sure that John Day would have agreed with that drastic conclusion or that his beloved Greeks made Aphrodite into a frivolous sex object, he would have rejoiced in the scholarly work of his pupil. The book is dedicated to him.

Another amiable unicorn still pawed the Barnard turf in the early 1950s: Gladys Reichard, the anthropologist. For sheer beauty I would rank her illustrated volume on Navajo sand painting not far below the *Book of Kells*. She had her office near mine in the basement of Milbank, where I often chatted with her at her long-legged writing table built tall so she could work standing up like a bookkeeper in a Dickens novel. Legend had it that when she was younger she had been discovered in flagrant fault with a Columbia professor, a situation that in the opinion of some trustees called for her immediate dismissal. Dean Gildersleeve asked if the Columbia professor was to be dismissed. No? She passed on to other matters.

In faculty meetings, Gladys Reichard would get up to talk at great length along lines that few but she could follow. She looked and sounded like the screw-loose old party you would see today in television situation comedies. At one meeting, both the president of the college and the dean of the faculty both happened to be absent. Almost unprecedented. In such circumstances, faculty statutes required that the senior member of the faculty preside. To nearly everyone's dismay, it turned out that Gladys Reichard had more years' service at Barnard than anyone present, so she presided that Monday afternoon in the College Parlor. Nothing was accomplished. But then, whatever *is* accomplished at a faculty meeting?

It is to Gladys Reichard that I owe the unique experience of lunching with royalty. A Javanese princess, making a tour of American institutions of higher learning for women, was lunching with the distinguished anthropologist, and Gladys invited me to make a third at table. There sat the princess, as tiny as Ravel's Empress of the Pagodas, whose courtiers played on theorbos made from walnut shells and for whom all the silver temple bells rang when she took off her silken robe and stepped into her bath. Gladys's royal guest wore a robe of pale silk and silver sandals, and to my romantic fancy her voice sounded like the soft treble notes of a gamelan. I imagined that back in old Java she could order an offending subject strangled on the spot.

> *Asia, Asia, Asia*
> *Ancient land of marvels in old nurses' tales*
> *Where fantasy dwells like an empress*
> *In her forest full of mystery.*

During the war years, Gladys Reichard brought the anthropologist Claude Lévi-Strauss to offer a course at Barnard. A refugee in

New York, he was writing his formidable study *The Elementary Structure of Kinship*. That was before I came to Barnard. But nearly thirty years later, in the spring of 1972, Lévi-Strauss returned to Barnard for a lecture on Structuralism and Ecology. The Barnard gym was packed. In his introduction he paid tribute to Gladys Reichard (she had died in 1955) and told us how her major work *Navajo Religion* was written during the time when he, Roman Jakobson, and a small group of friends and colleagues gathered at her house near the Barnard campus. "She was a great anthropologist," he said. The structuralist master then recalled his first class at Barnard:

> When I entered the classroom and started lecturing on the Namik-wara Indians, my fright grew into panic: instead of taking notes, most of the girls were knitting until the hour was over as if they were utterly unconcerned with what I was saying or rather trying to say in my clumsy English. They did listen, though, for after the class was over, a girl (I can still see her: she was slender, graceful, with short and curly ash-blond hair and she wore a blue dress) came to me and said that it was all very interesting but she thought I should know that *desert* and *dessert* were two different words. Her remark, which left me quite dismayed, deserves recalling not only because it took place in these premises but also for another reason: it shows that in these remote years I was already interested in ecology and mixing it, at least on the linguistic level, with the culinary art to which I did turn much later for exemplifying some of the structural ways along which the human mind works.

A younger unicorn, rather skittish, was Ursula Niebuhr, the first woman to take a First in theology at Oxford. Sometimes that intelligent Englishwoman would bring her husband, Reinhold, to lunch after he had talked to her small religion class in the basement of Milbank between Gladys Reichard's old office and the philosophy department preserve. Reinhold talked and moved slowly, for he had recently suffered a stroke. He and I shared enthusiasm for the tele-vision program "Our Miss Brooks" starring Eve Arden as the wise-cracking blonde schoolteacher in love with Mr. Boynton, the unper-ceptive biology instructor. I was puzzled by Niebuhr's peculiar mix of Calvin and liberalism. His charismatic preaching of original sin and social reform has touched the minds and hearts of many gifted people, including W. H. Auden and Jimmy Carter, poet and president. But I never had much chance to discuss philosophy of religion with Niebuhr. For one thing, Ursula Niebuhr had the fixed idea that I was your basic R.C. with the usual package of fixed beliefs to which she would refer at table (arch glance in my direction) in her high Oxford whinny: "But Mr. Brennan, in this post-*Freudian* era, even *your* Church . . . etc."

Ursula, hunter of lions, snagged the poet Auden—invariably referred to as "Wystan"—to lecture in the Barnard religion department in the spring of 1947 and again briefly in 1956. I have a confused recollection of a session of Ursula's with Auden present. Someone held forth earnestly on Dialogue, but Auden just sat silent as if plunged in deepest gloom. But optimist Ursula spoke flutingly of "the upsurge of religious interest" on the part of the students.

Auden was a charitable man with an eye for fallen sparrows. About that time he read in the newspaper that Dorothy Day, radical Catholic and friend of the poor, was being forced to evict the derelicts she sheltered in her House of Hospitality down in the Lower East Side. She also had to pay a fine of $250 for violating the city fire laws. On her way to court she was accosted by a rumpled man who gave her a bit of paper, saying, "I have just read about your trouble. I want to help out a little toward the fine. Here's two fifty." Miss Day thanked the man for what she thought was a contribution of $2.50. Only later when she looked at the check did she see that it was for the full amount of the fine and signed by W. H. Auden.*

Years earlier he had married Thomas Mann's daughter Erika, though his sexual preferences did not lie in the direction of women. It was a brief union, the whole thing arranged by telephone and cable, and Auden saw his bride for the first time on the day of the wedding. It was a generous act on Auden's part to get Erika a British passport so she could leave Hitler's Europe.

Often I wondered why I never cared for Auden's verse as much as I was told I should. Maybe it was all those echoes of Yeats:

> *The earth is an oyster with nothing inside it,*
> *Not to be born is the best for man;*
> *The end of toil is a bailiff's order,*
> *Throw down the mattock and dance while you can.*

* Ursula Niebuhr and others have set down their recollections of the poet in Stephen Spender's *W. H. Auden* (New York: Macmillan, 1975).

His ballad about poor Miss Gee, too timid to live, has some kick to it, but then like so much twentieth-century art, it has to rely on parody, in this case the tune "St. James Infirmary":

> *They laid her on the table,*
> *The students began to laugh,*
> *And Mr. Rose the surgeon*
> *He cut Miss Gee in half.*

> *Mr. Rose he turned to his students,*
> *Said, "Gentlemen, if you please,*
> *We seldom see a sarcoma*
> *As far advanced as this."*

Auden said, "Read *The New Yorker!*" and "We must love one another or die." I could never read the one nor believe the other.

Ursula Niebuhr cultivated Lionel Trilling, another lion of woeful countenance, and those of us who dwelled in Ursula's corridor saw nearly as much of the gloomy face of Columbia's star English professor and literary critic as we did of Auden's crenellated brow. At that time (the mid-1950s) Trilling's book *The Liberal Imagination* was widely discussed. At first I did not care for Trilling's critical writings, and to this day I find his style hard going. I objected to his Freudianism, a sympathy which in those days I uncharitably considered the substitute religion of the New York Jewish intellectual paraculture. Trilling's concentration on certain English writers— Jane Austen, Matthew Arnold, E. M. Forster—seemed excessive. I still believe there's a grain of truth in Jonah Raskin's claim that Trilling may have lived on Claremont Avenue but his real home was Oxford 1870. Some found Trilling's personality hard to take. In my few contacts with him, he seemed agreeable and interested in what was going on in philosophy.

Philosopher Ernest Nagel, who like Trilling achieved the top rank of University Professor, thought his colleague's high manner derived from the snobbishness many professors of English tend to affect. Nagel and Trilling had been good friends in the old days but parted intellectual company on the subject of Jacques Barzun, for whom Trilling had an inordinate admiration. Nagel had read Barzun's *Darwin, Marx, and Wagner* and one day said to Trilling that he thought the book pontifical and ill-informed. To Nagel's surprise, Trilling remained huffily silent. Whereupon the mild-mannered Nagel, for once annoyed, proceeded to tear the book apart. After that, Trilling's friendship with Nagel cooled, though it never ceased.

Very late in the day I was brought around to esteem Trilling as a critic by a Columbia College student, Jeff Sawyer, my advisee. Two years before Trilling's death in 1975, Jeff turned up in my Philosophy and the Novel course and soon became friend and confidant. Curly-haired and pink-cheeked as his namesake in Mark Twain's story, Jeff had two passions: literary criticism and squash. (I'm not counting girls.) In class Jeff asked generic and unanswerable questions like, "How much can psychology tell us about the motivation of a novelist's characters?" and "What do you really think is the position of the artist in society today?" In his senior year Jeff did special philosophy readings at Barnard at the time he was taking his second course with Trilling. Each of our meetings in my office ended with a discussion of Trilling's classes. I quickly felt the powerful effect of Trilling's mind on this perceptive though still somewhat naïve student. Because of Jeff, I turned back to Trilling's older essays and then read through more recent ones like *Sincerity and Authenticity* of 1972. No question about it. A critical intelligence like Trilling's was a very good thing to have around at a time when so many were finding their pet subjects for art and entertainment in disorder, unreason, and outright madness—a time when from grade school on up students absorbed and fixated the belief that feeling and personal individualism were what counted most. To so many souls, to be simply what one *is* seemed quite enough by way of credentials for absolution and admiration. Trilling said it well, though I wonder about that spelling of "favor":

> The doctrine that madness is health, that madness is liberation and authenticity, receives a happy welcome from a consequential part of the educated public. . . . The falsities of an alienated social reality are rejected in favour of an upward psychopathic mobility to the point of divinity, each one of us a Christ—but with none of the inconveniences of undertaking to intercede, of being a sacrifice, of reasoning with rabbis, of making sermons, of having disciples, of going to weddings and funerals, or beginning something and at a certain point remarking that it is finished.

In his admiration for Trilling, Jeff tried to arrange a personal conference with the great man. Not much use. He was busy. The phone was ringing. Other professors looked in. He had an appointment. He could give Jeff five minutes. Poor Jeff, not knowing how best to exploit this brief encounter, blurted out some question about Trilling's single novel, *The Middle of the Journey,* only to be cut short by a curt, "I never discuss that. It's too personal." Strange that the author of "Of This Time, Of That Place," one of the most perceptive tales of the relation of professor and student, should be remembered for such a brush-off. A little less strange, perhaps, when the following year the novel was reissued with a sixteen-page introduction by the author. It was one of the last things Trilling wrote, and maybe he was planning it when he declined to talk about the novel to Jeff. In Jamesian style, with *"nouvelle"*s, *"donnée"*s, and carefully modulated expressions of cultivated distaste, Trilling says clearly what had been well known for years: that he modeled the character of Gifford Maxim after Whittaker Chambers, whom Trilling knew as a fellow student at Columbia in the 1920s. If you haven't read *The Middle of the Journey,* you might try it. Apart from its widely publicized tie to the incredible Hiss–Chambers case of the late 1940s, the novel has a quiet little life of its own.

When Trilling died in November 1975, I sent Jeff Sawyer, then living in Paris, the obituaries and other relevant articles about his late teacher. He wrote in acknowledgment:

> Trilling offered me more inspiration, more perspective, more truth (or what was for me truth) than anyone among the great novelists and philosophers. He exists in the literature of our civilization as inherent proof of the evolution of humanity toward maturity. But while I owe everything to him as a teacher, I owe nothing to him as a person. He was rather cold and without humor, abrupt, inaccessible. I think of Professor ———— [another of Jeff's teachers], who has also had much intellectual influence on me, but warmly, as a friend. I ask myself if Trilling, with all his spirit, was capable of that. Perhaps he could find it only in heaven, in his proper social rank, and it may be that he is already united in firm friendship with *le bon Dieu.*

One last unicorn of the 1950s—Rosalie Colie. She was also a literary scholar, brilliant too, but as erratic as Trilling was ordered and calm. Posie, as she liked to be called, taught in the Barnard English department for many years. She read several languages, including Dutch (she had been briefly married to a Hollander), and her interests and skills cut sharply across departmental lines, a fact that did not make her position in the Barnard English department any easier. Rosalie Colie had the double talent of attracting a few close friends and of repelling large numbers of her colleagues. "An impossible person!" they chanted antiphonally of Posie. She had an array of mannerisms that irritated people, including the harmless one of walking her dog on Broadway while she, abstracted, Hamlet-like, strolled reading on a book. She grappled certain admiring men friends to her with hooks of steel until they, exhausted by her insatiable desire to run their lives, unhooked themselves gasping.

Rosalie Colie's was the unique case of a question of retention of a faculty member openly debated on the floor of a Barnard faculty meeting. It was wild. Apparently the English department simply could not stand her—brilliant though she was. She had been nasty to the department long enough; she could now go and be nasty to people somewhere else. They had no objections to her staying on at Barnard in some other department—history perhaps, but not English. All kinds of people got up to speak about Posie, ranging from old Cabell Greet, professor of Anglo-Saxon and consultant to the Columbia Broadcasting System on how to pronounce words, to economist Bob Lekachman, who skillfully defended Posie, arguing that a college or university organized along traditional departmental lines should always provide a couple of nondepartmental professorships to accommodate versatile scholars like Posie who were both brilliant and (as Mrs. McIntosh used to say) "administratively difficult."

As things turned out, Posie was let go, and her scholarly talents were lost to Barnard. In time they were secured by Brown University where she became Nancy Duke Lewis Professor of Comparative Literature. Her major works appeared late—*Paradoxica Epidemica* in 1966, a volume on Andrew Marvell in 1970, and *The Resources of Mind,* a study of Renaissance genre theory published posthumously in 1973.

Rosalie had a history of depression, and at least once she had taken pills in a suicide attempt, then spent a while in a psychiatric nursing home. One day in the summer of 1972 Rosalie Colie took a small boat out by herself from the Connecticut shore into Long Island Sound. She never came back. It was given out that the cause of death was a boating accident.

BARNARD: STUDENTS, 1950s

℘ On the wall of my office at Barnard there used to hang a large reproduction of Jules Breton's painting *Song of the Lark*. It's an old-fashioned picture of the anecdotal type, showing a peasant girl on her way to the fields at sunrise pausing to listen to the notes of a bird. Early in the century Willa Cather saw the painting in the Chicago Art Institute and later gave its title to her novel about Thea Kronborg, the young singer from Moonstone, Colorado, whose struggle for artistic success and her achievement of it is the subject of the story.

In her preface to a later edition of the novel, Willa Cather says that a story of effort *toward* achievement is far more interesting than any chronicle of professional success itself. To her that was particularly true of the artist, a type that fascinated her from early youth in Nebraska, a type she herself wanted to become and did. On rereading her *Song of the Lark* Cather made the point that when a talented person reaches that period of life where one defines oneself by career, one's personal life—at least in the telling of it—becomes somewhat dry and preoccupied. She recognized that the first part of the story of Thea's struggle for success in the world of music carried much more interest than the later chapters, which are taken up by the account of her heroine's success as an opera singer, making it to the Metropolitan in New York, her days taken up with rehearsals, fittings, coachings, booking agents, and all the rushing to get ready for matinees and evening performances.

The same rule holds in the case of a college or university teacher who has made nearly all of his or her career in the academic world. Who wants to hear about lectures, research, books written, professional meetings attended, papers read, the awards, fellowships and sabbaticals that mark off one teaching cycle from another? Oh, one can go on at length about what's wrong with the education of young people today or how science and technology have transformed the world by solid-state circuitry or why we must preserve the humanities and instill in our students a Deep Sense of Human Values. But all that is *about* education—meta-education, as they say in the journals—and most of the time it's pretty dull stuff. When someone who has made a good career in education starts generalizing about things like that, he's usually a little tired of teaching, and the story of his exertions will seem arid and devoid of interest even to himself.

Willa Cather took a dim view of teaching as a career (she had done some herself) and warned her young friends against it. In *My Mortal Enemy,* the aging beauty Myra Henshaw hears that the narrator is teaching and protests:

> Ah, but teaching, Nellie! I don't like that, not even for a temporary expedient. It's a cul-de-sac. Generous young people use themselves all up at it; they have no sense. Only the stupid and phlegmatic should teach.

There's a bit of truth in Myra's dictum. Many who are unbelievably stupid go in for what Gilbert Highet calls the Immortal Profession, and many who are bright and gifted burn themselves out in their eagerness to meet the insatiable demands of their students. That's why in midcareer so many teachers find themselves gone stale, sour, drained, repeating themselves. An old French scholar-priest said to a group of *aspirants* preparing for the teaching profession, "Give the light of your lamp to your students, but do not give away all the oil to them as well. Try to keep some of that for yourself."

Pessimism and discouragement overtake us teachers at times, particularly as one gets on a bit. Nothing wrong with that. Although most people think we have it easy, teaching can make you feel, as an Irish professor once put it, as if your soul had been drawn out through your toenails leaving you so weak you couldn't pull the socks off a dead man. For myself, I have a good cure for such moods. I think of my former students, those that stand out in memory. Some bright, some not so. Some who have made brilliant careers, others whose riches are known best to themselves and those close to them.

Sometimes I remember happily all the bright Jewish students of the 1950s who came to Barnard from the upper 10 percent of the graduating classes of their New York City high schools. What philosophers they made! Education-oriented by family tradition, trained in the methods of subtle argument by their Jewish studies outside of regular school hours, they were the best philosophy students in the world. Maimonides says that the first question on Judgment Day will be whether one has fulfilled the duty of study. They fulfilled that duty. Those young women came from a culture that revered books and study. Learned dispute was second nature to them. From conning the Talmud under the sharp eye and tongue of some scholarly rabbi, they had already experienced the intellectual joy of analyzing and questioning a difficult text. They did not need to have the study of philosophy defended or explained to them. How could anyone come to college and *not* want to study philosophy?

I must confess that some of them surprised me by their rudeness—or what appeared to be rudeness—to one another. These were the daughters of Eastern European Jews walled off in their Brooklyn ghettoes from social amenities others could take for granted. Their lack of manners often distressed the more sophisticated Jewish girls, whose families lived in the East Seventies or on Central Park West. "Why didn't they go to *Hunter?*" they would whisper when one of their classmates from Flatbush hurled an occasional "So shut up, already!" across the lecture room.

Though I would tell myself that my business was to teach philosophy, not social graces, sometimes I would dream about giving a lecture on courtesy or (I can't think of a better word) manners. The lecture would be for all the students, for those Jewish girls were not the only students who seemed not to have learned the rules of common politeness. Here is an abstract of the lecture. Very pedantic:

> The German philosopher Kant taught that each person is autonomous. That is, a being of good will and right reason capable of making moral judgments for himself or herself. As such, each person is sovereign and of unconditioned dignity and worth. Hence persons should be treated as ends in themselves. Never as means only. One's neighbor is a person, a rational being, and as such worthy of attention as an end, not an object to be kicked, a tool to be used or a hummock of earth to be ignored or walked on.
>
> Now this teaching of Kant is but a philosophical version of a doctrine implicit in the religious tradition of Judaism and Christianity, that the human is an ethical being, inviolable, each equally object of God's love. Without benefit of such philosophy or reli-

gious teaching, simple common-sense ethics recognizes this principle: other people are human like ourselves and so we should respect them.

Hence [a real pedant's word, like *now* above] courtesy, or true politeness, is not just an affair of what proper Bostonians used to call "good breeding." Courtesy is, rather, the external sign of our recognition of the independence, importance, and sovereign worth of another, a sign that we regard the other as a being intrinsically *worthy of attention,* not an object in the way to be brushed aside or looked through as if he or she did not exist. Simone Weil says, " 'You do not interest me.' No man can say these words to another without committing a cruelty and offending against justice." True morality lies not in judgment, but in attention. And what is courtesy, even in the modest form of greeting someone in passing, but the outward sign that the person is worthy of attention, that his or her existence is recognized.

Enough, already. I never gave the lecture.

Not all of the Barnard philosophy students were of Jewish ancestry. There was Ave Maria Brennan, who gave me a bit of a problem, for we usually called our students by their first names. When she raised her hand I felt I was starting a prayer rather than recognizing a member of the class. Tenki Tenduf-la, a young Tibetan woman, touched briefly at Barnard, wearing the wrap-around robe and colorful striped apron of her native land. When I asked her how she liked to be addressed, her exotic eyes gazed at me from her inscrutable Mongol face as she replied, "M' friends call me Peggy." I recall girls with Jugoslav, Hungarian, French, and WASP names who became professors of philosophy. For the many Patricia Greenspans who went to Harvard on a fellowship for the Ph.D. in philosophy, there would be one or two Eileen O'Neills off to Princeton for theirs. Mary Gallagher, one of the outstanding students of the 1950s, shared the Montague Prize in philosophy with Rhoma Mostel, niece of the actor Zero.

Mary Gallagher, daughter of a prosperous Chicago contractor, came to Barnard after a year at St. John's College, Annapolis, and a year at New York University, which did not completely satisfy her either. From the outset it was clear that in Mary we had a personage on our hands. The upward movement of her eyebrows made it plain that she was not accustomed to being addressed by *her* first name. On her arrival, she informed the faculty of the philosophy department that she was not only interested in learning what this or that philosopher taught, but whether what they taught was *true*. This caused some of us to re-think our courses a little. She expressed astonishment to me as chairman of the department that there was no philosophy club at Barnard. She proceeded at once to form one, and it was a success. At one meeting of the club under Mary's imperious eye, Mark Van Doren was the speaker. The College Parlor filled early on and people drifted up and down the aisles looking for seats. Just before Professor Van Doren began his talk, there appeared on the other side of the shut glass doors Columbia philosophy professors John Hermann Randall, Jr., Horace L. Friess, Ernest Nagel, and their wives. Usher Rhoma Mostel saw them and reported to Mary Gallagher that there were some people out there who wanted to get in. Mary glanced at them and said in her loud upper-class voice, "Well, Rhoma, we just can't let the whole *neighborhood* in."

After Barnard, Mary Gallagher went on to take a Ph.D. in linguistics, after studying with Chomsky and others at M.I.T. and Illinois. She became coauthor of a book on the teaching of English, taught linguistics as assistant professor, got tired of that, went to Harvard Law School, took her degree from there, and joined the Justice Department in Washington. There today her keen mind and intolerance and shoddiness trouble the repose of many a government bureaucrat. She reminds them that Justice, after all, was the end and purpose of Plato's Republic and that its Guardians had the high responsibility of achieving and preserving it.

Mary loves sailing. When you turn the tiller, she explains, the boat doesn't say, "Oh, we haven't any of those left," or "That's not part of my job," or "I'm planning to do it tomorrow"—the boat just *goes*.

As an undergraduate, Mary Gallagher attracted the attention of Judith Jarvis, at that time an instructor in the Barnard philosophy department. Their mutual respect for high standards and small patience for sloppiness soon made them friends. I first knew Judy Jarvis as an undergraduate philosophy major at Barnard—a quick, well-groomed New York girl with dark hair and snapping black eyes, who could solve four technical logic problems while I was doing one. Work being done at the time by English philosophers interested

Judy, and I was happy to take her and Betty Rubinstein, another major, to visit A. J. Ayer's class at New York University where he was visiting professor for the term. Judy had some sharp questions for the author of *Language, Truth and Logic,* at that time still a notorious book. For a time she attended a very exclusive seminar that Lionel Trilling and Jacques Barzun had laid on for a select group of Barnard and Columbia students. She gave it up when one of the professors asked the class to imagine that they were not in a Columbia seminar but in an English drawing room.

As senior majors, Judy and her friend Virginia "Janie" Potter gave Helen Parkhurst, then still head of the Barnard philosophy department, the impression of not taking the philosophy requirements as seriously as they deserved. After the final comprehensive examinations that year (1950), Helen came to me in a troubled state. She had just read Miss Jarvis's and Miss Potter's examination papers and was seriously considering flunking them both, thus preventing their graduation. They had been *flip* in certain parts of their papers and had practically *ignored* the important question on aesthetics which Helen herself had devised. I said that was deplorable, but I thought two such talented students should not be held up. Other members of the department concurred and Miss Jarvis and Miss Potter went forth into the world with their degrees, both to make a name for themselves (as Judith Thomson and Virginia Held) in the world of American philosophy.

After graduation, Judy went to England on a Fulbright fellowship and studied philosophy at Cambridge with John Wisdom. Upon taking a degree, she returned to this country and went into business for two years. Wisdom had discouraged her from going into philosophy. This astonished me, but I gathered later that Judy had run into that perfectionism then fashionable at Cambridge, perhaps part of the heritage of Wittgenstein who disliked the very idea of a professional philosopher. He was particularly unhappy with the thought of anyone's becoming a "lady philosopher," although he admired the work of Alice Ambrose and Elizabeth Anscombe.

Judy returned to philosophy and completed her work for the Ph.D. at Columbia, while an instructor at Barnard, junior member of the department that included Jean Potter and Stan Thayer, later of Bryn Mawr and City College of New York, respectively. She wrote her dissertation on "Necessary Truth," and her defense of it at her final examination (I was present as a member of the committee) was brief and brilliant. Not all of us could follow it in every part, for Judy's mind was so oddly subtle that she could think in quarter tones, in the cracks of the piano, so to speak, while the rest of us straggled after her in our homely diatonic. Even Ernest Nagel, senior member of the committee, admitted he couldn't keep track of Judy, but cheerfully joined in the unanimous vote of approval.

It was characteristic of Nagel that during Judy's defense he kept out of sight his lack of sympathy with much of the English philosophy of the day. He considered a lot of it no more than "a priori psychology." While at Cambridge on a Guggenheim fellowship in 1935 Nagel had been encouraged by G. E. Moore to sit in on any course he liked, provided he spoke to the instructor first. He was welcomed to all courses save Wittgenstein's. At their first meeting, Wittgenstein told him that he didn't like "tourists" coming to his lectures, then added, "You would not understand my philosophy." Finally, on Nagel's gentle persistence, Wittgenstein said, "When I teach my philosophy I *suffer*. When I see a strange face I suffer *more*. You wouldn't want me to suffer more, would you?" The compassionate Nagel gave it up.

Judy left the Barnard faculty after she married the English philosopher James Thomson (they are now divorced) and with him joined Massachusetts Institute of Technology's philosophy department. A brilliant series of articles quickly brought her to the front rank of younger American philosophers. Her writing for the journals often shows her gift for unusual metaphor. Here is an example. Like many of the younger philosophers Judy turned in the 1970s from purely technical questions of philosophy to moral issues of the day. In an essay on abortion she invited those who consider the fetus to have a person's right to life from the moment of conception to consider whether there might not be some similarity to the presence of an unwanted fetus in the womb and the hooking-up of a famous, critically ailing, violinist to your kidneys without so much as a by-your-leave:

> The director of the hospital now tells you, "Look, we're sorry the Society of Music Lovers did this to you—we would never have permitted it if we had known. But still, they did it, and the violinist is now plugged into you. To unplug you would be to kill him. But never mind, it's only for nine months. By then he will have re-

covered from his ailment and can safely be unplugged from you."
Is it morally incumbent on you to accede to this situation?

Reading this, you may say that Judy's analogy, if it holds at all,
is valid only for justifying abortion in cases of rape. But she believes
the analogy can be extended to a broader range and proceeds to explain why. Yet she does not favor indiscriminate abortion. Judy
worked for a long time on a book about ethics. "But I threw that
out," she writes in a recent letter, "in a fit of common sense." She
turned from ethics to complete her book *Acts and Other Events.*

Pamela Moore '57 wrote novels, not philosophy. She too was a
native New Yorker and as well-brushed as Judy Jarvis, whose first
term as instructor coincided with Pamela's senior year at Barnard.
But the younger writer came from a more WASPish background. She
graduated from Rosemary Hall School (now gone coed with Choate),
wore Brooks Brothers shirts, smoked Gauloises, and spoke somewhat
theatrically in the accents of the privileged. Pamela had the art of
successful self-dramatization, and with some right. At eighteen, she
had published her first novel *Chocolates for Breakfast,* a chronicle of
sad young love among the rich. Her heroine fights running battles
with her divorced actress-mother, experiments with alcohol and wrist-
cutting, has her pink Brooks Brothers shirt unbuttoned for the first
time by a smooth Hollywood type. *Chocolates* hit the best-seller
charts and was quickly reprinted in paperback and translated into
eleven foreign languages.

Although Pamela majored in English rather than philosophy,
she often came to our seminar room after class hours to listen to
records from the departmental collection played on our high fidelity
phonograph. The first time she appeared I was sitting alone in the
deserted seminar room listening to a recording of a choral group
singing a motet. It was Josquin Des Prés's *Misericordias Domini,*
one of those masterworks of Renaissance polyphony of unearthly
beauty, the kind that lifts us up above the urgency and venom of
the world and bestows a few moments of tranquillity. An authorita-
tive voice at the door broke the silence that followed the last ca-
dence: "Only once before in my life have I heard music of such
purity."

I turned to see a smallish dark-haired student with a blue cigarette pack in her hand.

"When was that?"

"When I first heard the chorus of the Red Army!"

She came nearer, stared at me a moment, then said, "Do you know that you have a very Irish head?"

Friendly critics thought Pamela Moore was America's answer to Françoise Sagan. After graduation she tried to live up to the part by writing variations on *Bonjour Tristesse,* but didn't quite make it. When she wrote her last novel, *The Horsey Set,* she was living with her husband and nine-month-old baby in a Brooklyn Heights apartment. One day she laid down her writing, put the barrel of a .22-caliber rifle in her mouth, and pulled the trigger. A page of the diary beside her contained a reference to Ernest Hemingway's suicide. Pamela was twenty-seven when she died. I still have the record *Misericordias Domini,* but it's badly scratched.

By the way, funds for that record collection and phonograph, together with new furniture and expensive draperies for the philosophy seminar room, had been contributed in memory of Gertrude Rich by some members of her Barnard class after her death in 1953. Gertrude was an assistant professor when I joined the Barnard philosophy department and very much under the thumb of Monty and Helen Parkhurst. When she took her Ph.D. at Columbia "the people across the street" (euphemism for the Columbia philosophy department) said she should not expect to rise above the rank of assistant professor. Gertrude had a friendly and cheerful manner. She spent endless hours counseling students. Active in church work (Riverside), she set store by her social position on Morningside Heights. Her husband became well known as a patent lawyer and later achieved a federal judgeship. Gertrude doted on her adopted daughter, Verity, who went on from Chapin to Radcliffe. When Helen Parkhurst retired, Mrs. McIntosh named Gertrude chairman of the philosophy department and promoted her to associate professor despite "the people across the street." The big office, once inhabited by Monty and Helen, blossomed now in bright paint. A fine new desk appeared as a gift from Gertrude's husband, and all was gotten ready for the occupancy of the smiling new department head in the fall. Early in July I had an urgent telephone call from Newtown, Connecticut, where the Riches had their summer place. The night before, Gertrude had put herself to sleep with a massive overdose of barbiturates. She did not wake up.

Happier fates awaited many Barnard students of the fifties. By way of a correct New York school for girls, Francine du Plessix brought wit and intelligence from France as well as all the courtesy that the particle of nobility in her name implied. Although she received only an *assez bien* in logic, she got a *très bien* in metaphysics. Francine expressed well-bred surprise that American professors, particularly certain ones in philosophy, were not the bourgeois types she had expected. After graduation she married and wrote as Francine du Plessix Gray, her material appearing in *The New Yorker,* the *New York Review of Books,* and other right places. In *Divine Disobedience,* Francine looked at radical movements in the Church following Vatican II, her far-out priests were rather funny, and she became upper-class Catholic chic. Her recent semi-autobiographical *Lovers and Tyrants* quickly became a best-seller. Decked out with fashionably explicit sexual arabesques, Francine's novel suggests what might have become of Erica Jong's Isadora had she possessed an aristocratic French father, a Russian mother, and had oscillated between Paris–St. Tropez and New York–Cambridge, dealing with husbands, lovers, sexually liberated priests, and occasionally recalling a friend from her undergraduate years at (not Barnard) Radcliffe. Nothing bourgeois about heroine Stephanie. Well, almost nothing. In the early days of her marriage in the 1950s, she spends five whole hours unbourgeoisely making a single *pâté en croute* to please her husband and even buys some of ". . . that bourgeois finery I've always detested, china, monogrammed towels, a little silver even," to reassure the creature. Then she says "I hung his Harvard summa-cum degree over his desk." But wait! You can't hang a degree over anything; it's a rank, not an object. Just as "home" is bourgeois for "house," so is "degree" for "diploma." (Francine: "I take it back. He was bourgeois all along. Only a bourgeois could be that pedantic!")

Alessandra Comini '58 had no *particule de noblesse* to her name. She came from Texas. When she arrived at Barnard, Alessandra (I liked to pronounce her first name, drawing out the vowels) looked like your basic American girl, very young, bright merry eyes, round childlike cheeks, brown hair cut short Catholic schoolgirl fashion. She played the flute, sang folk songs, and occasionally came out in class with remarks that showed unusual familiarity with European high culture.

After she graduated from Barnard, Alessandra turned professional folk singer for a while, opening her own café in Dallas and later in San Francisco. She wrote many of her own songs and recorded some of her compositions. Then she worked for the Columbia-Princeton Electronic Music Studios on 125th Street, a job that sent her to Europe to collect more folk songs and to demonstrate electronic music. In Czechoslovakia she experienced a sort of epiphany while demonstrating a five-string banjo to interested, if sullen, groups. She wrote to me that she was overtaken by a sense of protective interest in the humanities, a vague but consuming wish to take the part of the West and its civilization against what seemed to her the zombie dehumanization of the Communist East. This brought her back to graduate study first at Berkeley, then at Columbia, where she taught for a number of years in the department of art history as well as at Berkeley, Yale, and Princeton. Eventually she returned to Dallas, where she became professor of fine arts in the Meadows School of the Arts of Southern Methodist University.

In 1974 Comini's *Egon Schiele's Portraits* appeared, a monster sixty-five-dollar-a-copy job from the University of California Press, a blockbuster of a book with fascinating text and beautiful, terrifying reproductions in black-and-white and in marvelous color. Alessandra's Schiele volume had much the same kind of shock effect produced in me by Alan Trueblood's noble tome on Lope de Vega—the two were published in the same year. How *could* mere mortals whom I had known as young Navy ensigns in North Africa and France, or Barnard students with Catholic schoolgirl haircuts, turn into magicians, metamorphosize into demiurges capable of creating works like these? No answer, but a wonderful feeling. It warms the entrails, as the Spaniards say.

Egon Schiele was an Austrian painter, a tormented Kafka-like genius who died in 1918 at the age of twenty-eight. Amid a treasure of other works, he left behind an astonishing series of self-portraits, absolutely hair-raising in their extremity of self-obsessed romantic agony. Schiele's father was a syphilitic railroad employee who died mad at fifty-four. His son drew pictures of trains rushing through the night. As a sex-tormented adolescent he made nude drawings of his twelve-year-old sister, and once took her on a train ride to Trieste that duplicated their parents' honeymoon itinerary. In 1906 at the age of sixteen he was admitted to the Vienna Academy of Fine Arts, the prestigious institution that a year later would reject a less-talented aspirant named Adolf Hitler.

In Vienna, Schiele was befriended by Gustav Klimt, grand master of the *Jugendstil* tradition, whose sumptuous paintings, gilded and flowered, transformed Viennese society ladies into femmes fatales. At first, Schiele tried to paint in the style of Klimt, who got him a job at the Vienna Werkestatte as he had already done for Klimt's comrade Oskar Kokoschka. But soon Schiele groped his way to a tormented style of his own, a naked Expressionist ugliness, a brutal autosexuality that horrified an elite accustomed to the idealized eroticism of Klimt. A series of frightening self-portraits streamed from Schiele's workroom in the years just before the 1914 war. Standing naked before a full-length mirror, the artist painted himself as a skeletal figure barely covered with flesh, torso twisted by unbearable inner pressure, bony fingers on the ends of hands cutting hatchet-like toward his own genitals, face twisted by a suppressed scream of pain, hair standing on end like that of a man undergoing electrocution.

In a village where he had a studio, Schiele was arrested for painting children in a room hung with his own erotic pictures. The judge burned one of his drawings before his eyes and sent him to jail for twenty-four days. Poor Schiele could not believe it. How could anyone lock up an artist? He wrote in his diary:

> Not very far from me, so near that he would have to hear my voice if I were to shout, there sits in his magistrate's office a judge, or whatever he is. A man, that is, who believes that he is something special, who has visited churches, museums, theatres, concerts, yes, probably even art exhibitions. A man who consequently is numbered among the educated class which has read or at least heard of the life of the artist. And this man can permit me to be locked up in a cage.

In the great influenza epidemic of 1918, Schiele caught influenza from his wife. As she lay dying he drew her picture and, when she could no longer talk, put a pencil and paper in her hands. She managed to scrawl that she loved him endlessly. Four days later, Schiele himself died. His last words were, "The war is over. . . . and I have to go, Mama."

Alessandra's big book on Egon Schiele (she has since brought out a smaller one, as well as a companion Klimt volume) proved too much for the critic of the *Times Literary Supplement* who reviewed the book with deep respect up to a point. Further than that he could not go. He gave unstinting praise to Professor Comini's scholarship, but could not understand her curious detachment in the face of such "perverse unmaskings," could not accept her strange calm, "the relentless way in which Professor Comini examines the convulsions and contortions of Schiele's artistic and psychological development." Perhaps, he suggested, she had become infected by the spectral X-ray vision of Schiele himself.

When Alessandra Comini was at Barnard with her Catholic schoolgirl haircut, examinations were given under the honor system, an arrangement that held until the early 1970s when complete cross-arrangement between Barnard and Columbia forced a changeover to the Columbia system, in which examinations are proctored by faculty members or their surrogates. Under the old Barnard system, the instructor handed out the examination papers, stayed a bit for questions, then left the room to return only at the end of the exam to pick up the blue books. Students were on their honor not to cheat or plagiarize. The system worked pretty well over the years. Barnard's internal structure was rather familial, and a student honor board handled irregularities. Most Barnard students had enough sense to see the long-range profitlessness of academic cheating. To some, it was a matter of individual conscience, and in Alessandra Comini's case that conscience declared itself in a rather sweet and touching way. To a note I wrote her about the Schiele book in 1976, she replied, "How extraordinary that your letter should arrive on the very day I recounted to a class of 184 students the same *JGB Story* I have related to countless classes for the past decade as a Warning Not to Cheat on the Final Exam." She enclosed a copy of the following:

Parable

AC came to Barnard College, following her mother's footsteps, in 1952. She came from a Catholic high school in Dallas where she had a thought-provoking course during her senior year called Logic. Studying the Barnard catalogue, she found a course given under the Philosophy Department called Symbolic Logic. She was elated to recognize the second word in the title and gave little thought to the first word—*symbolic*—it must be something like *religious,* since hitherto *Logic* had been, for her, the property of Catholics. And so she signed up for the course quite pleased that she would be able to steal a march on the other students since she had already studied Logic.

Another encouraging factor, she discovered on the first day of class, that the course was given by a soft-spoken cello-playing man called PRO FESS OR BRENNAN. Soon AC was not only enjoying the syllogisms, in which she played a minor premise, but also the pronouncements of the Major Premise, the PRO FESS OR, on subjects outside the realm of Logic, such as Brahms and Schubert.

BUT! Two weeks deep into the course conditions changed. The "Logic" disappeared and the "Symbolic" emerged. Gone were the verbal syllogisms and their obvious conclusions; instead PRO FESS OR B. now covered the blackboard with algebraic formulas like

$$(\exists x)\ Fx\ .\ Gx$$

Now AC also followed her mother's footsteps in another sense: she had absolutely no head for, no potential for comprehension of MATH in any shape or form. Despair! Only now did AC notice that her classmates were all pre-med or science students! Horrors! What to do?

An agitated confession of noncomprehension to the kindly PRO FESS OR produced encouragement and sympathy, leaving AC determined to pass the course or die. She did not want to disappoint the Humanist Who Also Knew and Understood Math. The semester wore on. AC took voluminous notes and faithfully copied down every recipe (or "Formula," as the Humanist called them) presented in class. She could not determine how much of the code represented the question, and how much constituted the solution, but she took down EVERYTHING! In the meanwhile PRO FESS OR expressed such genial confidence in AC that she did not dare to tell him again that she still had absolutely no idea of what was going on in class. At last the end of the semester came and a date was set for a final exam. AC spent days staring at the Greek formulas in front of her. What to do? Coaching from her mathematically inclined roommate did not help to fill the great BLANK of AC's mind as she gazed at her 125 boxcars of chugging formula trains. Using a verbal syllogism (ah! the good old days of humanoid language) AC arrived at the dismal *conclusion* that she was going to fail the exam, the course, and worst of all, fail the expectations of the Humanist Who Also Knew and Understood Math. What to do?

A *solution* presented itself: an evil, but practical Voice whispered into AC's ear, "Cheat." So AC prepared a "cheat sheet." A dozen or so of the longest boxcar ensembles were copied down on a piece of paper and on the day of the exam this paper was neatly slipped underneath the regulation Blue Book. AC sat in the very back of the room, conforming to a symbolic logic all her own, which pinpointed her as the lowest of the low, the WORM in the bottom of the bucket. She even felt slimy, but desperation postponed total self-repugnance.

The exam was being given on the "honor" system. AC was ready to save *her* honor, so all was harmonious if tense. The Humanist made a few final remarks to the class, walked over to AC, and said, reaching for her Blue Book, "Well, A les *san* dra! Let's see how you are getting along." The Blue Book was in mid-air; the cheat sheet was falling out! "OH, NO! PRO FESS OR BRENNAN! I want to *surprise* you!" shrieked AC, throwing her body on top of the Blue Book and restoring it and cheat sheet to the desk top. Sweet accord illuminated the features of the HUMANIST and he left the room.

Whew! That was close! And now to work. AC worked the two human language syllogisms and then turned to the recipes. Deftly she slipped out the cheat sheet so that she could compare the hieroglyphics with the ones on the test. Ah, so craftily, so silently. She checked the backs of the heads of her fellow students. Everyone was absorbed in "solving." AC lowered her eyes to the cheat sheet, pen poised and ready to transfer data.

And then something totally unexpected happened. The moment AC focused on the correct formula, her vision *blurred*. Blurred so much that she could not read the formula. She looked away, surveyed the room, and gazed back down at the redemption sheet; it immediately went out of focus. At the same time someone began beating a large drum in a steady but agitated rhythm. Oh dear, it was not a drum after all, but a tell-tale heart; AC's own pounding heart! Odd that none of the other students turned to stare at her. How could they ignore that noise?

For the next sixty minutes AC attempted—in vain—to read the formulas on the cheat sheet. Each time she looked, the formulas stubbornly went out of focus. Each time she looked back at her still-blank Blue Book, everything came clearly into focus. What frustration! That guilt could be so powerful! But guilt, Guilt, that is, wasn't through with its victim yet. A new physical defect beset AC. All at once her eyes started blinking rapidly and involuntarily. Now, not only was her vision blurred, but her eyelids blinked and SQUEAKED loudly as they did so. The squeaks compounded the drumbeat of the heart and AC thought that the final hour had come. Other students were leaving the room—the exam was almost over! Two hours had been spent in squeaking and blinking!

AC balled up the cheat sheet in disgust and threw it away. Immediately the squeaking and blinking and blurring stopped. The drum ceased its beating and AC felt an enormous sense of relief. Guilt had retreated. She was on her own again. She wrote out a few recipes as best she could from memory and that was that. Somehow she did not fail the course. I think she even got a C.
The moral? DO NOT CHEAT.

The most atypical Barnard student I ever encountered had the unlikely name of Sue-Sue Ellen Cable. She arrived at the college in the early 1950s from a small place in tidewater South Carolina where her father was a prominent local "Dimocrat." She had enormous dark eyes, black curly hair, natural scarlet flush on high cheekbones in a delicate heart-shaped face, and an unbelievable accent. Very slim, she carried herself so straight and yet so easily that she seemed taller than she really was. Sue-Sue Ellen enrolled in my section of Introduction to Philosophy with mixed results. She was quite intelligent, but given to bursts of strange scattered thoughts; her writing often came unstuck in the middle. On one test she interrupted her explanation of the distinction between analytic and synthetic propositions by drawing a doomed bird, with title:

THWARTED INTELLECTUAL GYRATIONS

When I asked Sue-Sue Ellen later what this inserted artwork had to do with the point at issue, she kicked up her scarlet flush a couple of degrees and said,
"Oh, ah jist stuck it in fer the *hail* of it. Hope yew din' *mahnd!*"
Of course, I *did* mind, but what, as Sue-Sue Ellen would say, the hail.
Sue-Sue Ellen's informalities on test papers ran into a brick wall in the person of a visiting French scholar in whose class she enrolled.

A test paper she wrote for him made him angry and, as I happened to be passing by after he read it, he showed me her blue book. On the last page she had added a message:

Cher professor. Je regret que j'ai fait cette examen si mauvaisement. Mais j'etais une peu malade hier soir et je ne pouvait pas etudier for votre examen. Merci pour votre gentil consideration. Affectionatement,

Sue-Sue Ellen

P. S. Votre course fait me un grand plaisir.

"I cannot believe it," the scholar said, batting the blue book with the back of his fingers. "I make a simple test on La Fontaine. And this young woman from the South, herself of a name that makes the sound of alligators slithering in the Florida swamps, writes me a little note. The grammar! And not an accent! Tell me, do ALL American students write little notes to their professors in their examination papers? *Affectionatement,* donc? I tell you, my dear colleague, I do not know what to do with such a paper. It passes the understanding."

"All the same," I said, "it's nice to know she is enjoying your course."

One day in the West End, a big noisy eat-and-drink place on Broadway crowded with students, I noticed Sue-Sue Ellen sitting at a table with a Columbia boy I recognized from my classes: Marvin Kalish, a junior Phi Beta Kappa, destined to a Ph.D. at Harvard in (I think) comparative literature. Since Marvin and I were musical amateurs we sometimes talked music as well as philosophy together. At this moment Marvin was bending on his companion that look of mingled pride and awe a young ornithologist might direct to some rare, elaborate bird he has discovered, a species hitherto unknown to science. As I passed their table, Sue-Sue called out in her weird accent: "Halo, perfesser, hair yew? We'd lak f'yew t' jine us. We're drinkin' bare!" Hospitably she pointed to the half-filled pitcher on the table. Unwilling to disturb Marvin's enchantment, I went on with a smile and a hand-wave.

Sue-Sue Ellen did not graduate from Barnard. One day she left college and returned to South Carolina. She was never heard of again, by me at least. Marvin received one garrulous Christmas card. The rest was silence.

"Her mouth," Marvin confided to me one day when I thought it no more than friendly to invite him to the West End for a sandwich and drink, "her mouth was so soft, and her smile—you remember she was always smiling—it was a smile only an unbearable sadness could erase.

"There's a piece of music, not very great maybe, by William Barlow—*The Winter's Past,* a rhapsody for oboe and orchestra. Do you know it? Well, for his first theme he uses a sort of transposition of the old folk song, 'Black Is the Color of My True Love's Hair.' Only you wouldn't recognize it, if you weren't looking for it. Now that theme, the way the oboe plays it first, is *exactly* the way Sue-Sue Ellen . . ."

Marvin went on in the same exalted vein. I said nothing, but nodded sympathetically from time and time and sipped my bare.

HOFSTRA: F. M. FORD & BIALA

Hofstra University is in Hempstead, Long Island, about twenty-five miles out from Manhattan. To augment my Barnard instructor's salary back in the old Levittown days, I joined the Hofstra faculty to teach part-time. The college (as it was then) turned out to be such a pleasant place—good faculty, able and unusual students, excellent research facilities—that I remained on the staff as special lecturer after the pressing need for money to support a growing family had passed.

Beginning as a small commuter college, Hofstra expanded wildly as masses of war veterans returned to seek or complete their higher education. My first classes were taught in the evening in Quonset huts taken over from the Air Force across Hempstead Turnpike in Mitchell Field. Young businessmen and -women, recently moved out to the Island, wanted evening courses, and Hofstra provided them. A youthful and fertile population needed schoolteachers, and Hofstra had education programs to train them. Today nearly half of Nassau and Suffolk (the two Long Island counties) school superintendents, principals, and teachers have a Hofstra degree.

In the 1960s, Hofstra became a university, with graduate schools of education, business, and law. Residence dormitories appeared, their concrete towers rising nakedly from the Hempstead plain in contrast to the modest Dutch-adapted architecture of the earlier permanent buildings. By the 1970s, like so many other private colleges and universities, Hofstra found itself overexpanded and in trouble because of inflation, rising costs, a tenured-in faculty, and massive draining away of its students by the growing number of low-tuition public community and state colleges close by. In 1976 Hofstra's financial condition forced the resignation of its president, Robert Payton, former U.S. ambassador to the Cameroons, now head of the Exxon Education Fund.

But in the 1950s when I first lectured there Hofstra grew and flourished under the leadership of John Cranford Adams, a college president of the handsome silver-haired type you used to see in the movies. An Elizabethan scholar, Adams constructed a replica of the Globe Theatre on campus and sparked off the college's tradition of annual Shakespeare festivals. Hofstra's faculty was mostly young and energetic; many would move on to higher places or do unusual things. John Senior reorganized the comparative literature program at the University of Kansas. Henry Acres headed a midwestern association of ten colleges, then became simultaneous chancellor of two eastern ones. Bernard Beckerman of the drama department went on to Columbia as dean of the School of the Arts. Geritt Judd IV of the old Hawaiian dynasty taught history as did Myron Luke, chronicler of old Long Island. Dan Lawrence took his editorial work on G. B. Shaw from Hofstra to N.Y.U. Elie Siegmesiter made music and Broadus Mitchel did biographies of famous Americans. Years later, anthropologist Colin Turnbull told the world about the disagreeable Ik.

Typical of the atypical was Frank Keefe, member of the Hofstra English department, of Jose Limon's ballet company, and lieutenant of lifeguards at nearby Jones Beach. The young admired his powerful build and genial bellow in accents that veered from New York-ese to Irish and back again. After a performance of the extravaganza *Arabian Nights* at Jones Beach's floodlit Marine Theater, he took my children backstage to give them a ride on the big mechanical whale that swam into the stage-front lagoon at the production's high point. They loved it. Frank fancied himself the archetypal Irishman, and one night he had a vision of Brendan, ancient Hibernian saint and navigator, beckoning to him from his curragh—a sign that Frank must stop teaching at Hofstra and go to Ireland. He went and stayed there in the damp until he became broke and ill, returning to this country a semiderelict, sleeping on park benches and under bridges, from time to time producing a fine poetic work like his *Ballet of Saint Francis.* At last report, Frank was teaching crowded classes of open-admissions students in one of New York City's community colleges, where he shouted Yeats and Hopkins to admiring blacks.

Most of my evening students were family men in business or teachers in training. Army and Air Force officers also attended, including a black major later promoted to general. Odd types, some gifted, turned up: a Persian film actress, a Finnish fashion designer, an electronics specialist and photographer who made a logic machine for me. Later he went to jail for running a porno shop in the basement of his house as well as for more serious related offenses. (I visited him in an upstate prison to find him teaching classes in computer science to his fellow inmates.) A pale older woman wrote poems she would press on me after class, asking for reading and criticism—long poems with titles like "Soul's Ecstasy" and "Cataclysmic Surge." A semiprofessional astrologer volunteered to do my horoscope free, but she needed the exact hour of my birth to complete it properly. Docile, I wrote to my mother, then still living in Boston, who replied that she did not know; after the event, she had done her best to forget the whole thing.

Venerable Mrs. Thomas from Colorado—she attended class as an auditor with her thirtyish daughter—*had seen electricity.* We were discussing perception and its relation to the external world, the way we often reason to the existence of something we cannot see by observing its effects—electricity, for example. Mrs. Thomas spoke up:

"I've seen it."

I asked Mrs. Thomas what she had seen.

"Electricity!" she said.

Respectfully I suggested that perhaps Mrs. Thomas had seen the sensible *effects* of electricity—the lighting of a bulb, or sparks. Or had heard a crackle. Or felt a small shock.

"No sir, I'm not talkin' about any effects," she said. "I've seen Electricity itself. I was settin' in my kitchen out there in Colorado one day durin' a thunderstorm watchin' the lightening and, glory, all of a sudden Electricity came in through the winder. It was three inches long, and gun metal in color."

"The Thing-in-Itself," I thought. "Kant's *Ding-an-Sich.*"

Two students from foreign lands I count memorable as well as one from Bowling Green, Ohio. Monique Severin was a tiny Belgian actress married to a prosperous businessman with a house on Long Island. In the course of his official duties, Frank Keefe had met her sunning herself at Jones Beach and had recommended my class to her. Monique drove to Hofstra in a beautiful white convertible fitted out with red leather. More than once when my feeble old car lay disabled she rode me home—a terrifying experience, for she drove pedal flat to the floor, hanging out in the left lane of the Southern State Parkway at seventy-five all the way. Monique soon left Hofstra for California, divorced her husband, and made Phi Beta Kappa at Berkeley and a career in television in Los Angeles.

Marian Weller had less flamboyant gifts—a quiet English girl of lovely mind and looks. Her brother Eric majored in philosophy at Hofstra and today is dean of faculty at Skidmore College. I recommended Marian to Columbia's Lewis Leary for graduate work in American studies. As her advisor he assigned A. Walton Litz, at the time visiting professor at Columbia and today professor at Princeton and one of the country's top literary scholars. He saw her through her master's essay on Wallace Stevens, then married her. And who could forget blonde Judy Baird, from Bowling Green, Ohio, mother of two, lover of Walt Whitman, *Tristan and Isolde,* and Mohammed Ali? Her eyes were so incredibly blue that I mentioned them one day to her adviser, Dean Hyman Lichtenstein. He said she wore colored contact lenses. Did she see the world a lovely blue, I wondered.

Once at Hofstra I taught an eight o'clock morning class on days I had no Barnard or Columbia duties. I offered my course in Philosophy and the Modern Novel, and it was at this point that Maria Kazantzakis showed up. Maria was a wild type, slim as a spider monkey, hair brown, thick, untidy, eyes the color of Nauplia harbor on a bad day. She had slightly bowed legs, but this anomaly only added to the general positive effect she produced on nearly all who knew her. Maria was the granddaughter of a Greek army general who ran a military dictatorship in Athens for a year or so after the Smyrna disaster following World War I. Her parents missing or dead, she was put into an orphanage in this country and later farmed out to a foster home.

Maria grew up in the borough of Queens, the terror of her street, beating up all the nice boys, including Malcolm MacKay who, by astonishing coincidence, happened to be in this very Hofstra course with his old enemy. (Later he became a successful teacher of French literature.) Maria came on as a sort of poor man's Lady Brett Ashley: she swore, chain-smoked king-sized Kent cigarettes, drank sturdily, and knew where to get what was not yet known as pot. She did not use it herself. Maria edited the college undergraduate newspaper *Chronicle* and wrote effective and correctly spelled prose. Once in her editorial column she called upon the entire student body to stand up at a particular hour wherever they were, in class or not, and to howl. This was to protest some administrative ruling Maria did not care for, and the howl, duly carried out, constituted a rather effective protest for those days, a decade before the great campus revolts of the sixties. Speaking of howling, Allen Ginsberg's cousin sat in that unbelievable Hofstra class and she inscribed to me her own copy of *Howl* that Allen had sent her. She said she didn't want it.

Maria's official young man was an ex-Marine who had won the Navy Cross in Korea, but, like Lady Brett, she trompéed him all over the campus with one or another of her following. Altogether that year she had a dozen men faithful to her, including two junior full-time faculty members and an aging homosexual Hamlet whom the college had imported from Canada to play in the annual Shakespeare festival. Nor did her own sex hold all this male attention against her; the young women of her class admired Maria and hurried nervously to execute her wishes. She had many.

If she decided to come to class, Maria would waver in twenty minutes late, usually dressed in a tight skirt, imperfectly buttoned blouse, and dark glasses to cover her eyes, which at that early morning hour were not at their best. When she had settled herself in her chair, Maria would read a page or two of her current *Mad* maga-

zine, of which she was said to own a complete collection, then nod
off for a brief nap. After that she became alert and attentive. Occasionally she would show impatience. One day after a test on which
she had done badly, she picked up her copy of Kafka's *The Castle*
and threw it out the window. She got a kick out of the stories I told
of the sufferings and greatness of the writers whose works we were
reading. Marcel Proust particularly intrigued her. "His sentences are
so goddam long," she said, "but you make it sound interesting." Inspired by the description of Baron Charlus's hostel for male inverts
in *The Past Recaptured,* she composed and circulated an unprintable set of verses to the old pop song "There's a Small Hotel." Her
line about the lacustrine dreams aroused in the sad old faithful lech-
ers by the kilts of the Scottish troops in wartime Paris would have
earned praise from Charlus himself.

Academically, Maria was in constant and boiling hot water.
A senior the year she took my 8:00 A.M. course, she came very close
to not graduating. She constantly cut classes and turned in papers ir-
regularly. During spring semester that year she did not attend more
than six classes of a French course she needed to fulfill her foreign
language requirement for graduation. One late afternoon in May
I walked through the Hofstra cafeteria on the way to my car parked
by the hawthorne bushes at Holland House. The cafeteria had emp-
tied save for people with mops, and Maria sat alone at a far corner
table, her Phaedrus-like epicene head bowed over a disordered pile
of books and papers. As I passed, I heard enraged mutterings in the
idiom of a boatswain's mate.

"What's the trouble, Miss Kazantzakis?"

As a rule with Maria I tried to be formal. She addressed all faculty she knew by their first names, and it was not until after the
Columbia revolt of '68 and subsequent claims of equal first-name
rights that I got used to the familiar mode of address from students.
To her I was "Joe" and nothing could be done about it. At a president's reception, she addressed Dr. John Cranford Adams as "Jack"
until someone on the receiving line stepped firmly on her foot.

Now she had problems, serious ones. She owed her professors a
total of four term papers, including one of five thousand words to
Professor Hull on Joyce's *Ulysses.* All were overdue, none written.
Friday was the last day she could get them in for credit. Those of
her friends who might have helped her were taken up with their

own late papers. I sat down at the table, looked over the assignments, and saw that Maria was in bad trouble. To graduate she needed all the points of these courses. She could not get credit in any unless she handed in the assigned papers, hopelessly overdue.

"*You* wouldn't believe it," she growled. "But more than anything else in the world, I want to graduate. From the time I was a kid I wanted to graduate from college. And now—I even bought this ring . . ." She stuck out an ink-stained paw to show her class ring with its handsome blue stone. "I want to graduate with my own class and now I *can't*, goddammit, I *can't!* And it's my own [obscenity] fault that I can't!" She angrily brushed away a single tear.

As Sartre says, when you deliberate the chips are down. For the first, and I profoundly hope the last time in my career, I threw my professional integrity out the window. Out that cafeteria window as easily as Maria had defenestrated Kafka's *Castle.* I told her that if she could find three other sympathetic professors on the faculty to help her with the smaller assignments, I'd assist with the Joyce paper. Had she done anything at all on it? Well, a few notes. I took them home and that night laid them beside my typewriter, inserted a blank sheet of paper, and glanced at her topic. Dr. Hull had assigned Maria the topic Metempsychosis in *Ulysses.* Duck soup. With one eye on my old Random House 1934 edition open before me and the other on Maria's notes, I began to click. No blurred vision like Alessandra of the blinking eyes:

Metempsychosis?
Yes. Who's he when he's at home?

In four hours I had finished, not forgetting to leave in a few characteristic touches of her editorial style. Next morning I drove around to the elderly crone's house near campus where Maria rented a cheap room in the attic. After a while, she came downstairs, body sagging, shadows under her eyes like soot. She had pulled a man's tattered shirt over her jeans. Her bare feet were imperfectly clean. From her lower lip hung the first king-size Kent of the day.

"Here's your Joyce paper, Miss Kazantzakis. I've looked it over, and aside from a few too many staccato sentences, I think it's all right."

She was gruff, but her eyes filled a little.

"Thanks. I didn't think you'd do it."

The *Ulysses* paper got an *A*— from Professor Hull. I was a little miffed at the minus. Her shorter pieces came around later in the day. Three full-time faculty members (not Hull) had worked on them each by each until well into the morning hours. Such was the chthonic power of this mad Greek woman that they too, for the first and last time I am sure, had committed an infraction of academic integrity on her behalf. Those instructors—who, of course, had no idea they were writing papers for each other—were a little harder on their respective colleagues' efforts than Bill Hull had been on mine, but no matter. All grades were well above passing. The French professor gave Maria an *F* for her final examination, but a *D* for the course—a bad grade but still passing. So Maria got her credits and turned up at commencement with her class.

After graduation, Maria became a reporter for *Newsday,* Long Island's big daily, and soon had her own byline. She dived in the ocean with Jacques Cousteau and parachuted with Jacques Coustel, just missing a fatal streamer at Orange, Massachusetts. The U.S. Space Agency laid on for her a series of tests in simulated space conditions. With John Glenn watching to see that she came to no harm, she withstood three and a half G's. For a while she was a news reporter for one of the large networks and we could watch her at home on television asking people questions about murders and street accidents. But her voice was too husky for her to stay long at that. From her travels she would send an occasional postcard (from Eleuthera: "Only the good ones come here. Brett"). She had always wanted to go to Greece to seek out the home of her grandfather, who hanged six men with his own hand. One day she did. From Athens there arrived a pair of cufflinks with the owl of Minerva hammered into them.

She married a professor from Rutgers and learned from him the art of making films. A nationwide chain store hired her to do their documentaries. Recently I heard she was thinking of filming the opening of a MacDonald's in Athens.

Hofstra has an excellent library. Poking through the stacks one day in the early 1950s I stumbled into the daft and wonderful world of Ford Madox Ford, the English novelist, author of *The Good Soldier,* who had spent some time in this country before returning to

Europe to die in 1939. When asked to do something for Hofstra's "Friday at Four"—afternoons when faculty gave poetry readings or put on little shows—I adapted in drama form two scenes from Ford's novel sequence *Parade's End,* dragooned some faculty and students to do the parts, and put on the production with just one rehearsal. It was great fun.

Do you know Christopher Tietjens, the hero of *Parade's End?* He was a young squire of Yorkshire landed gentry, a sober Edwardian, a kind of archetypal Good Man who draws down upon his head the unreasoning hostility of nearly everyone he meets. (Graham Greene's Scobie is a lineal descendant.) A lumpish St. Sebastian, Christopher accepts the arrows of his enemies without complaint. Like Socrates's just soul in the first book of Plato's *Republic* he is thought by all to be evil, yet remains steadfast in his goodness. His beautiful wife, Sylvia, can't stand him and plays all sorts of dirty tricks: cuckolds him, tells his superiors he stole two pair of her best bedsheets, throws a plate of salad all over his uniform as he stands before her, a lieutenant ordered to duty in the trenches in France, 1915. Tietjens's true love, a young woman with the unlikely name of Valentine Wannop, is the only heroine of a great modern novel who is a physical education instructor as well as an accomplished Latin scholar and suffragette.

The first bit we did at Hofstra was the Duchemin breakfast scene from the novel sequence's first volume, *Some Do Not.* The time is just before the outbreak of World War I. Tietjens's protégé MacMaster, an ambitious Scot who works with Christopher in the Imperial Department of Statistics, has taken his friends to an elaborate breakfast at the country home of Mr. Duchemin. He is a rich Anglican clergyman afflicted by intermittent fits of madness during which he shouts obscenities in Latin. Among others present at the breakfast is Valentine Wannop, there to help Mrs. Duchemin, a pre-Raphaelite type who will that day succumb to MacMaster. Mr. Duchemin himself is flanked at table by his curate, the Reverend Mr. Horsely, and Parry, a professional boxer who acts as Mr. Duchemin's valet-attendant.

All goes well until Duchemin persuades himself that Tietjens and MacMaster are medical men sent to observe him. That gets him on his feet shouting unspeakably in Latin which the company, classically educated as they are, understand only too well. Duchemin is rising to the point of comparing John Ruskin's wedding night to his own when MacMaster saves the situation by ordering Parry to punch his master in the kidneys with his thumb while reminding him politely that it is time to prepare his sermon. Exit Duchemin followed by Parry and eventually the rest of the company, all save MacMaster and Mrs. Duchemin. Her languishing gratitude brings them together in a pre-Raphaelite kiss, silently observed by the returning Tietjens, as they recall Rosetti's awful lines:

> *Since when we stand side by side*
> *Only hands may meet,*
> *Better half this weary world*
> *Lay between us, sweet.*

Professor Bill Hull made a marvelous Duchemin. A native of Georgia hill country, he combined high culture with a natural Appalachian madness; his personal erudition could handle classical as well as contemporary scatology. Bernard Beckerman's actress wife Gloria languished beautifully as Mrs. Duchemin and John Senior was perfect as Tietjens. Frank Keefe's immense voice was just right for Mr. Horsely, the curate, though he tended at times to drift off into a rich Irish brogue. Georgia Dunbar, official grammarian of the university, broke up the house with her gravel-voiced delivery of a single line Ford allotted to the deaf Miss Fox when Duchemin rises to begin his erudite obscenities:

"I think we shall have thunder today. Have you remarked the number of minute insects . . ."

In preparing the script I had doubts about some of the classical learning that Ford gave to many of his characters. Ford himself was something of a mythomaniac and needlessly fattened his pedigree. For example, he gave out that he was a Balliol graduate, though he had left school at eighteen. He probably did not sit on Tolstoy's knee as a child, as he relates in his numerous memoirs. He did know and publish the aged Thomas Hardy, often called on Henry James at Rye, collaborated on four novels with Conrad, worked hard with Wyndham Lewis and Ezra Pound, earned the sardonic admiration of James Joyce, and employed ungrateful Ernest Hemingway as assistant editor of his *Transatlantic Review* in Paris. But as man and writer, Ford oscillated between genuine kindness and humility, and a pose of I'm Mr. Know-It-All and Have Met Everybody.

In *Parade's End* he paints the lily of his own learning. The encyclopediac information with which he endows Tietjens—a man, like Sherlock Holmes, who *knows everything*—bristles with inaccuracies. Though most of the classical references in the Duchemin breakfast scene seemed all right, I thought it best to check one passage with Gilbert Highet. Highet jumped out of his tree:

> This is a tissue of ignorance and falsification. There is no such work as the *Trimalchion* of Petronius. One part of Petronius's book, which by the way is called the *Satyrica* or *Satirica, not* the *Satyricon,* describes a dinner given by a rich Oriental ex-slave whose name is Trimalchio. (The French version of this name is Trimalchion, but that is not its form in Latin or English.) The dinner of Trimalchio is characterized by almost every social and moral error except hot licentiousness. *Festinans, puer calide* does not appear anywhere in Petronius's extant works. The word *festino,* from which *festinans* comes, does not appear anywhere in Petronius and the form *calidus/ calide* will hardly go into iambics without shoving, and there are few iambics in Petronius, if any. Wilamowitz-Moellendorf spelt the first part of his name with one "l" not two, and virtually all his work was in Greek, not in Latin. I do not know that he ever touched Petronius. No one but an idiot would translate "puer calide" as "youth of tepid loves."

The smaller of the two scenes I took from *No More Parades,* the second novel of Ford's tetralogy. It needed only three characters: Captain Christopher Tietjens; General Campion, his division commander; and Campion's aide, Colonel Levin, a devout admirer of Tietjens. It's an informal military court of inquiry, and the build-up to it is delightfully loony. Tietjens's wife Sylvia wangles her way to an inn just outside the base camp in France where Christopher is stationed and invites him to spend the night there with her, ostensibly to discuss their future. But to get some fun out of it, Sylvia has invited an old lover, one Major Perowne, to drop in at bedtime. As Tietjens and his wife are undressing, the eager Perowne arrives and is ejected by Tietjens. The disturbance attracts a bibulous provost marshal, General O'Hara, who makes the mistake of ogling the near-naked Sylvia and is himself thrown out of the room. Next morning the irate O'Hara demands that Tietjens be court-martialed, hence the informal court of inquiry.

After questioning by Levin, all sympathy for his hero, Tietjens is brought before General Campion, who happens to be an old friend of the Tietjens family. Campion acquaints Tietjens with a number of charges against him, ranging from putting a general officer under arrest without due cause, adultery with both Valentine Wannop and Ethel Duchemin, being a Socialist, and confusing himself with Christ. Such men unsettle things. Under guise of promotion, Campion sentences Tietjens to death (in effect) by ordering his transfer to a front-line battalion that the Germans are cutting to pieces. Tietjens dreamily recalls an occasion he was in London and had to look in at the War Office, where in a room he found an officer devising the ceremonials for the end of the war. For the disbanding of a Kitchener battalion

> the adjutant would stand the battalion at ease; the band would play *Land of Hope and Glory,* and then the adjutant would say: *there will be no more parades.*

Through Tietjens, Ford prophesied the end of a great empire and of an era where each knew his place and did his duty, and where a man's honor meant something.

At Barnard we put on the shorter Ford piece a number of times —the Duchemin breakfast scene needed too large a cast and too many actors—with Adolphus Sweet as Tietjens, followed by Kenneth Janes, who succeeded Dolph as director of Barnard's Minor Latham Playhouse.

Dolph Sweet had a pro football build, a gentle voice and touch. As a POW during World War II he staged his own productions of *The Front Page* and *Juno and the Paycock* in Stalag Luft Number 3 after his B-24 went down near Cyprus. He left Barnard in 1961 for Broadway (remember his marvelous snorting metamorphosis from man to beast in Ionesco's *Rhinoceros?*), then went into movies and television. Through the mid-1970s he played Police Lieutenant Gil McGowan in the television soap opera *Another World.* He returned to Broadway in the role of Cokes in David Rabe's *Streamers.*

During his Barnard tenure, the rock-shouldered Dolph was both actor and director. When he put on George Etherege's comedy *A Man of Mode,* Dolph himself played Diamant and peopled the boxes with Columbia students as Restoration fops clawing lecherously at the female actresses on stage. He let me play with him in a couple of Chekhov one-acters. I remember his gentle refusal to let me improvise to cover a misremembered line in rehearsal. It had to be done over again—exactly as written. Dolph asked me to play Tim Finnegan in someone's adaptation of scenes from Joyce's *Finnegan's Wake,* but since the role called for me to lie silent and dead in a coffin through most of the play, I declined. I wanted a small part with good lines like "Three quarks for Musther Mark!" or "Pass the fish for Christ's sake!" Dolph's reading of the Tietjens part was more robust than Ken Janes's, but both were good.

In late 1954 Frank MacShane was looking for material for his biography of Ford, and I sent him copies of my stage adaptations from *Parade's End.* At the time Frank was teaching at Williams College and had done a thesis on Ford for the Ph.D. at Oxford. That was long before he headed the writing division of Columbia's School of the Arts. Frank responded by inviting me to a Christmas party he gave at the Gramercy Park Hotel for some old friends of Ford. Ford's last love, Janice Biala, was there, and Leonie Adams, her husband William Troy, and Edward Naumburg, Jr., patron of the small New York Ford coterie and owner of a large collection of Ford material. Leonie Adams, Barnard alumna and poet, had known Ford in Paris and talked with me at length about that and Ford's summer writing conferences at Olivet College, Michigan, during the late 1930s.

William Troy, Leonie's husband, sat down beside us and held forth loudly on various matters. He was rather drunk. Leonie made sure I knew that he was a man of letters in his own right. I had heard that Troy had been friendly with Joyce and that the Irishman got Bill briefly into *Ulysses* at the outset of the "Cyclops" episode, where the reader is tipped off that some Dublin Polyphemus is to be blinded for a moment at least. ("I was just passing the time of day with old Troy of the D.M.P. at the corner of Arbour Hill there and be damned but a bloody sweep came along and he near drove his gear into my eye.") As I listened to Troy's insistent ramblings, I could sense some irritation between Leonie Adam's protectiveness. Perhaps her "Lullaby" (I had it in my old Untermeyer anthology) was not, after all, written for a child, but for old Troy of the D.M.P.:

> *Your eyes*
> *In sleepy fever gleam,*

Your lids droop
To their dream.
You wander late alone,
The flesh frets on the bone,
Your love fails
In your breast,
Here is the pillow.
Rest.

Now Janice Biala raised her voice angrily, and Frank brought me over to change the subject. She looked like a little fighter with rough skin and sharp black eyes that gleamed under a crop of close cut pepper-and-salt hair. She painted large flat pictures in buff and ocher of faceless humans and brave bulls. When I spoke to her warmly about my admiration for Ford's writing she said, "I'm so moved. For Ford," and asked me to come to her house for a weekend visit in rural New Jersey.

Ford loved women and liked most of those he loved. In their turn women—talented women—were drawn to him. Four of his loves stood the test of years. The four do not include Rene Wright or the novelist Jean Rhys. Ford had affairs with both. Rene Wright divorced her husband and would have married Ford, but declined to be his official mistress, the best position he could offer her, since his first and only wife never divorced him. Jean Rhys sheltered with Ford and Stella Bowen for a while in Paris. Her novel *Quartet* (earlier titled *Postures*) reflects her time in Paris with Ford and Stella, whom some say are the models for the faintly sinister Heidlers of Rhys's novel.

Now then, the four: first Elsie Martindale, his legal wife, whom he married when he was twenty. For years they lived quietly in the south of England, with Ford dividing his time between writing and farming in a small way. They had two children, both girls. The idyll broke up over Violet Hunt, a novelist who had a bohemian salon in London where Ford's work as editor of *The English Review* often took him. Ford traveled to Germany with Violet and on his return told reporters she was Mrs. Hueffer, which was Ford's name before he changed it after the war. Elsie read the papers and sued her husband for restoration of conjugal rights. Ford balked and was sent to Brixton jail for ten days, where he complained that his jailers would give him no reading matter but young women's magazines.

Violet Hunt became increasingly violent and Ford escaped by going off to the 1914–18 war at the age of forty as a subaltern in the Welsh Regiment. It is said that a colonel, watching Ford mess up a platoon at drill, asked his aide incredulously, "Did you say he wrote *The Good Soldier?*"

After the war Ford lived in Paris and the south of France with the Australian artist Stella Bowen. They had a daughter named Julie, for whose Catholic baptism James Joyce bit the bullet and stood as godfather. Ford had suggested "Work in Progress" as temporary title for Joyce's *Finnegan's Wake* and had published an excerpt in *the transatlantic review*. Joyce in turn commemorated Ford's effect on women with a parody of the Irish tune "Father O'Flynn":

> *O Father O'Ford you've a masterful way with you*
> *Maid, wife and widow are wild to make hay with you,*
> *Blonde and brunette turn-about run away with you*
> *You've such a way with you, Father O'Ford.*

Both Violet Hunt and Stella Bowen recalled their lives with Ford in memoirs: Violet in *Those Flurried Years* and Stella in *Drawn from Life,* a fact that angered Janice Biala. She could not stand women who wrote books about their dead lovers who were geniuses.

When I first visited her, Janice Biala was living in a big stucco house in Peapack, New Jersey, with her husband Daniel Brustlein, a big, gentle, red-bearded Alsatian who drew cartoons for *The New Yorker* under the name of Alain. Janice served an excellent dinner; she admitted to being a good cook "for cuisine bourgeoise." In the morning she showed me some paintings she was preparing for a coming New York show. She had no pictures but her own, save for a de Kooning which she prized. Reluctantly she showed me an early portrait of Ford she had painted while he was convalescing from an illness in the early 1930s. She didn't like it—"Too soft," she said.

She told me she first met Ford at his "Thursdays" on the rue Vaugirard. She had come hoping to meet Ezra Pound, whose poems she loved, particularly "River-Merchant's Wife" and "Bowmen of Shu." When Pound came briefly to the United States before the outbreak of World War II, she said, he visited Ford but wouldn't speak to her nor she to him. By that time Pound's fascist anti-Semitism had gotten out of hand. And Biala was a Polish Jew.

Janice believed that Ford was, like the victim-heroes of his novels, a Good Man. She said that Ford belonged to the company of great and good men like Socrates and Jesus. "Why not say it?" she insisted. "In for a penny, in for a pound. He was like Christ." That was why she went wild when young men came to her to ask permission to write books about Ford and his "wives." As for scholarly books about Ford's work, she thought they were quite unnecessary. People interested in Ford, she said, should go to his books, not to books about them by somebody else. She violently objected to Mac-Shane's projected biography of Ford, about which I had made sympathetic noises. MacShane was a nice young man, she said, but he missed his vocation; he should have been a private detective. (Odd that MacShane's best book should be his 1976 biography of Raymond Chandler, creator of Philip Marlowe, who was exactly that.) She had read two or three chapters of his Ford manuscript and thought them pedestrian and academic.

MacShane's book did not appear until 1965, ten years after I had tried to persuade her to tolerate it. Frank's preface regretted that he was unable to use material to which Biala held the rights. Janice saved her permissions for Arthur Mizener. His biography of Ford was a better book than MacShane's. Far more complete, since, among others, Janice Biala and Mrs. Charles Lamb (Ford's second daughter by his wife Elsie Martindale) had given him access to the Ford material in their possession. Even so, Janice Biala's *imprimatur* was reluctant. In his acknowledgements, Mizener had to record Janice's belief that his portrait of Ford did the master an injustice, as well as Mrs. Lamb's conviction that Mizener's portrait of her mother was unfair.

The last time I saw Janice was at the Naumburg's apartment in Manhattan. That night I won a dollar bet from her over the authorship of a favorite poem of hers:

> *So, we'll go no more a-roving*
> *So late into the night*
> *Though the heart be still as loving,*
> *And the moon be still as bright.*

> *For the sword outwears the sheath*
> *And the soul wears out the breast*
> *And the heart must pause to breathe,*
> *And love itself have rest. . . .*

She couldn't *believe* Byron wrote that. We looked it up right there in Naumburg's library and she gave me a dollar on which she wrote a kind word or two. I have it still. Shortly afterwards she and her husband moved to Paris, and I saw her no more until twenty years later when I ate a sandwich with her in New York after her winter 1977 show at the Livingston-Learmonth Gallery. She hadn't changed much. To her, the Mizener book on Ford was almost as bad as MacShane's.

Once at Peapack I asked Janice about Ford's death, for I knew she had been with him at the end. She did not want to talk about it. Anything to do with people suffering pain or injustice, strangers or no, brought angry tears to her eyes. She came to Barnard once, crying because she had to visit a woman ill with cancer. I could imagine the effect of Ford's death on her. In the spring of 1939 they had sailed for England aboard the *Normandie*. Ford, who had long been ailing, came down with uremic poisoning en route. They debarked at Le Havre, stopped at Honfleur for a while, then she took him to a hospital in Deauville. He died in her arms. Ford wanted a small funeral ceremony with Catholic rites. He had been baptized a Catholic at eighteen, and had thought of himself as a Catholic all along, though not a believer, never *croyant*. Whenever Ford was in church, Janice told me, and happened to pass a statue of the Blessed Mother, he would always bow. Why? Because she was a lady, he said, and had been in trouble.

PART

IV

SARAH LAWRENCE; IRELAND, JOYCE; FRANCE, GIDE, DELIUS

&ᴥ In 1965 Esther Raushenbush became the sixth president of Sarah Lawrence College, and Jacquelyn Mattfeld—who would succeed Martha Peterson as Barnard's head eleven years later—joined Sarah Lawrence as dean. I had served with Esther on a committee to make recommendations for an experimental college at Hofstra— New College. That acquaintance plus the fact that a new book of mine had been reviewed with mild favor in the *Times* led to an invitation to join Sarah Lawrence for a year as visiting faculty member.

Sarah Lawrence is in Bronxville, New York, a twenty-minute drive north of Manhattan in Westchester County. Traditionally known as a rich girls' school like Bennington, its tuition and costs ran substantially higher than more conventional women's colleges such as Barnard or Bryn Mawr. Sarah Lawrence's small clientele came mostly from the privileged classes, although as early as my year there the school was beating the bushes for deserving scholarship blacks. Sarah Lawrence described itself then as an experimental liberal arts college for women. (Some men were admitted in the 1970s.) Classes rarely exceeded a dozen members, and individual conferences and tutorials took precedence over lectures. Long student papers called "contracts" counted heavily for course credit. Teachers were "dons." Professorial rank as such did not exist, though tenure and salary differentials did. Since I now held the rank of full professor at Barnard, Sarah Lawrence offered me such a good sum of money for my services that I ran out to buy a new car, a lovely red Dodge with black bucket seats and a chrome stick-shift. I couldn't drive to that smart college in a beat-up old '59 Chevy Belaire, could I?

Sarah Lawrence's curriculum listed heavily toward the "arts"— theater, dance, painting, sculpture, music, poetry—a fact that did not sit well with my Barnard friend and colleague Kate Millett. As chairman of the Education Committee of the New York chapter of the National Organization of Women (NOW), Kate was investigating women's higher education in the United States:

> According to the prevailing American assumption that the arts are "feminine" or "effeminate," Sarah Lawrence and Bennington specialize in an arty "female" milieu of theater, dance, and music. Despite its rather prestigious and apparently unfounded reputation, Sarah Lawrence is weak both in chemistry and physics, its economic and political science are unimpressive and it offers no advanced course in Russian.*

Kate was a little hard on Sarah Lawrence. Though it did tilt toward the arts, the college had good offerings in other fields and many able teachers on the faculty the year I was there—novelist Harvey Swados and poet Muriel Rukeyser in writing, for example; Kurt Roesch in painting; Bert Lowenberg in history. On board too were Rudolf Arnheim, the gestalt analyst of aesthetic perception, and Joseph Campbell, myth-*Psychologue* and archetypist, and key maker to *Finnegan's Wake*.

Sarah Lawrence methods of instruction made for good teaching and learning, provided the student wanted to work and there were enough competent dons available so that students were not squeezed out repeatedly from courses they wanted to take. But the system was

---

* Results of the survey were published as a monograph, *Token Learning: a Study of Women's Higher Education in America* (New York: 1968). Kate Millett was listed as chairman of the committee that did the study, the dismal term "chairperson" not yet having come into required usage. Kate's report relied heavily on the Gourman report ratings, published by the Continuing Education Institute for 1967–68 in which Sarah Lawrence got a score of 350 compared to Barnard's 520.

Kate Millett taught at Barnard from 1964 to 1970. She was what Mrs. McIntosh used to call "an administratively difficult person." The English department declined to reappoint her for the academic year 1968–69 and she taught her last year in Barnard's Experimental College under the sponsorship of our department, Philosophy. Mary Mothersill, our department chairman, was very good to her. Kate could be rather grim until she knew you were well disposed toward her and her interests. Like a stern-faced Mother Superior, she would march her freshmen girls into pornographic movies about the Times Square area so that they might see samples of a business that made high profits out of the degradation of women. Kate occupied the office next door to mine for a year, and we had long chats about Bachoven and his *Mutterrecht* and longer telephone conversations when the English department gave her the deep six. Kate liked Barnard and took it hard at the thought of leaving. Her *Sexual Politics,* originally offered as a dissertation for the Columbia Ph.D., appeared just after her departure from Morningside Heights.

expensive and hard on the teachers. With each student needing weekly or biweekly individual conferences and supervision of "contracts," the faculty labored like mother St. Bernards with litters of a dozen each. Work under that kind of pressure could not but drain away energy and time for research and writing. Class sizes rarely exceeded twelve, and students laid siege to dons' offices to get accepted before the desired class closed out.

Student urgency permeated my first day on campus. Registration was going on and that required holding a sort of levée in one's office while students lined up outside, then pushed in individually, asking to be admitted to the course. On my invariable approval, the applicant would look dismayed and say, "But don't you want me to tell you more about *myself?*" No need, I'd say, and cheerfully signed in all these nice people until Esther Raushenbush blew the whistle. What she had said about a limit of a dozen students per course was no joke. Since I had already signed thirty-five enrollment slips, I produced a Homeric foul-up in the registrar's office, causing that ancient official to erupt igneously at me from her den.

Sarah Lawrence at the time had little in the way of physical plant. The whole college was crammed into a shoebox-sized campus on the Bronxville-Yonkers hillside border. The library cried scandal (they have a new one now as well as other buildings) with a staff gone old and tremulous, physical space hopelessly unequal to the needs of students who had to do staggering amounts of individual reading for their courses. Faculty offices were tiny cubicles jammed into overheated dormitory basements where the students came down mornings, many still in their nightgowns, to do their laundry.

When I arrived at Sarah Lawrence the campus still buzzed about the last year's firing of two dons for dalliance with students, one affair allegedly lesbian, the other vigorously heterosexual—the sort of thing that ten years later would evoke a mild waggle of the finger from most eastern college administrators if it were not ignored entirely. I could sympathize with the errant dons, whoever they were, and wondered why such incidents were not more frequent. Except in winter, the undergraduates usually came barefoot to their individual conferences, wearing shirts and shorts. The dons' hot little offices were so cramped it was difficult to avoid literally knocking knees, and the girls were amiable and healthy.

There were fifteen students in my principal course. The young ones conducted themselves well, manners friendly yet respectful; they appeared for conferences with scrubbed faces, hair neatly brushed, and feet washed. Two were women in their thirties: Myra Russell, a keen Jewish housewife from New Rochelle who went on to be a college teacher herself, and Christine Stiassni, daughter of John Illingworth, the English yacht builder, whose firm designed and fitted out Francis Chichester's *Gipsy Moth IV* for his round-the-world solo voyage in 1966. Of the regular undergraduates, one was Greek and one an American black, Alice Walker, later well-known as poet and novelist. The rest were young women from affluent families of Boston, New York, St. Louis, Washington, Los Angeles, or suburbs thereof. Most were intelligent and conscientious about their work. About half had some conspicuous talent. Two or three showed academic weakness.

Sarah Lawrence students were not awarded conventional grades of *A, B, C,* and so on. Instead, each don at term's end had to write out an evaluation of each individual student's work. The registrar then collated this report with the student's other two dons' evaluation (undergraduates usually took no more than three courses a term) and sent the resulting composite evaluation sheet to the student with copies to each of her three dons. Here is one of mine a little touched up:

SARAH LAWRENCE COLLEGE
FACULTY REPORT

Report of COURTNEY BLAKE.

Philosophy and the Modern Novel (Mr. Brennan)

> Courtney Blake is a vigorous student who has pursued her work with a real desire for accomplishment. Her contributions in class have been interesting and her conference work—with the exception of the two weeks she spent on her archaeological dig in Crete in November—was regularly carried out. Her contract for this term, The Whiteness of the Whale in *Moby Dick* as Symbol of Heidegger's *Dasein,* struck me as overambitious, but Courtney would not be dissuaded from proceeding with this unusual study. Courtney shows some anxiety when subjected to conventional academic pressures, but her work will improve, I am sure, with added experience. Since

she wishes to work spring semester on Black Phenomenology, I am suggesting that she take the course in Urban Studies.

Theatre of the Absurd (Mr. Rosenblatt)

Court's approach to experimental stage work is visceral and positive. She shows no insecurity and does not shrink from new experiences in the theater. Typical of her gut response was her reaction in our recent staging of Pasch's "Occurrence #3" when she stepped by mistake into a bucket of lard onstage. Instead of letting the mishap throw her, Court turned it to positive advantage by kicking the lard bucket into front row center with a kind of Peter Weiss élan. Her contract on Artaud, on the other hand, seemed weak and excessively Jungian.

Pre-dance Group (Miss Pettigrew)

Courtney is in serious danger of failing *both* Flamenco and Yoga. Sometimes she seems full of interest and energy. More often the flame of life seems to burn low in this attractive young woman. Perhaps she is simply too tired out by her Princeton weekends. But unless definite improvement is noted in the second semester, Courtney will not be encouraged to go on to Advanced Listening and Intermediate Watching. Her choreographic design *Morning Milkers with Alienated Cow* was *far* too sketchy. Courtney *must* learn to express herself with greater clarity and discipline as well as to try to control her loud and intimidating laugh.

But things were already changing at Sarah Lawrence in the mid-sixties. The better students protested the finishing-school image of the college. They wanted to go on to graduate school, and those evaluation forms were meaningless or worse to admission offices of graduate faculties. Responding to student and faculty pressure, the registrar devised a code system by which the student evaluation could be translated into letter grades so that a conventional transcript could be sent with a graduate school application. A certain restlessness could be felt in the air. Many students agitated for academic reforms to bring Sarah Lawrence's curriculum more in line with those of the graduate-study-oriented colleges of the Ivy League.

Socially conscious student activists joined the picket line of striking workers at the Bronxville hospital. Others gave time to good works with the neighboring poor, including tutoring of ghetto chil-

dren from nearby Mount Vernon. Pressure for interracial activities
and increased minorities' representation on campus was building.
Anti–Vietnam War demonstrations began to stir things up. Disturbances on distant campuses attracted attention. Berkeley had
erupted just a year before.

In the fall term of my year at Sarah Lawrence, Adda Bozeman
laid on a cocktail party in my honor. I thought this was a very nice
thing for her to do, for nobody had ever given me a cocktail party
before in my life. Mrs. Bozeman seemed to be head of the influential
conservative wing of the college faculty. A specialist in International
Relations, she had acquired added prestige as mentor of whispery-
voiced Hope Cooke who, after graduating from Sarah Lawrence,
married the Crown Prince of Sikkim and thus became the first
American-born woman to be crowned a queen—if in fact a Gyalmo
is the equivalent of queen.

Shortly after five o'clock on the evening of the appointed day,
the Sarah Lawrence hierarchy, led by President Raushenbush and
Dean Mattfeld gathered in the Bozeman drawing room, which stood
brilliantly illuminated against the gloom of the November evening.
First round of drinks in hand, we crowded together smiling and
talking when suddenly all the lights went out. People rushed to
windows and saw no light at all in the street or in neighboring
houses. The lights were out and stayed out. Resourceful Mrs. Bozeman produced lighted candles and a transistor radio. The latter
began to crackle forth alarming announcements. A massive electrical
power failure had occurred. The lamps were going out all over the
northeastern United States and part of Canada, and no one was sure
we would see them lit again in our lifetime. Something unknown
struck southern Ontario and western New York at 5:16 P.M. and
New York City went dark at 5:27. The great northeastern U.S.–
Canada power grid had failed and other systems fed by it were
collapsing one after another like falling dominoes. Ominous specula-
tions emanated from the transistor, and the guests stood in the
candlelight transfixed with fear and uncertainty. An invasion from
outer space—ridiculous? The Russians—nonsense! All the same . . .
they thought of the exits, their cars, their homes, their families. Led
by president and dean, calling apologies over their shoulders, the
Sarah Lawrence hierarchy precipitously fled, leaving me holding my

first and as yet untasted cocktail. The party had been killed dead by the Great Blackout of November 9, 1965.

My Sarah Lawrence year was pleasantly followed by two summers in France on the faculty of the college's summer session in Paris. Mary elected to stay home the first summer but suggested I take Ainslie along. Since it was her first trip abroad, we decided to cross the Atlantic by ship rather than plane, choosing the most glamorous vessel we could think of, the *France*. Ainslie was sixteen at the time and stood five foot eight in her bare feet. When we mounted to the bridge on the captain's invitation (he had been in the *débarquement* at St. Maxime in 1944), Ainslie's commanding height, prominent freckles, and Elvira Madigan straw hat made the ship's officers look to their charts and instruments with that idiomatic smile of faint amusement that only Frenchmen can achieve. On the third day out, we passed the *United States* on its way to New York and heard the deep distant growl of the great American ship's siren in response to the *France*'s salute. That summer was twilight for the giant transatlantic liners, and we had the luck to make the crossing before their day drew to a close.

By chance, my Barnard colleague Patricia Graham and her husband, Loren, of the Columbia history department were aboard with their small daughter. Pat was director of Barnard's teacher training program, a post she would hold until she left the college in 1974 to become Radcliffe vice-president and dean of the Radcliffe Institute as well as professor in the Harvard Graduate School of Education. Ainslie and I extricated her little Meg from the nursery section of the *France* so she could have her meals with us like a grownup—her parents' table had no room. It was a happy voyage. By day the cool gray sea to look at, by night *Le Club des Noctambules* for talk, drinks, music for dancing. Loren Graham, an attractive man in his early thirties, had just signed with Alfred Knopf for his big book on science and philosophy in the Soviet Union (it would be six years in the making), and we talked in *Le Club* interminably about dialectical materialism and Copenhagen physics. Pat Graham (her blonde hair and ice-blue eyes came from her Danish Albjerg ancestors) could more than hold her own with dialectical materialism, but liked to give dancing equal time. That trip on the *France* marked the beginning of a friendship with the Grahams, the closest I enjoyed in my thirty years on Morningside Heights.

Leaving Ainslie in England with Dick Dale, my Royal Navy opposite number in Naples '45, I headed for Dublin to see what Bloomsday was like. June 16 is the day Mr. Bloom of James Joyce's *Ulysses* recaps the twelve-year voyage of Homer's Odysseus, compressing it into sixteen hours of a single troubled day and night in Dublin, 1904. Long banned in his native Ireland, Joyce's works had now entered a period of cautious approval that slowly grew in the following years. On that Bloomsday of 1966, some of Joyce's books, including *Ulysses*, stood quietly in the windows of Dublin bookshops like Browne and Nolan's with no particular notice drawn to them by advertisement of the occasion.

By the 1970s, the rehabilitation of Joyce in Ireland had been nearly completed. Then I was serving on an international advisory committee attached to a joint U.S.–Republic of Ireland research project on educational testing in the Irish schools. Meetings were held at Saint Patrick's, the Dublin equivalent of Teachers College. At one of these conferences I asked to visit classes at Belvedere College, Joyce's old Jesuit prep school. There Father Rector still maintained a certain reserve about his school's most famous graduate. But one night I went downtown to the Gate Theater to see something unthinkable in Dublin a few years back: a full-house performance of *Ulysses in Nighttown,* an adaptation for stage of the "Circe" scene from *Ulysses.* In 1958, Alan McClelland's *Bloomsday,* scheduled for performance in the Dublin Theatre Festival, had been dropped without explanation; the Catholic Archbishop of Dublin thought inclusion of this play inappropriate. But now for *Ulysses in Nighttown* there were priests in the audience, Jesuits in fact, smiling benignly at the antics of Joyce's hallucinated Dubliners. To be sure, Molly Bloom and the bawdyhouse women were decently clad and their lines bowdlerized—more than can be said of Burgess Meredith's version with Zero Mostel as Leopold Bloom. I had seen the Meredith–Mostel *Ulysses in Nighttown* off-Broadway in 1958, staged almost as respectably as the Dublin production—Vassar girls as Nighttown whores tried to act tough and sound Irish. But in the show's 1974 revival at New York's Winter Garden, Zero Mostel was upstaged by Fionnuala Flannigan lying quite naked in bed auto-erotically misbehaving as she recited choice bits from Molly Bloom's soliloquy. None of that in Dublin!—for a long time at least.

At our Bloomsday 1966 a minor Irish official from the government division of sanitation and sewers read a scholarly paper on Joyce. Next morning the fans—about twenty in all—piled into a small bus run by Mr. Fitzsimons, later location advisor for the filming of *Ulysses,* and drove out nine miles along Dublin Bay to the Martello tower at Sandycove, where Joyce lived for six months or so with medical student Oliver St. John Gogarty and made it the landmark of the novel's opening scene. On the way back from the tower, the bus stopped outside downtown Dublin and we transferred to elegant carriages like the one Mr. Dedalus senior and Martin Cunningham rode in with Bloom to Paddy Dignam's burial at Glasnevin cemetery. Off Grafton Street we got out at Davy Byrne's Moral Pub where Bloom had his lunchtime sandwich of Gorgonzola cheese (with its feety smell) and a glass of burgundy, its taste recalling the old days when his wife thought he was a fine fellow.

Davy Byrne's had changed since Bloom stopped in there sixty-two years before. All chrome and pink lights now, it awaited tourists; we had on the house a venomous drink called a "Ulysses Cocktail." The only pub that seemed untouched by time since Joyce's day was Mulligan's in Poolbeg Street, the "Burke's" of the novel where the medical students from the maternity hospital in Holles Street rushed with Mulligan and Stephen Dedalus after the birth of Mrs. Purefoy's baby. In the dark of Mulligan's, rough-looking medical students still sat over drinks, their voices quiet now.

Americans made up most of the Bloomsday troop, though I recall one Yugoslav and an Irish mother with small child. Mr. Fitzsimons assigned Muriel Wiessner as my bus and carriage partner. Her husband, Fritz, had led the ill-fated 1939 expedition to the Karakorams that tried to reach the summit of K-2, second highest peak in the world and at that time still unconquered. Wiessner was beaten back just short of his goal, and four lives were lost in the descent. I knew about the Wiessner expedition, for my first reading of Ruttledge's *Attack on Everest* back in the 1930s had converted me to mountain literature. No climber myself, I could not look over a gentle slope without turning green. When Mary and I ascended Mont Blanc by *téléferique* the following spring, 1967, I stood with my eyes closed the whole way up, clutching her arm for dear life. At the eleven thousand-foot stop-off she had to get me a brandy to restore my courage.

Next day Muriel and I visited the National Library in Kildare

Street, where Stephen Dedalus had held forth on *Hamlet*. (The play is autobiographical, but it's the Ghost, not Hamlet, that speaks with Shakespeare's own voice; cuckolded by his wife up there in Stratford, the bard composed his injured feelings by writing a drama of brooding and delayed revenge.) Muriel, an expert photographer, asked the head of circulation if he would mind rolling back the desk calendar to the day before so it would show THURSDAY JUNE 16. The original Bloomsday had been a Thursday too. Smiling, the librarian obliged. In sweet France where I was going, how different! One would have been tossed out of the Bibliothèque Nationale for daring to ask such a thing.

The Irish are an obliging race, though it may be only their curiosity that makes them so. On the way from Dun Laoghaire to downtown Dublin, I stopped to visit the church of Mary Star of the Sea, whose choir Mr. Bloom heard on that warm June night as he sat on Sandymount strand watching Gerty McDowell. The cab driver knew the church well. When I asked him to wait, he shut off his engine, got out, and followed me in, saying, "Ah, I might as well go in and say a bit of a prayer meself." Inside the church I wondered what he would charge for the waiting time. He charged nothing. On the way in to Dublin he commented on the Irish (Gaelic) language examinations which must be passed to obtain government jobs, particularly teaching posts. "I had it in school with the Christian Brothers," he said. "But I never learned it. It always seemed such a baby language."

Few of those old types survive in Ireland today. Once in a pub where I was listening to a man play the ullenharp—a very Irish instrument, almost totally inefficient, that emits its mournful plaint through a set of pipes by air awkwardly pumped by the player's elbow—an old tad pushed his glass next to mine, kept a minute of silence, then turned with his opener: "In thirty words, no more, no less, tell me: What's wrong with the world?" I agreed it was in a terrible state of chassis, but didn't know the ultimate causes of its disarray. American tourists now often wonder what has happened to the archetypal Irish of their dreams. Those of Hibernian ancestry are particularly disappointed when they don't get the old "God love you!" treatment they expect on arrival. They announce in the shops that their name is Bogan or O'Brien and that their ancestors came from County Cork or Mayo, only to receive a cool and brogueless reply, "How nice. I hope your stay is very pleasant. Now is there anything else I can show you?"

I took the direct Aer Lingus flight from Dublin to Paris and settled in the Hotel d'Isly near the church of St. Germain-des-Près. I had stayed at the d'Isly when I made my first trip to Europe in 1934 playing cello in the third-class orchestra of the White Star liner *Majestic.* Now the rue Bonaparte crawled with people and cars; tourists packed the outdoor tables of the Café Flore, Deux Magots, and Brasserie Lipp, long since abandoned by existentialists. Mornings I'd take the Metro to the Porte d'Orléans, walk up the Boulevard Jourdain to the Cité Universitaire, and teach my small classes in the Pavillon Néerlandais.

After class I'd have lunch with a few students at Columbia's Reid Hall on the rue de Chevreuse in Montparnasse—a fine old house with a flowering courtyard that had once been the hunting lodge of the Duc de Chevreuse. Afterward we might have an iced Burgundy at the Dôme (they had read Hemingway), then walk through the rue de Fleurus, where Gertrude Stein had lived with Alice B. Toklas. Then I'd take them through the Luxembourg Gardens up the hill to the university, where we'd sit through a lecture in the peaceful Sorbonne, the shattering riots of '68 less than two years away. How about a stroll over to the Collège de France? There they could see Bergson's lecture hall with a bronze relief of the philosopher hung outside, as well as a more recent tablet with the names of the faculty killed by the Germans. Then we'd take the elevator up to the observatory roof to enjoy a view of Paris, the sort that drew from Rastignac his cry to the great city: "It's between you and me now!" Afterward we'd call in at the library of St. Geneviève, where young James Joyce had poured over the gorbellied works of Aquinas on an empty stomach. Once we were ejected by a librarian hissing in Gallic fury because I had led my students into the catalogue room without *written* permission. On the return trip, I'd point out where Pascal had lived, then leave them at the metro stop, reminding them of their assignments in Merleau-Ponty due that week.

Some students wanted to see where Proust was buried, so I took them to Père Lachaise, to the wall where the Communards were shot, had them look at the stone inscribed, "Ici repose Colette," then to the cemetery office to ask where Proust's grave was. The woman at the counter turned to the man working beside her:

"Marcel Proust—est-il ici?"

"Proust? Oui."

She looked up the name in a card file and filled out a form:

```
Formule N° 28                                    1°  le·  N  14818

            PREFECTURE DE LA SEINE

         CIMETIERE  PARISIEN
         DE L'EST - PERE - LACHAISE

            SITUATION DE SEPULTURE

Nom : ...Proust Marcel...

Date de l'inhumation : ...1922...
...85... · Division ...............................
.......1.· ligne  a gauche du chemin...
N· ...386...

        10027 -- La Productrice    5.000 ex.  - 1-1964

                              19 PA _ 1908/
```

Among many Prousts, all lettered in gold, we found Marcel's flat slab of black granite, the kind the French call *noire de Suède*. It was close to the crematory and columbarium where Truffaut placed his cameras to film the final scene of *Jules et Jim*.

Àpropos Proust, I took Ainslie to a more cheerful place his spirit haunts. On free weekends I'd visit her at Villers, near Deauville on the Channel, where she was staying with a French family. The summer of '66 was cool and rainy, and Ainslie and I had to walk along the beach at Villers huddled in our trenchcoats against the thin, steady rain, the kind that gets sucked in with every breath and soaks through your pores into your entrails. But when the sun came out just a little we'd take the local train from Villers to Cabourg along the same track that Proust's Marcel took "the little crawler" to Balbec, sometimes with his girl Albertine, sometimes with Mme Verdurin's vacationing little clan.

We'd get off at Cabourg and have lunch at the Grand Hotel if we had money enough. As we ate a mediocre lunch in the dining room (at fifty-seven francs each) I'd tell Ainslie that this was the very room that Proust wrote about in his novel where Marcel, bored with food, would let his eye wander from his plate to look at the sea through the window, except on those days when the waiters set down on the table some gigantic fish, a marine monster, "whose body with its numberless vertebrae, its blue veins and red, had been constructed by nature, but according to an architectural plan, like a polychrome cathedral of the deep." But Ainslie was thinking of the black kitten we had met in a Cabourg grocery store on our way to the hotel. We had stopped in to buy a newspaper, and she had picked up the kitten to pet it. Roaring with affection, the little beast butted its velvet head into her nose.

"Oh, whose is it?"

By the pleasant expression on the storekeeper's face, I knew she had asked the wrong question.

"But it is yours, mademoiselle!"

That summer Ainslie and I visited Nicole Bouffet, owner of the big country house at Cuverville that had once belonged to Andre Gide and his wife Madeleine. Gide used the lovely estate as setting for *Strait is the Gate,* his favorite story based on his love and court-ship of Madeleine Rondeaux, Gide's other-worldly first cousin. Cuverville lies about twenty miles east of Le Havre, not far from the sea at Étretat. It's a little place, no more than a few small houses, a tobacco store, a Catholic church where the writer and his wife lie buried in the churchyard's "Protestant corner." A little beyond the church stands the two-storied white house that the Gides inherited from André's mother. Locals call it "the Château."

Nicole Bouffet was twice widowed and very rich. With her first husband she had gone out to equatorial Africa to manage a coffee plantation. After his death she married a man who became chief of police in Paris under the Vichy régime. He died some time after the Liberation, having paid for his sins in prison. His widow bought the house at Cuverville from Gide's double cousin Dominique Drouin. He had inherited it from Gide but could not keep up with the expense of maintaining it.

Mme Bouffet had remodeled the interior of the house to her excellent taste, restoring some of the original eighteenth-century pieces, replacing other items according to her fancy. In the salon she kept Gide's piano, on which he practiced his favorite Chopin. (She once played for me a recording of Gide giving a piano lesson to a young girl.) In the smaller living room, Mme Bouffet had preserved the original wainscoting of white and gold, but had done the room over in coral and almond green. Blue Delft tiles framed the big fireplace. She had covered the easy chairs with red *velours de laine* and put an English boat-table of polished wood in the center of the room.

From the hall, a door led to the large back garden dominated by a towering copper beech tree, a favorite of the poet Paul Valéry, Gide's friend. Ainslie and I were led to the outer garden beyond the walls through which Jerome of the story used to make his way to Alissa in the inner garden. Alissa had passed through that narrow gate with its hidden latch after she had sent away her beloved Jerome for good. She had renounced his love in accord with Christ's counsel of perfection, to give up all and follow Him—"Strait is the gate and narrow is the way, which leadeth unto life and few there be that find it."

On another occasion I came down from Paris with a colleague to Cuverville for a small luncheon with Mme Bouffet and a few of her friends. Dominique Drouin was one of the guests. After lunch Mme Bouffet took us up to her own room by the main staircase, slippery with wax, that dated from Madeleine Gide's time. Drouin said that the clergyman who read the service at Gide's funeral in 1951 had amused the mourners by sliding down half a flight. Nicole Bouffet's room had been Madeleine's own. There was the fireplace in which Madeleine had burned her husband's letters to her when she found out that he had gone to England with his young lover Marc Allegret.

Madeleine Gide knew of the homosexual side of her husband's life and kept silent. If she were not the object of his desire, at least she knew she had his love. But she drew the line at young Allegret, son of an old family friend, when Gide began to court him in the years of the First World War. She knew they were planning a honeymoon in England at war's end and long before their departure she made it clear that she saw through her husband's attempts to pull the wool over her eyes. Gide wrote to her from Paris complaining that she misunderstood him, that he really loved her, that she was his life, his breath, and so on. She replied from Cuverville:

> André dear,
>
> You are mistaken. I have no doubt of your affection. And even if I had, I would have no cause to complain. My share has been

very beautiful. I had the best of your soul, the tenderness of your childhood and of your youth. And I know that, living or dead, I shall have the soul of your old age.

I have always understood as well your need of movement and liberty. How many times in your moments of nervous suffering, the price of your genius, have I been on the point of saying to you, "But leave, go, you are free, there is no cage door to hinder you." (I did not say it for fear of grieving you with too hasty an acquiescence in your departure.)

What causes me anguish—and you know it without need of open avowal—is the road to which you have committed yourself, a road that will lead you and others to destruction. I pity you the more because I love you. It is a terrible temptation that rears itself before you, one armed with every seduction. Resist.

> Adieu, au revoir
> Your MADELEINE

Gide did not resist. He went off to England with young Allegret. She burned André's love letters to her. One day after his return he asked for them, for it was his wont to dip into them for a bit of fine writing to use in his work in progress. She confessed that she had burned them in her fireplace, after rereading them one by one, crying. Gide himself wept (he says) for a week. He hoped that she would come around to saying she was sorry she had destroyed those letters "into which I had put so much of the best of myself." But she did not, and his absences from Cuverville became more prolonged. In 1926 he went off to the Congo with Allegret who had been commissioned by the French government to make a documentary film. Gide had just finished *The Counterfeiters,* a complex novel with pederasty at its center: the young hero Olivier is modeled on Marc, while Edouard, the older writer, shares much with Gide himself.

Years later, after Madeleine's death, when he himself was approaching old age, someone asked Gide if he did not have regrets about certain things in his past life. "Regrets?" he wondered. "I regret only not having yielded to certain temptations," and added that when we are young, at the time our desire is keenest, our souls, youthful and austere, too often hold back desire from fulfillment. Like the old man in Cavafy's poem, the author of *The Immoralist* pondered:

> . . . . how Wisdom had deceived him;
> and how he always trusted her—what folly!—

the liar who would say, "Tomorrow. You have ample time."
He recalls impulses he curbed; and how much
joy he sacrificed. Every lost chance
now mocks his senseless prudence.

After Mme Bouffet's elegant luncheon, I walked out in the garden for a while. A sea wind from Étretat stirred the leaves of the great copper beach. At that moment it seemed that Gide must still be wandering—as he recalled he did once at Cuverville in harvest time—like a madman amidst a peace as arid to him as the desert.

Another lovely house, quite different from the château at Cuverville, belonged to Mme Robert Merle d'Aubigné at Grez-sur-Loing, not far from Fontainebleau. It had been the home of the English composer, Frederick Delius, who with his wife, painter Jelka Rosen, lived there from his marriage in 1903 until his death in 1934. Delius had composed most of his major works in that old sandstone farmhouse with its beautiful garden reaching down to the quiet river Loing. Shortly after the end of World War I, the composer fell ill from a syphilitic infection acquired years before, and became blind and totally paralyzed. For the rest of his life he had to be carried like a large rag doll upstairs and down, from house to garden, by a husky manservant.

Delius's last years were brightened by the presence of a young English musician, Eric Fenby, who took down notes at the composer's dictation for his final compositions. Fenby has told the fascinating story in his memoir *Delius As I Knew Him,* the book on which Ken Russell based his moving film portrayal of Delius, *A Song of Summer.*

When Christine Stiassni—of Sarah Lawrence and the boatbuilding Illingworths—heard I was teaching in Paris, she asked me to visit an old family friend who had a summer place in Grez-sur-Loing. As a Delius fan, I jumped at the chance. But it was not until I arrived at Grez that I found Christine's friend owned the very house that had belonged to the composer. It fronted blind on the village main street next to the church of St. Lawrence with its old Norman tower. Heavy wooden doors closed over the entrance through which haywagons once were driven to the field beyond the courtyard, now a terraced garden stretching down to the river.

Mme Merle d'Aubigné—or "Bibka," as she liked to be called—was a personage in her own right. Of Russian-Jewish ancestry, she had married Dr. Robert Merle d'Aubigné, a noted orthopedic surgeon, but now lived apart from him in Paris and Grez. An ample, mild-faced woman in her late sixties, she would talk for hours over tea in the garden about great writers and their work. Her daughter Catherine, a biochemist, said that it was all very well to talk about Tolstoy until sunset, but there were times when one wanted to know where the car keys were. I quickly caught on that Bibka did not care to be reminded that this house and garden had once been the property of Frederick Delius. She strongly believed that houses, wives, and other attachments of great artists should be only of minor interest to lovers of their art. Compared with Delius's music (I don't think she particularly cared for it), what did it matter that he happened to live in this house? Though the aging Fenby was always welcome, she refused to allow the Delius Society in England to affix a plaque to the side of her house identifying it as the composer's.

Mme Merle d'Aubigné lived the life of an amiable matriarch in Paris and Grez, entertaining her children and grandchildren, as well as her own good friends. At Grez I met her contemporary, Mme Louis Joxe, nee Halévy. Her husband, Louis Joxe, former French ambassador to the Soviet Union, was de Gaulle's Minister of Justice until his dismissal after the crisis of June '68, when the student revolts almost toppled the Third Republic. (Joxe had taken a hard line, refusing to intervene in any way for the students imprisoned after the May riots at Paris and Nanterre.) Bibka enjoyed the company of young people, particularly students, and in later years welcomed any of my own from Barnard and Columbia who might be passing through France. One of her visitors was our son Mario, who stopped off in Paris as he was returning to Vietnam after Stateside leave. But how, she asked, could one of my sons be fighting with the American Army in Vietnam, while another, said to be a pacifist, worked in the Peace Corps in Colombia? Was I sure that "Peace Corps" was not just an American euphemism for a Special Forces unit bent on armed intervention in South America?

Bibka mellowed a little on Delius when I wrote to her how some of us shed a tear as we watched Ken Russell's film about the composer on television. And she was pleased to get reports of Frank Corsaro's new staging of Delius's opera *A Village Romeo and Juliet* that I saw at its first run in the John F. Kennedy Arts Center in Washington in the spring of 1972. She also wanted a full account of the Delius festival in Jacksonville, Florida, earlier that year, where I had read a paper at the local university.

Jacksonville music-lovers have a special interest in Delius, for as a young man he lived in that part of Florida for a year and a half, a period that marked a turning point in his life. When Delius's tyrannical father despaired of his son's ability to make his way in the family wool trade in Yorkshire, Fred persuaded him to buy an orange grove on the St. John's river a few miles below Jacksonville so that he, Fred, could manage it and market the fruit. But once installed in his riverbank cabin at Solano Grove, Delius succumbed to the subtropical evenings and the local blacks' singing; he forgot about the oranges. On a trip to Jacksonville to buy a piano, he met Thomas Ward, organist of a Jesuit church in Brooklyn, whom the Fathers had sent south to recover from tuberculosis. Delius had the piano moved down to his cabin and brought Ward along as his professor of harmony and theory. A number of Delius's early compositions recall his American stay, especially his suite for orchestra *Florida* and his tone poem for orchestra and chorus *Appalachia*.

My paper read at the festival was on Delius and Whitman—an easy subject, since the composer set much of his music to Whitman's texts, particularly those with a Long Island sea and shore theme. *Seadrift*—Delius's tone poem for orchestra, baritone, and chorus set to Whitman's "Out of the Cradle Endlessly Rocking"—celebrates the poet's recollection of two mockingbirds he saw on the beach as a boy. One of the birds vanishes, maybe killed, leaving her mate to seek her in vain in the waves. Delius is a master of the dying fall and it is hard to forget the final cadences of *Seadrift:*

> *But my mate no more, no more with me,*
> *We two together no more . . .*

Percy Grainger's widow, Ella (née Ström-Bandelius), showed up on the arm of Stewart Manville, forty-five, handsome archivist of the Percy Grainger Library Society, headquarters at White Plains, New York, where the Australian pianist-composer had lived with his Swedish wife for many years before his death in 1961. Ella was 83 at the time of the 1972 Delius festival, and still beautiful. The eccentric Grainger (fanatic booster of everything Nordic and blue-eyed, and a lifelong self-flagellant) had befriended Delius who admired the pianist's art and rich hoard of folk tunes he had collected over the years.*

---

* Delius borrowed the melody of "Brigg Fair," an old tune Grainger had picked up in Lincolnshire, for his orchestral piece of the same title. (Grainger had heard the

Percy and Ella were frequent guests at Grez-sur-Loing. I was surprised to find that my harmless ruminations on Whitman seemed to affect Stewart Manville deeply. I had mentioned Delius's *Idyll* for soprano, baritone, and orchestra, text from the poet's "Once I Passed through a Populous City," on which the composer had tacked other lines of Whitman, somewhat altered:

> *Day by day, night by night we were together!*
> *I hear her whisper*
> *"I love you, before long I die,*
> *I have waited long merely to look at you*
> *For I could not die till I had once looked on you."*

"Impossible," said Manville, "impossible not to dissolve in tears upon hearing the Whitman texts you cited. I cannot help thinking of Ella and myself in those lines from the *Idyll*. Later I found that the Delius festival coincided with their marriage. Today, as of this writing, Ella survives in White Plains, near ninety, blind and deaf. Her husband cooks for her, helps her, drives her to pleasant places like Shenandoah Valley National Park.

After the paper readings at Jacksonville, the festival participants were taken by bus down to Solano Grove, near Picolata, where Delius had his plantation and cabin by the river. The cabin no longer stood there, having been knocked down and rebuilt on the campus of the University of Jacksonville. (It would have been much better to have left it there overlooking the broad waters of the St. John's.) Pilgrims had to hike in to the site from the main highway about a mile along a lane shaded with moss oak. My partner on the walk was nine-year-old Jane Warren (daughter of the president of the Delius Association and professor at the university). Jane convulsed the people walking in front of us by telling me in a loud clear voice details of obstetrical complications that had attended the birth of her little brother. Jane was a solid citizen. Patiently she endured hours of Delius songs and sonatas. When I got back to New York I sent her a limerick by way of thanks for her company:

---

melody sung by Joseph Taylor, a seventy-two-year-old bailiff who won a Lincolnshire folk-singing contest with his moving rendition of "Creeping Jane.") Sir Thomas Beecham, Delius's ardent promoter, never cared for the composer's rhapsody on "Brigg Fair." When Sir Thomas was asked by reporters in an American midwestern city what he had programmed for his upcoming concert in Cleveland, Beecham replied, "I'm going to conduct Delius's *Brigg Fair*. It's a very bad piece of music. The people of Cleveland will love it."

A candid young lady named Jane
Said, "I'll give you my estimate plain,
   The music of Delius
   Should speak to the really us,
But some of it gives me a pain."

COLUMBIA REVOLT, 1968

&ª *"Up against the wall, motherfucker, this is a stickup."*

So Mark Rudd, Columbia College junior and leader of Students for a Democratic Society (SDS), ended his letter to Grayson Kirk, president of Columbia University. He took that complimentary close —as the nuns of St. Joseph's School taught us to call that part of the letter—from LeRoi Jones, now Amiri Baraka, then patron saint of SDS. Mark's communication pronounced our society sick, Kirk and "his capitalism" the sickness.

Next day at noon, Tuesday, April 23, SDS held a rally at the sundial on College Walk between Low Library, Columbia's administrative headquarters, and the grassy approaches to Butler Library. That rally set off a series of wild events that led to the take-over of five university buildings, occupation of Kirk's private office, fruitless negotiations involving administration, faculty, students, community leaders, city officials, and finally the violent clearing of buildings by New York police, resulting in the arrest of hundreds of students and many injuries. The shock was not the first to strike the Columbia campus since the Berkeley revolt of 1964, but it was by far the worst. Since 1965 there had been earlier incidents—demonstrations against the NROTC, against campus recruiting by the Marines, the CIA, and the Dow Jones Chemical Company. But these were all comparatively minor scuffles. None had led to the riotous building occupations, strikes, mass arrests, beatings, and near shut-down of the university that bloodied the crisis of April–May, 1968.

At normally tranquil Barnard, two mild premonitory symptoms of unrest manifested themselves about a month before the explosion detonated by the April 23 rally. The first was the Linda LeClair incident. Then came the unsuccessful attempt by the Barnard philosophy department to get the Barnard faculty to consider a resolution against the Vietnam War. The first had its funny side and got wide publicity in local and national news media. Everybody but the Barnard faculty ignored the second and they themselves quickly forgot it in the rush of following events.

Early in March 1968 the *New York Times* ran a feature article about female college students living off-campus with their boyfriends. It described, among others, the life style of an unnamed Barnard student whom the college easily identified as Linda LeClair, a twenty-year-old sophomore. At the time, Barnard housing regulations stated that no student under twenty-one could live in nonuniversity housing off-campus, apart from her family, unless the student had a bona fide live-in job with an approved household. Under an assumed name, Linda arranged a nonexistent job that met these conditions and was happily living in an off-campus apartment with a twenty-year-old Columbia dropout, Peter Behr. Yielding to pressure from her housing director, Martha Peterson, the new Barnard president, took steps to bring Linda to book. This was a mistake. Noisy protest from a small parade of Barnard and Columbia students snowballed into a *cause célèbre* with lines drawn and sides taken by students, faculty, administration, and alumnae, the news media gleefully reporting all the accompanying silliness.

Martha Peterson, a large woman of commanding height with silver-white hair and a pleasant face, came to Barnard after long service as a dean at the University of Wisconsin to succeed Rosemary Park, who resigned as Barnard president in 1965. Not the trustees' first choice, Miss Peterson turned out a good one, as subsequent events showed. A native of Kansas, Miss Peterson became the first president of Barnard to come from the Midwest. Her manner was friendly and informal. Her critics described it as cutesy, and regretted her lack of a good French accent. But to keep Barnard College from flying apart at the seams, as Columbia did, something more than a good French accent was needed, and amiable Martha Peterson possessed this something more.

On the Linda LeClair case she was badly advised. She listened to the outraged college housing director and to certain other administrators who objected (they said) less to Linda's sexual irregularities than to the fact that she lied to the college housing authority. Then

Miss Peterson consulted the President's Advisory Committee, a small group of senior faculty whose chief business was to pass on promotion and tenure, but whose counsel the president sought on other matters as well. As a member of the committee at the time, I suggested not making an issue of the affair. Columbia and Barnard students were already in springtime heat (in the 1950s they used to work it off in panty raids) and now stood eager for an excuse to take a high moral posture against the administration on a matter of principle. Too late. Proceedings had already started against Linda—a very casual student who rarely came to class or handed in assignments, who was thinking of dropping out of college anyway. Administrative steps against Linda were mild enough, but, as predicted, the students saw a principle at stake and jumped to her defense. Three hundred of them signed petitions that Linda herself mimeographed. Some Barnard faculty got into the act, supporting student demand for an open hearing before Judicial Council, a joint student-faculty-administration hearing board. Columbia's Jewish and Protestant chaplains supported Linda's complaint of outmoded rules, though not necessarily her right to cohabitation. Sound trucks double-parked on Broadway outside Barnard Hall; news photographers and television cameramen moved in. LeClair headlines and photo captions sprinkled local and national press in the following weeks:

HEAD OF BARNARD ASKS PARENTS OF DEFIANT GIRL FOR THEIR VIEWS

SEX AND THE SINGLE COLLEGE GIRL

BARNARD UNIT AGAINST EXPELLING GIRL WHO LIVES WITH BOYFRIEND

FATHER DESPAIRS OF BARNARD DAUGHTER

SIXTY COEDS OFFER TO ADMIT BREAKING BARNARD HOUSING REGULATIONS

BOARD SENTENCES LINDA TO LOSS OF CAFETERIA AND SNACK BAR PRIVILEGES

BARNARD PRESIDENT DELAYS ACTION ON DEFIANT GIRL

GRADES ARE KEY IN LECLAIR CASE

LINDA LECLAIR CLIMBS INTO PRESIDENT KIRK'S OFFICE IN STRIKE

BARNARD EASES ITS RULES FOR OFF-CAMPUS HOUSING

Linda LeClair's loss of cafeteria and snack bar privileges startled the staid editorial page of the *New York Times* into a Flatbush interrogative: "THIS IS PUNISHMENT?" Good for a laugh in *Newsweek* and *Time* as well. But Judicial Council's action had a serious purpose: to apply minimum discipline for an infraction of an outdated college rule and to call into question the right of a college or university to stand any longer to its students *in loco parentis,* or—as Linda put it—*"in loco grandparentis."* College youth's new sexual morality was here to stay.

Whatever personal feelings one might have against the more Tantric aspects of undergraduate sexual behavior in these and the years to come, one couldn't deny some logic to the new freedom. College students had enough of postponement of sexual activity for the ever-lengthening intervals between sexual maturity and the time society considered them qualified to enter the job market and conventional marriage. The availability of effective contraceptives removed much of the old fear of pregnancy and, if pregnancy did occur, abortion was available if wanted.

Rejection of the Vietnam War by college youth—a crucial factor in the campus unrest of the 1960s—had its own logic too, though its forms of expression may have been sometimes offensive and unfair. From grade school, young Americans had been brought up to believe their country a democracy, a government in which important things are done with the consent of the governed. Now in 1968 the nation had for four years been engaged in a hot, brutal war halfway around the world without so much as a by-your-leave toward the people, especially that part of it needed to fight it, the nation's youth. Young men were being drafted into the war without their consent, a significant number of them middle-class and of college age. Our Vietnam enterprise broke on determined resistance of bourgeois American youth to being forced to take part in it. You can't draft an unwilling middle class.

Barnard College became the first of Columbia's schools to bring an anti–Vietnam War resolution before its faculty. Our philosophy department offered it *before* Lyndon Johnson announced he would not seek renomination, before the assassination of Martin Luther King, a month before the massive outbreak on the main campus across Broadway. After the Columbia explosion in April such resolutions became a dime a dozen. But in March 1968 the idea of a Columbia faculty passing a *political* resolution was still a disturbing novelty. My colleagues in philosophy—Mary Mothersill, Sue Larson, Malcolm Brown, and Ilmar Waldner—joined me in presenting the resolution for the department:

> RESOLVED,
>
> that the faculty of Barnard College declare its opposition to the policy of our government in prosecuting the war in Vietnam. We ask that steps be taken immediately to secure a negotiated peace, and that these steps be such as will bring the fighting to a speedy end. Our plea is addressed to every individual and institution with power to help in achieving this goal.

I was no pacifist. I esteemed the profession of arms, and was glad to keep my commission in the Naval Reserve. Socrates performed his military service and did it well; he saw action at Potidaea and Delium, and passed up a decoration for valor so another man could get it. So long as the world is organized as a system of nation-states, the use of political power to secure a nation's own good is not inherently evil. War is an extension of political power that can, at times, be legitimate, even meritorious. But the Vietnam War was all wrong. In the cynical words of Napoleon's lieutenant—it was worse than a crime, it was a mistake. The amount of destruction the American war effort had produced over the years in the form of suffering, death, disruption of social order, and demolition of property and natural resources had insanely passed the bounds of whatever dubious good this effort may have been intended to bring about. If it were improper for a faculty to take a stand on the question of Vietnam on the ground that such an issue lay beyond our legitimate concern as a faculty, then for what desolate event had we to wait before making a protest?

Miss Peterson, presiding, said she would neither declare my motion in or out of order and turned to the political scientist she had appointed as parliamentarian of the meeting. While he gravely juggled the concepts of order and out of order, the chairman of the psychology department rose to point out that by tradition a vote of the faculty is binding and when evoked on a question of this sort presents a challenge to academic freedom. He therefore moved that no discussion of the admissibility of the motion be entertained. The Kafkaesque idea of a motion not to discuss whether a resolution could be discussed in advance of its being moved so confused the parliamentarian that Miss Peterson good-humoredly dismissed him on the spot. Not until six weeks later did the faculty decide the resolution was in order, but voted not to consider it anyway. By this time nobody cared much one way or the other, for the entire Columbia campus steamed in turmoil and Barnard classroom buildings were being picketed by our own students.

Major disorder on the Columbia campus had begun at noon on April 23 with a mass meeting at the sundial. Mark Rudd urged a demonstration against the university's affiliation with the Institute for Defense Analysis (IDA), a government agency that sought advice from universities on matters of interest to the military. Columbia's IDA involvement was slight, but President Kirk had, intentionally or not, given the impression that there were no ties at all.

There was also the prickly issue of the building of a new Columbia gymnasium, a project that members of the Harlem community now violently objected to on the ground that gym construction encroached on Morningside Park, a public area in their territory. Feelings were not soothed by the university's argument that Harlem community leaders had agreed to the arrangement with the city back in 1958 when Columbia announced its plans to invite the community to use the gym and facilities through a separate entrance from Morningside Park. No good, said the new activist community leaders, 1958 was not 1968. Right-on, said Columbia's Student Afro-American Society (SAS) and demanded that construction on the gym site be stopped.

As excitement grew, Mark Rudd urged the students to carry the anti-IDA demonstration into Low Library, ignoring a written invitation from David Truman, vice-president and provost of the university, to meet with the demonstrators in McMillin Theater, Columbia's largest auditorium. But Low Library—the domed Columbia landmark that houses the university president's office and those of other high administrators—had been shut tight and locked by campus security police. The crowd milled around aimlessly until someone shouted "To the gym!" and two hundred students marched to the site overlooking Morningside Park where they broke down fences, stopped the bulldozers, and charged the outnumbered police on hand. One policeman was knocked down and kicked in the face. Others arrested one student and took him away.

At the sundial, the demonstrators who had been turned back from Low Library regrouped, then marched into Hamilton Hall, a large classroom building nearby with offices of the administrators of Columbia College, the university's undergraduate school for men. White SDS and black SAS declared the building occupied and imprisoned Henry Coleman, acting dean of Columbia College, in his office. Apart from a few rude epithets hurled his way, Dean Coleman's detention, lasting twenty-six hours, was moderately civil. His captors did not interfere with sympathetic colleagues outside who sent him in towels, shaving equipment, and two bottles of whisky.

At dawn next morning (Wednesday, April 25) the blacks asked the whites to leave Hamilton Hall. After some discussion, they did. A spin-off group now broke into Low Library and occupied President Kirk's office, where they roamed about, sipping his sherry, sampling his cigars, and rifling his files. Shortly before 8:00 A.M. police entered Kirk's office but made no arrests. Campus security officials removed a Rembrandt painting for safekeeping. As the morning wore on, the occupiers got hungry and outside sympathizers began to pass in peanut-butter-and-jelly sandwiches and soft drinks. Demonstrators climbed in and out of Kirk's office by the windows at will. CORE and other Harlem community organizations sent cartons of food into Hamilton to sustain the orderly blacks.

Meanwhile segments of the Columbia faculty were doing what they could to bring about a peaceful resolution of the conflict. Some senior professors met at Lionel Trilling's apartment on Claremont Avenue, and a larger number of faculty began gathering in the Graduate Students Lounge in Philosophy Hall. An emergency faculty meeting held that afternoon in Havermeyer Hall passed a resolution calling for the establishment of a tripartite university body with representatives from faculty, students, and administration. Faculty strongly urged administration not to use police to clear the occupied buildings. Dean Coleman walked in and got a standing ovation. He had just been released from Hamilton Hall.

Despite faculty efforts to cool the situation, trouble spread. The blacks in Hamilton turned down administration efforts to compromise, and on that rainy Wednesday night a line of faculty wearing white armbands improvised from handkerchiefs stood guard outside

Hamilton to prevent student violence. A sizable antistrike group of conservative students, later known as the Majority Coalition, threatened counteraction by force. Activists called them "jocks" because of the large number of athletes in their ranks. They in turn christened the demonstrators "pukes."

By Thursday, Avery and Fayerweather Halls had been occupied, the latter mostly by graduate students of architecture. Mathematics Hall's turn would come later. Earlier that day, a body of liberal professors calling themselves the Ad Hoc Faculty Group met and passed a resolution expressing sympathy with many of the demonstrators' aims and asking peaceful evacuation of the buildings, with a promise to interpose themselves to prevent forcible police entry. The demonstrators politely turned down the proposal. On Thursday night a crowd of one thousand students listened to Harlem activists harangue them on Broadway just outside the closed gates of College Walk. Police allowed one of the orators, Mau Mau–helmeted Charles 37X Kenyatta, a relative moderate, to walk peaceably through the campus to Hamilton Hall to talk to the brothers. Counterdemonstration athletes tried to break into occupied Fayerweather, but a line of faculty turned them back, urging patience and nonviolence. The spectacle of philosophy professor Sidney Morgenbesser hanging pleadingly on the neck of an indignant jock was a sight not easily forgotten.

Over the weekend demonstrators settled in the occupied buildings and made themselves as comfortable as they could. Many floors had only men's toilets. These were promptly declared "liberated" so that young women strikers and sympathizers could use them too. Strike Central in Ferris Booth Hall arranged to distribute food donated by neighborhood grocers and community citizens to those hungry souls in occupied citadels. Strikers sought out commodious offices, particularly those with floor rugs. In Hamilton Hall, the occupying blacks kept a regimen of tight discipline with a schedule of meals, showering, cleaning-up, and sleeping, strictly adhered to. White students in the other occupied buildings lived in more easy-going fashion.

Visitors and entertainers popped in and out of the occupied buildings. Street actors put on guerrilla theater. My Barnard colleague, Otto Luening, pioneer in electronic music, soothed savage beasts in Low by playing a piano he found there. A small Sarah Lawrence contingent helped Barnard girls fix hot meals and sandwiches for the strikers. Few seemed to be bothered by the usual male expectation that food preparation was a job for women. But in Fayerweather, held by an odd mix of extreme radicals and relative moderates, a posted sign reminded women that they were liberated and, as such, should reject the traditional housekeeper role unless they found personal creative fulfillment in it. Most strikers refrained from pot smoking for fear of giving police added grounds for hostile action. Some informal sexual activity ensued, but less than might have been expected in the circumstances. The heady joy of communal togetherness seemed enough. One young couple was married in candlelight on the steps of Fayerweather by Reverend William Starr; the bride wore white jeans and a veil.

The word now was Amnesty. Vice-president David Truman declared himself opposed to it and stated in public that none of the offenders would go unpunished. Sorely tried, he showed impatience with faculty attempting to act as honest brokers between strikers and administration. According to reporters from the Columbia *Spectator,* Truman complained that Lionel Trilling "was running around spouting phrases like *de facto* and *de jure* which he did not understand." Groomed to succeed Grayson Kirk as Columbia's president, Truman rightly sensed that bright future slipping away from him. His stonewalling hardened the demonstrators' resolve, and the weekend dragged by in a series of futile attempts to negotiate. Mayor John Lindsay sent up Barry Gottehrer as his personal representative to try to bring some measure of compromise among the embattled factions, but to no avail. Gottehrer stood speechless at the sight of professors crying and hysterical.

Finally in the small dark hours of Tuesday morning, April 30, New York City police moved onto the Columbia campus, smashed through the barricades, and cleared the occupied buildings. One thousand police under the command of Chief Inspector Sanford Garelik were used in the operation, the largest police intervention in the history of higher education in the United States. The blacks in Hamilton allowed themselves to be led out quietly. White students in other occupied buildings put up various degrees of resistance. Some 712 Columbia students were reported arrested, including 104 Barnard undergraduates. There were 148 injuries, but unlike certain forgotten American college disorders of the nineteenth century, there were no fatalities. Most of the injured were student demonstrators. A few faculty got roughed up; some bled from clubbings. A number of policemen suffered beatings and kickings, and a few were bitten by Barnard girls. A Sarah Lawrence student aimed a kick at a policeman's face, overreached herself, and fell painfully on her back. The son of Professor Dupee of Columbia's English department was kicked by a police horse.

Held on leash for days, the New York police had little sympathy for the Columbia boys, whom they considered an overprivileged, ungrateful lot—in two printable words, young punks. As for the Barnard demonstrators, the mayor's man said later:

> The police found it even harder relating to Barnard students. A dirty-looking girl who uses bad language can't be a good woman; she must be a whore. A girl would yell, "Go f—— yourself, you pig," and the cops were very upset. The longer they were there, the worse they felt. When the bust finally came, when they had their chance, some cops were very hard on the women.

Arrested demonstrators were processed through seven different police stations, then all were taken for arraignment down to 110 Centre Street. A Barnard trustee stood ready to provide bail money so that no Barnard student would have to spend a night in jail. No need, since a new day had dawned and representatives of the college administration who went downtown had little trouble securing the release of those Barnard women still held.

Barnard received scant mention in subsequent published reports on the Columbia events of April–May 1968, although the proportion of Barnard students taking part in the first "bust" was only a little less than the proportion of Columbia *College* active demonstrators to the total student body of their own school. Various reasons for this, most of them obvious: the 1968 explosion erupted as a Columbia thing, its sources entirely on the Columbia side of Broadway. Significant numbers of Barnard students joined the action only after Columbia broke loose. Barnard College had no history of discontent comparable to the growing rancor that soured the Columbia atmosphere since 1965, nor did Barnard students play any important part in the sporadic demonstrations against the various military-related outfits recruiting on the Columbia campus during the long build-up to the outburst. Barnard women were not subject to military service. Prospects of ultimate draft into the Vietnam War ate away at the nerves of Columbia men.

Due in large part to its peculiar history and Topsy-like growth, Barnard College had a flexible familial structure that helped hold it together in high winds, in contrast to the loosely articulated university of the main campus, each school a separate academic village except Columbia College, open at the top with no well-defined faculty of its own and a poor sense of identity. Nearly every Columbia College teacher engaged in or aspired to graduate school courses, and their qualifications for tenure were usually judged in that light. In contrast, Barnard College had clear boundaries, well-closed top and sides, its own campus, president, library, faculty, trustees, and endowment, yet it had open access to university courses and other facilities. Barnard was small enough (about 1,800 students, 150 faculty) so that the students knew who their teachers were, and most faculty in turn had some awareness of the students in their classes. Instruction by graduate students, common at Columbia, rarely occurred at Barnard.

Nevertheless when Columbia flared up, Barnard went wild with excitement. Between two and three hundred Barnard students swept onto Columbia's campus the night of the bust, although just over a hundred were arrested. A number of Barnard's younger professors joined the faculty lines that interposed themselves between the police and the occupied buildings. Activists picketed Barnard buildings as roving bands of demonstrators marched chanting "On strike! Shut it down!" People rushed around doing important errands. Faculty caucused all over the place. Columbia and Barnard couriers, both faculty and students, raced messages from Strike Central to outlying headquarters in other parts of the university. Black armbands worn by those mourning the arrested and injured gave way to red ones for strikers. Nonstriking students and faculty who favored amnesty wore green armbands. Stubborn conservatives sported light blue, Columbia's color. Ad hoc groups proliferated like rabbits and faculty meetings, overlapping, tripped over each other's toes.

Nearly all schools of the university suspended classes until the dust settled. Campus oratory rose to unprecedented eloquence. Students and faculty bounded with the exhilaration Jean-Louis Barrault described in the fever of the near-simultaneous revolt of French universities, that "vertigo which everyone experienced in those feverish weeks, exhausted, harassed, drunk like everybody else with words."

At Barnard, Martha Peterson was splendid. Although she had assumed the Barnard presidency in the fall, her formal inauguration coincided with the spring Columbia eruption and some traditional formalities of her investiture went by the board. Almost gaily she took on the maelstrom, making no irreversible stand on principle, behaving like a sensible tree in a storm, bending with the wind rather than debating it. She calmed overstimulated students who wanted to ride off in all directions at once. She steered faculty meetings like Captain McWhirr of the *Nan-Shan* in heavy weather. Some professors supported the students of the radical Left; conservatives jumped up to disown them. Departments split down the middle. When a senior professor made her strenuous protest against proposals to cancel classes—"But I was just coming to a climax in my Colonial America course"—a disrespectful young colleague remarked audibly, "I'll bet that's the first she's ever had." Mild pedagogues turned in a flash into flaming revolutionaries. Few beings are more difficult to control than a dionysiacally excited professor, and Miss Peterson had to deal firmly with some. Whenever a professor rose, choking, "I've seen my students hit over the head . . . ," Martha would interrupt, "We've all had our students hit over the head, so please sit down."

Campus disruption forced cancellation of Barnard's traditional Greek Games, an annual ritual in which freshman and sophomores, clad in classical costumes of varying length, competed barefoot in dances, ode-reciting, javelin- and discus-throwing, torch- and chariot-racing. The games were never resumed. Instead the Barnard gym opened its doors that spring to impromptu teach-ins, sing-ins, revolutionary assemblies, and celebrations from all quarters of the university. A black group staged a booming African tribal dance. A white Columbia professor joined the stomping ranks, thrusting out his pelvis with the rest to the rhythm of pounding drums.

In May, campus tension again reached the boil-over point when the university tried to reopen classes against the will of more than 1,000 students and 200 faculty members supporting the continuing strike on the main Columbia campus. Classes were boycotted or disrupted and lists of counterclasses posted. A sympathy sit-in on behalf of neighborhood tenants in a Columbia-owned apartment building was broken up by police, who arrested about 50 students. On May 21, just a month after the initial bust, students once more occupied

Hamilton Hall, this time to protest impending disciplinary actions against SDS leaders of earlier demonstrations. Small fires broke out in some buildings. Police cleared Hamilton and charged student barricades on campus. Nasty beating, kicking, and clubbing ensued with injuries on both sides. Some 138 students were arrested. In the next two weeks, the university suspended 73 demonstrators.

On June 4, commencement exercises were held, not outdoors on the steps of Low Library, but in the mammoth cathedral of St. John the Divine a few blocks from the university campus. President Kirk did not show. About three hundred candidates for graduation, most of them from Barnard or Columbia College, put on red armbands and walked out during Professor Richard Hofstadter's address to join various countercommencement exercises bubbling on the main campus. On one group of students whose consciences (during those days so many people discovered they *had* consciences) prevented them from accepting Columbia diplomas, Harold Taylor, former Sarah Lawrence president, conferred the "degree of happiness and freedom," by virtue of the authority invested in him by "the trustees of the human imagination." At Barnard's traditional precommencement diploma ceremony, three candidates for graduation made dissenting speeches. Some graduates refused their Phi Beta Kappa keys; overnight those trinkets had turned into symbols of Establishment oppression.

After commencement, everyone who had not already gone home left Morningside Heights. Building repairmen moved in and placid summer school students soon followed. In August, Grayson Kirk arranged his early retirement. Sad to see him so badly mauled. Apart from a lunch or two in the Barnard deanery, I had few contacts with him during his Columbia tenure. I did write a citation for him to read when he conferred an honorary degree on philosopher Susanne Langer. And he asked me to deal with correspondence from a New Jersey man protesting the use of my logic book at Columbia on the ground that the book took no account of the correspondent's personally invented philosophy of Organics, a system of thought based on the "naturalization of the syllogism, nonsymbolic and nondescriptive, dealing with veritable truth and providing insight into the future." Kirk was a good man who had the bad luck to look like a stuffed shirt. His hands full dealing with business corporations and money-raising, he had little contact with students, leaving them—

particularly the sensitive Columbia College undergraduates—pretty much in the hands of his subordinates. When he saw the mess in his office after the occupiers had been driven out, he stammered, "My God, how could human beings do a thing like this?"

The Columbia revolt of 1968 neither began nor ended the campus disturbances of the decade. Berkeley, Michigan, Wisconsin, Stanford, Howard, and others preceded it; Harvard, Cornell, Michigan State, Dartmouth, and others followed. Some campuses, like San Francisco State, erupted like Old Faithful year after year. Columbia itself suffered another building occupation and police assault just a year after April '68. The U.S. invasion of Cambodia detonated a new go-around of campus upheavals in the spring of 1970, the worst Ohio's Kent State confrontation with the National Guard when four young people were shot dead.

Across the Atlantic, just a month after the initial Columbia uprising, French militant students at the University of Nanterre, led by Daniel Cohn-Bendit, set off the catastrophic spring revolution, in which labor unions joined. That crisis paralyzed France, dejobbed ministers of state, and undermined the de Gaulle government. Compared with Columbia's social-dynamite explosion, the blast at Nanterre and the Sorbonne was thermonuclear. French students had much to complain of. In the spring of 1967 I visited classes at the Sorbonne, the faculty of letters of the University of Paris. Classes were dreadfully overcrowded. Students had to arrive at large lecture halls nearly an hour before class to secure a seat. The professor appeared on the platform, delivered his lecture, and vanished.

After World War II, France liberalized her university admission policy and French higher education lost something of its air of élite preserve. But despite the massive postwar increase in the number of students, there was little or no corresponding rise in the number of teachers. Building construction lagged shamefully.

Columbia University students did not share the miserable physical conditions of their French comrades, yet the Cox Commission, summoned to investigate and report on the causes of the Columbia disorders of 1968, made much of the poor physical shape of the Columbia College dormitories. The commission noted as well the proximity of the university to a major "ghetto" area, Harlem, a constant reminder to socially aware Columbia students that some enter at the portal—and some do not. Interesting that at Nanterre, the population of that working-class suburb of Paris included a mass of slum dwellers, Arab and Hispanic, living close to the sixteen thousand students that piled into the new, though unfinished, university buildings. Yet many of the major American campus disorders flamed at universities with no "ghetto" neighbors at all.

Causes, causes! What caused the student revolts on American campuses in the period 1964–72? Expert explanations of why all this happened flooded the market *after* the events, few or none before. For all the sophistication, real or alleged, of the methodology of the social sciences, I don't know any that *predicted* the disruptions. Not one Columbia sociologist in my ken offered early warning signals of the '68 earthquake on Morningside Heights. Over the cries of "Strike! Shut it down!" an eminent Barnard sociologist, former president of the American Sociological Association, asked her students, "Have I been with you all these years and know so little about you?" They replied, "We didn't know either!"

Unfair to expect predictability—the hallmark of the natural or "hard" sciences—of the social studies. Too many variables. All the same, for decades psychology, sociology, and allied disciplines had aspired to the condition of the natural sciences. For decades they had been surveying, comparing, analyzing, quantifying, charting, diagraming, tabulating, graphing, computerizing human behavior data. Their authority had mounted, their faithful proliferated, their doctrines spread and believed, their course enrollments swollen in proportion. Yet their preceptors stood as open-mouthed as the rest of us when students short-circuited campus generators and dumped reason and civility out of the house of intellect.

Bales of books, reports, newspaper articles, and essays appeared *after* the facts, offering laundry lists of causal explanation of the social disruption that social science was unable to predict. Among them:

Vietnam War and vulnerability of middle-class students to draft
Repressive character of corporate industrial society
Alienation of students from that society
Social injustice to blacks and other minorities
Irrelevance of college and university curricula
Relative affluence of students and consequent lack of interest in jobs
Insensitivity of universities to needs of working class

Political naïveté of students
Political naïveté of professors
Irrationalism
Misarchy (Nietzsche's word for "hatred of all rule")
Ressentiment (Nietzsche-Scheler term for rancor of oppressed)
Inflammatory effect of writings of Marx and Mao; of Fanon and
    Marcuse
Jews (Mark Rudd and SDS leaders at Columbia; Cohn-Bendit at
    Nanterre)
Philosophy majors
Sudden tuition increases
Generation gap
Spring sap rising
Other
Various combinations of above

Historians tried to comfort the world by reminding it that student revolts were as old as the universities themselves, dating back to the twelfth and thirteenth centuries, when medieval students expelled and beat up their professors and each other at will, at the same time making life miserable for the townsfolk by their drunken disorder and violence.

Identifying causes of any kind of human action is a complicated job. The idea of "cause" itself is a relatively crude tool to use to explain it. There are all sorts of causes—"push" causes, like winds knocking over trees; "unwinding" causes, as the revolving of my phonograph turntable allows a Mozart quintet or a Stevie Wonder song to move from start to finish; "spark" causes, as a lighted match produces explosion of a gas in a cellar. People speak of the gym construction at Columbia in '68 or the five-hundred-dollar tuition increase at Boston College in 1971 "triggering" the respective campus disruptions.

We tend to speak knowingly of the "causes" of "human behavior." But the very word "behavior" carries the assumption that human action is an event that occurs when we are *pushed* by something from the outside or inside, like billiard balls or dominoes. Yet human action can only be imperfectly understood in terms of such forces acting upon us. Human action can never fully be represented by models whose motions are described in terms of pushes and shoves —historical, social, economic, psychological—however delicately the pushes and shoves are thought of, however sophisticated the apparatus used to conceptualize them. That is why we are so often surprised, even shocked, by the unexpected things people do, individually or in groups. Human beings, as D. H. Lawrence said, are tricksy-tricksy. We are highly purposive and intentional beings, and what we do can never adequately be explained in terms of what is done to us.

That caution made, one can risk a bit of speculation. The democratization of college and university education, in this country and in Europe, crowded campuses with young people who were rather more aware than their less numerous predecessors of what was going on in the world. They knew more of what the social situation was, and of the contradictions between what was preached and what was practiced. By the mid-1960s, the American middle classes had grown mightily in number and affluence. Many of their children in college felt the contradiction between the idea of democracy and the reality of a dirty war in Indochina into which they were being netted—a war their government had committed them to with less consultation than took place in changing the date of Thanksgiving or George Washington's Birthday. Refusing to be drafted, the sons of the middle classes turned colleges and universities into forums of protest.

Of course, it was neither all that simple or virtuous. Much youthful activism was aimless, witless, and idiotically destructive. Great blocks of the militants had no real political experience, did not know what politics was, though they thought they were acting politically. Nothing in their sheltered background or upbringing prepared them to construct an ideology and carry it out in social action. In that respect, the black militant students were usually ahead of the whites, for they had a clearer idea of what they wanted, where they were going, and how to achieve the discipline necessary to get there. But the greater part of white middle-class youth had no ideology beyond a fervent personal individualism—the doctrine that what is most valuable in a human are those qualities that make that particular human unique, different, irreplaceable. From grade school on, they had heard teachers and counselors exalt ideals of self-discovery and self-realization. The big question was "Who am I?" ("I'm me, Natalie!") *Real* education, they were told, would bring out that hitherto-hidden individual self. One could face oneself, know it, and proclaim its reality and value to the world. That was the meaning of "To thine own self be true." That was Openness, Honesty, Sincerity, Expressing Your Feelings.

Now many of these bourgeois students failed to find their valuable and unique selves emerging as promised. Where was that self? Wasn't it the job of education to bring it forth? Yes, but it did not appear. So naturally the students held their teachers and curriculum to blame, the boring things! Any educational set-up that did not lead to discovery of Self, to an experience of Identity, seemed irrelevant. Disappointed and restless in college classrooms, some students dropped out of the bad educational scene. Some went home, others off to communes and the third world, still others remained to form a pot-smoking drop-out subculture that hung around universities while scorning them and the Establishment they represented. There were those who stayed at college, but withdrawn and peevish. Many took to protest and revolt when the opportunity rose. College or university made a convenient stand-in for society at large, the administration a handy target for harassment and abuse. All that was thought to be *political*.

A curious thing about the student protests concerned time-lag. Demonstrations peaked in a period when the authoritarianism of higher education, once real and heavy-handed, had been relaxed, step by step, in a series of liberal adjustments in the direction of student "needs"—often no more than easing up on requirements and providing trendy courses ranging from Art Deco to the Psychology of Revolt. Similarly, protests of white oppression mounted on campuses long after universities had eased admission of black and other minority students by way of scholarships and liberalized admission standards, as well as active recruitment of underprivileged groups near and far. An American Indian at Barnard, a freshman and a little weak academically, absented herself at length from Introductory Philosophy class to help the college recruit other Indians. She found none to recruit.

Academic year 1968–69 brought less than the hoped-for peace to the Columbia campus, though the university was neither successfully struck nor shut down. Again SDS tried to make racism their cause, but Columbia blacks ignored them, preferring to present their own demands and demonstrations. In mid-April blacks staged a two-day occupation of Columbia College's admissions office in Hamilton, demanding yet more minority recruitment, still further liberalized admission policies. Two days later a couple of hundred SDS demonstators fought their way into Philosophy Hall past a defending line of Students for Columbia University, a conservative group, and name-calling escalated to ugly fistfights. Over the screech of insults and the scuffing of feet against feet, the voice of University Proctor Kahn could be heard pleading, "Can we please not destroy the flowers?"

Next day my friend Loren Graham, professor of history, was showing a visiting Soviet scholar around campus. As they approached Pupin, Columbia's hard-science building, they suddenly encountered a small parade of student demonstrators, some of whom carried red flags. The Muscovite professor turned pale and whispered hoarsely to Loren in Russian, "Let's get out of here! Can't we go another way?" So much for the fraternal spirit of bolshevism.

A group called "The Crazies" invaded one of my classes in Milbank Hall. Dressed in bizarre costume, they distributed mimeographed sheets to the students with various "demands," while one Crazy stood at the front of the room and delivered an incoherent speech. I did nothing to interfere, but sat atop my desk and listened attentively. After five minutes, the Crazies ran out of steam and mimeos, and departed. We resumed our discussion of the ontological argument for the existence of God.

Various cross-patch groups invaded Martha Peterson's presidential office at intervals throughout the year, sometimes staging sit-ins there to reinforce their several demands. One uncomplimentary sign carried outside Barnard on Broadway accused her of pettishly plotting genocide. On certain days picket lines tried to prevent Barnard students and teachers from entering buildings, and many students, sympathetic or not, simply stayed away. Student and faculty counterdemonstrators tried their hand, among them Professor Julius Held, Barnard's eminent authority on Flemish painting, who carried a sign saying, "Students! Go to class!'" The Barnard Organization of Soul Sisters (BOSS) insisted on segregated living for themselves in the residence halls:

> It is a strain—academically, socially, and therefore psychologically —for us, Black Women, to live apart from one another in the dormitories. We have no desire to assimilate into the white society at Barnard. We want sections to be designated "for Blacks only" so that we may have the option of living instead of merely existing.

Martha Peterson did what she could to accommodate them, and for some years afterward, until the practice was declared illegal, most black students lived apart from the whites. Many of my liberal colleagues and students who had supported the black cause thought all that very awful and against everything they had worked and fought for. Indeed it was startling to confront frozen-faced blacks who declined to speak to you or told you to get your ass out if you trespassed on their turf in Brooks, Hewitt, or Reid. I tried to put a good social-Hegelian face on it by suggesting to my unhappy liberal white students that such black withdrawal might be socially and historically necessary. Think dialectically about it. Blacks needed to separate themselves from whites for a time, maybe a long time, establishing their own identity, by taking up a position contradictory to that of the whites (the first negation) before they could move back on a higher level (*aufgehoben*) to live and work with whites once more in friendly relations (negation of the negation).

Occasionally black students publicly berated the college, from which most of them were receiving some sort of aid. One young black woman, about to receive her Barnard diploma, declared over the microphone to the assembled faculty and graduating seniors that black women had been given a hard time at Barnard and she knew that today, Commencement Day, we were glad to get rid of her and her sisters. Faculty and students gave her a cordial round of applause. I sat on my hands.

But do you know something? Today frozen faces are melting and smiles are breaking through once again. And black smiles *are* beautiful.

For just a few years after '68 the word on campus was Change It! Tripartite committees pullulated. An ungainly university senate was constructed to which all constituent schools sent delegates, some of whom talked themselves to exhaustion, like marathon dancers. College requirements, already pared thin, were further reduced. Language requirements diminished. English majors dropped. If science had to be taken, let it be anthropocentric; the world of inanimate matter held little interest for the new humanists, whose Florence was the Inner City of Urban Studies. Students hunted for "exciting" courses. Barnard started a small experimental "college" where students could get a few points' credit for self-selected projects. Ceramics proved especially popular. For three years the spirit of learning on Morningside Heights took its cue from Tranio of *The Taming of the Shrew:*

> *No profit grows where is no pleasure ta'en:*
> *In brief, sir, study what you most affect.*

But all too soon the waters began to run the other way. Even before the recession of the early seventies, nearly everybody decided to go to law school. Passion for justice, egalitarianism, civil rights played its motivating part. But law school wanted high board scores, sensible transcripts, good grades. So did medical schools: relatively easy to enter during the sixties, they froze tight before the new onrush of applicants. Teaching jobs disappeared. As the economic pinch tightened, more Barnard students began to think of careers in business. The Women's Movement provided a cause which could be well served by serious study on Barnard's home grounds. Morningside Heights settled down as students faced the prospect of Earning a Living.

President Peterson of Barnard pulled out a few banderillas from her broad shoulders and sighed with (temporary) relief. One Christmastime, to mark a peaceful approach to the holidays, I dropped into her office with my cello and Jo-Ann Reif, a talented flutist from Scranton, Pennsylvania, mad about Mahler. That sort of impulsive informality delighted Martha and she beckoned in deans. We played a Bach suite and Jo-Ann encored with Debussy's "Syrinx."

Good Martha Peterson! She gave Barnard seven years of her generous life, but unlike Dorothy, her fellow Kansan, she did not quite find her Emerald City. Not in New York, anyway, though there were a few scarecrows, tin men, and cowardly lions on Morningside Heights. In the end, some members of the Board of Trustees made her position so uncomfortable that she took once more to the yellow brick road and found her modest Oz in the presidency of Beloit College, Wisconsin.

U.S.S.R. & DAVOS

§ Due to a sabbatical leave I missed the campus revolts of May 1970 that followed the U.S. invasion of Cambodia and the Kent State shootings. On my way to the Soviet Union, motherland of Revolution Itself, I expected to meet Loren Graham in Moscow at the Institute of Philosophy of the Soviet Academy of Sciences. Earlier that spring we had read over together a manuscript copy of his book on science and philosophy in the Soviet Union, and I looked forward to discussing it with him and to seeing the sights of Moscow and Leningrad in his company. Loren spoke fluent Russian. The Institute of Philosophy published *Voprosy filosofii* ("Problems of Philosophy"), the main philosophical journal of the U.S.S.R., and that periodical had given an oddly favorable review to a new edition of one of my books. Scanning the review in Loren's translation, I was amused to note how the Russian reviewer had coped with the longish volume. Apparently he had read very carefully the eleven-page introduction of the book and based his entire review on that, save for a skip to the back where he found "an excellently compiled reference-bibliographical *apparat*."

The institute itself seemed to be a well-ordered *apparat*. As Loren's guest, I was received with every courtesy on my brief visit. The institute took pride in its large collection of foreign philosophy journals, though to judge by the mint condition of most of them, they had not been read with fervor. Neither at the institute nor during any other time during my stay were we followed around. Much of the obtrusive guidance visitors to the Soviet Union mistake for spying stems from an almost hysterical anxiety that foreigners, not speaking Russian, will unwittingly find themselves in trouble or simply get lost.

The political element had a way of showing itself, however. On my entry at Moscow's Sheremetyevo Airport a customs official frowned at a book he picked out of my luggage, one Loren had asked me to bring so he could give it to a Russian friend. The book was a copy of Loren's study of the Soviet Academy that Princeton had published (in English) in 1967. My agent scratched his head over it, then called down a supervisory official, who turned the pages dubiously. Clearly they did not know what to do with the sinister red-jacketed volume until Loren himself, waiting for me on the other side of the barrier, spotted the book and shouted an explanation in Russian that satisfied them as to its harmlessness.

"Oh. Is present for your friend. Is okay." They put it back in my bag. Four years later, though, after Loren's *Science and Philosophy in the Soviet Union* had been published, the Soviet authorities denied him a visa to reenter the U.S.S.R. Strange, for the book expressed admiration for Soviet science and even for dialectical materialism. To this day it is not clear whether Loren's new book or something else caused the refusal. A few years later they admitted him for another trip, so whatever trouble there was must have passed.

In Moscow every intellectual *apparat* appeared to run smoothly; academic and urban tranquillity prevailed. Young people at the university chatted peacefully as they strolled with their friends to class, the crowded subways were spotless, walls shiningly free of graffiti; the atmosphere seemed pervaded by a sense of collective responsibility for civic tidiness and control. Despite the humid May warmth and women in light summer dresses, most men wore dark suit jackets and ties. In Moscow one comported oneself correctly. Once on the way home from the university library Loren had been stopped by a woman who told him that it was uncultured (*nye-kulturnyi*) to walk in a public street with a pencil tucked behind his ear.

Since Loren could not get me into his Hotel of the Academy of Sciences, I had to stay at the Ostankino, some miles the other side of Red Square, a second-class hostelry where they screamed "Tourist Brennan!" if they wanted me. Mornings I would take the Number 24 bus downtown to meet Loren somewhere near the Hotel Rossiya, equivalent of a Moscow Hilton. Beside the essential "please," "thank you," and "I'm sorry," I had learned a few survival phrases in Russian like "Where is the men's room?," "Which is the way to . . . ?" and "Should I get off here for . . . ?" Though I could understand hardly a word of the voluble replies, I found that by carefully watching the body tensions and choreographic gestures of my informants —who always took time out firmly to correct my bad Russian pronunciation of *Oktiabrskaya* or whatever—I could generally make a fairly logical construct of their meaning and act accordingly.

Bus fare downtown was five kopeks, the coin deposited in the center of Number 24's box unguarded except by the bus passengers themselves. One morning I found that the smallest change I had was a ten-kopek piece, so on boarding the bus I dropped that in the fare box, figuring I could afford to donate five kopeks to the cause of Socialist Justice. After all, wasn't it five kopeks that Tchitchikov of Gogol's *Dead Souls* offered to his old schoolmates, who were getting up a subscription for a former teacher who had fallen upon evil days, and didn't they fling back the five kopeks in his miserly face? Ten-kopek piece in the box, then. But it was a mistake. Instantly I found myself surrounded by a vocal group of bus standees informing me of my error and not very genially either. A stern-faced woman appointed herself head of an impromptu committee and when, at the next bus stop some good soul got on and tried to deposit his proper five-kopek piece, she snatched it out of his hand and pressed it into mine. Abashed, I mumbled an ineffective series of *"prostete!"*'s and *"spasebo bolshoe!"*'s to all Soviet citizens who had assumed collective responsibility for correction of my mistake.

People in the countryside also showed appreciation for the proper way of doing things. One day Loren and I took a bus to the end of its twenty-mile run outside Moscow, and from that point we hiked into the country. After some hours, we felt like having a bit of lunch and soon found a small *palatka,* a roadside food stand, where we bought a tall bottle of Georgian wine and two small loaves of delicious white bread. Our backs comfortably propped against the side of a grassy ditch, we finished off the bread, then settled down to enjoy the rest of the wine, passing the bottle back and forth to each other, tipping it up to our mouths, heads back. Now along the dirt road with her grandmother came a little girl who glanced fearfully at us in the ditch. She said to her grandmother (Loren translated), "Grandma, what are those two strange men *doing* there?"

Grandmother glanced at us briefly, then said to the little girl, "No need to mind them, my child. They are drinking well."

We rested for a while, starting up only when Loren, who had gone to sleep, suddenly awoke to find a goat eating his tie. As we went on our way across a meadowland we met a countryman eating his lunch and drinking from a large bottle. He greeted us and proferred his bottle. Loren politely declined for both of us. That offended our friend. He made a passionate speech concluding with words of deep Russian sadness. Loren translated, "As a fellow human, I *personally* am asking you to drink with me!" No more to be said. I took the bottle and downed a slug. Shattering, whatever it was! I had to gasp to get my breath back. As I steadied myself, Loren swallowed a little, and the man let us depart in peace in God's name.

My ticket entitled me to go to Leningrad by Aeroflot, while Loren took the overnight express train, the Red Arrow. At the airport, I found that only stand-by places for the Leningrad plane were available. After the regular passengers had boarded, the stand-bys were unleashed, rushed madly to the plane, and tried to fight their way up the ladder. This was not TWA or SAS. Aeroflot stewardesses kicked the stand-bys back, like sailors repelling boarders. Earlier one of the cabin attendants had told me to stand to the side and watch for her signal. When she closed one eye in my direction I made for the ladder while she punched out a path for me. Every seat in the plane was occupied, so my stewardess ordered a woman passenger to pick up her little boy and hold him on her lap so I could have his seat. His name was Andrushka and he cried timidly "Grom!" ("Thunder") as the plane roared down the runway.

In Leningrad I met Loren again but we had so little time that one afternoon we had to choose between the Hermitage and all that art, or going for a hydrofoil ride on the Baltic. Vote for the hydrofoil was unanimous and we spent the afternoon at Peterhof. Back in Leningrad that night, we had dinner in the old Hotel Europa, where waiters served some diners ice cream for dessert but refused to give us any. Two Swedish businessmen sat at our table and discussed automobiles with us. They assured us that the Saab was a better buy than a Volvo. When we asked what kind of automobile they owned, each replied Mercedes.

Next day it was back to Moscow for the institute and other events. One couldn't avoid the near-obligatory visit to Lenin's tomb. Once again we experienced the favoritism shown to foreigners from important countries. As Americans "with papers," Loren and I were pulled by a guard from the end of a queue that stretched half a mile along Red Square and pushed up front. There we quickly descended into the dark cool underground chamber where soft light plays on the wax doll propped up there; head and hands seemed oddly disarticulated. Brrrr! It was a relief to get out into the sunshine again where the pilgrim line filed along a path shaded by fragrant lilac bushes where lie the tombs of the Soviet honored. John Reed's was there. So was Stalin's slab, but he had no effigy. A little girl behind us asked her father (Loren translating), "Papa, why doesn't Stalin have a statue like these others?" Her father said they were making one. Unconvinced, the child pressed him, "Are you sure? Is it obligatory?"

That night we had dinner at the Ararat, where a wild Armenian band competed with wild Armenian food, then on to the Bolshoi for *Giselle*. The production was no more than routine, but oh! the richness of all those strings in the orchestra. By comparison the Paris Opera orchestra sounded like a vaudeville pit band; imagine doing *Daphnis and Chloë* with twenty strings! Afterward we went to the bar high atop the Rossiya, a luxury lounge with only eighteen seats so that one had to wait in line to get in. But, since we were hard-currency customers, we did get in, and enjoyed a lovely view of Moscow at night. We drank vodka and orange juice.

My visit to the Soviet Union that spring of 1970 coincided with the closing of the door over the cultural breathing space allowed by Khrushchev. In both Leningrad and Moscow I talked to a number of academic and professional people, sometimes in English, more often with Loren interpreting, surprised at the openness of the speech and the bitterness of their complaints. (Later it was explained that they took me on trust because I was Loren's friend.) Almost everyone complained of travel restrictions on Soviet citizens. "Look at all those Finns!" a Leningrad graduate student said. "Hundreds of them over on holiday from Helsinki every weekend. And *we* can't go anyplace outside our country. When we squawk, they tell us the Soviet Union is so big it has every kind of climate and scenery to be found in the world."

Academics and professionals were feeling increased pressure from the heavy hand of Soviet cultural bureaucracy. A highly placed writer for the Soviet Information Bureau spoke with disgust about the way the government used well-paid novelists to get antiliberal views across. He had just read an approved novel, newly published, in which an old Jew is made to say, "Maybe I'm bad, but I never wrote dirty stuff like Solzhenitsyn." A journalist friend of Loren sat with us as we visited him in the grounds of a Moscow hospital (poor Vitali, he is dead now from the kidney disease that brought him there) and told us about various repressive measures afoot. One was the closing of a small experimental theater, in Moscow, just a few weeks before. In a surrealist revue a sequence showed nothing on-stage but a large sun which slowly disappeared. Dangerous symbol-ism—the sun could be Stalin, Communism, the Politburo, or just an ordinary tired sun. But Soviet art should show things coming up, not going down.

Honor to the Soviet motherland—though as the day of my departure approached I found myself speaking of "getting out," an expression one would not find oneself using in Holland or Switzer-land where I was now going. For all its good-humored people, its lilacs and vodka, its *prospekts* so clean and unpoliced, its crazy church of St. Basil that looks as if it could pick itself up and dance across Red Square, Moscow still breathes an air of heaviness and gloom that cannot be blamed simply on the Bolshevik revolution or communism or even on Stalin, "Josef the Beautiful." That air seems to come down from the shadowed ages of Russia's past. One could not knowingly pass the place of the ancient chopping block for human heads on Red Square without feeling a bit of the weight of dark centuries of old Russia or catching the stale scent of that long history of oppression and blood. So, for all the Soviet Union's dear men and women (so like Americans in their love of informality and jokes), its technological marvels, its lovely meadowlands—I was "getting out."

Loren eased my passage through customs at Sheremetyevo so I wouldn't miss the KLM flight to Amsterdam and gave me a little blue and gold pin from Leningrad as souvenir of our happy stay there. *Do-svidaniya!*

A forty-minute stopover in Warsaw, then Amsterdam two hours later. A fast switch there to Swissair for I had an appointment to visit Odilo Trämer, rector of the Foundation School at the Benedic-tine monastery of Einsiedeln, about forty miles from Zurich. Father Trämer, who spoke Romansch as well as German and English, was holding down the job of Ludwig Räber, our onetime guest at the Barnard Educational Colloquium, until he returned from the Swiss University of Fribourg, where he was professor of philosophy of edu-cation and (in his last year there when I visited his seminar) dean of the faculty. A learned man, Father Trämer had little time for modern literature. When I touched on Hermann Hesse, mentioning that Einsiedeln had furnished the writer the model for the Benedictine abbey of Mariafels in his novel *The Glass Bead Game,* the Rector said amiably, "Hesse? Oh yes, he's a Protestant." Absent Father Räber knew rather more about Hesse for he had some acquaintance with Dr. Lang, Hesse's psychiatrist, who himself had a Benedictine education and in his later years studied theology and mysticism.* The novelist had endured seventy sessions with his psychoanalyst (a pupil of Jung) but begged him not to cure him entirely lest too-successful analysis take away his gift of art.

In Zurich I discovered that I had forgotten to make hotel reservations. There were no vacancies anywhere; a medical convention had taken every room. But wait, there was a maid's room available at nominal charge at the luxurious Dolder on the heights overlooking the city and lake. Would the Herr Professor object to that? Since normally the Dolder exceeded my price range as much as the Baur au Lac, I leaped like a salmon in spawning time and rode up the hill in the hotel's free (free!) limousine. Just one tiny disadvantage: the maid's room stood right off the main lobby, where at regular intervals six sturdy Swiss in short pants serenaded the hotel guests with alpenhorns. An alpenhorn is so long that its bell lies on the ground eight feet or so in front of the blower (they use them to call the cows up in the Alps) and six alpenhorns going at once sounds like the Entry of the Gods into Valhalla.

Next day I had lunch with Pat Graham on her way to join her husband in Moscow after visiting the Pestalozzi Institute, Zurich's center for research in special education. We talked about Davos where I was headed for a few days' walking along the gentler mountain paths, something I had done twice before. Pat's great-aunt Louise Parks had married the Indiana artist Samuel Richards, a tuberculosis patient at Davos at the time John Addington Symonds was nursing his afflicted lungs in the diamond-clear mountain air. In 1890 at Davos, Richards drew the handsome pen-and-ink portrait of Symonds that now hangs in the Herron Art Institute, Indianapolis.

For Davos you take the Chur express that runs along the Lake of Zurich, making stops further on at Sargans and Bad Ragaz, the latter close to the village of Maienfeld where Heidi and her goat

---

* In 1976, while mountaineering in Sicily, Ludwig Räber (he was a noble soul!) accidentally fell into the crater of the volcano Stromboli, the first philosopher I knew to die this way since Empedocles fell or jumped into the crater of Etna 2,500 years before.

lived. (There's a little "Heidi-spring" there with a small commemorative sculpture inspired by Spyri's story.) At Landquart you get off and cross over to the train for Davos that slowly winds its way up into the mountains, wheels squealing as it rounds the curves until, after Klosters, the train rolls out on the floor of the valley of Davos. Depending on the location of your lodgings, you get off at the Dorf or the Platz. The two centers, once separate communities, are connected by Davos's main street, a narrow mile-long thoroughfare lined with shops selling sports equipment, woolens, and all kinds of good things to eat. Davos has a famous fondue restaurant where gourmets come from all over, but since hot melted cheese is a little too olfactory for me, I prefer Rose Schneider's chocolate shop just down the street from the Hotel Schweizerhof; there you can sit over a cup of good coffee and watch the people or the scenery as you prefer.

Near the Dorf there's a cable car to take you up to the Parsenne (ten thousand feet); another by the Platz to lift you to the Schatzalp, from which you can walk back down by wooded paths to the village accompanied by small red squirrels with furry ears that search in your pockets for nuts. By Postbus you can ride to Frauenkirche or beyond, to the lovely valley of Sertig, where you can look at an unforgettable panorama of snowy mountain peaks. Or you can take the train from Davos to St. Moritz, switching there for a bus to Sils Maria where Nietzsche had his vision of the Eternal Return (sound Strauss's *Zarathustra* fanfare!) on the shores of the lake of Silvaplana. The house at Sils where the ailing philosopher spent ten summers is now the Nietzsche Haus with mementoes, a small library, and rooms for student lodging.

Davos has an international reputation as a winter sports resort. There's fine skiing on the Parsenn, a breath-taking run down to Klosters, and world skaters use the Davos rink for Olympic tryouts— in 1976 Sheila Young of Detroit set a world record there for five-hundred-meter speed skating. I've tried skiing on the kiddie slope of the Parsenne, but ended in a spill every time. I blame it on the altitude.

Long before the century's turn, Davos had acquired international fame as a fashionable cure for tuberculosis. Robert Louis Stevenson came there in 1880, just after his marriage to Fanny Osborne, whom he met during the first of three summers he spent at

Grez-sur-Loing. The author of *Treasure Island* stayed two winters at Davos, where he wrote "The Stimulation of the Alps," an essay about the feverish exhilaration the stimulating but fatiguing rarified mountain air produces in its visitors, particularly those with lung ailments like himself. Symonds was a fellow patient; the two rare birds met, tried their best to like each other, and failed. Stevenson hated Davos, complained of mental inertia there, found little interest in the spell of disease and death that immobilized the affluent tubercular community.

In 1913 the English poet James Elroy Flecker arrived at Davos and made the final revision of his play *Hassan* before dying there of tuberculosis. With incidental music by Frederick Delius, *Hassan* was a theatrical hit in London in the early 1920s. Dated and neglected now, *Hassan* has some wonderful lines, not least the epithet hurled by the captain of the military at the caliph's chief of police:

Thou dragger of dead dogs from obscure gutters!

Two years before Flecker's arrival at Davos, Thomas Mann turned up at the Alpine resort for what proved to be a momentous three-week visit. Unlike Stevenson, the German novelist found himself receptive to the macabre enchantment of the place and exploited it hugely for his next book. As for so many others, what first put Davos on the map for me was Mann's novel *The Magic Mountain*. El Caughey set me onto it while I was in college and the novel is still one of my absolute favorites, many times reread. Once long ago I made the acquaintance of its author.

THOMAS MANN

When I visited Thomas Mann the first time in Princeton, he shook my hand and said to me in careful English, "You are very humid." The time was January 1940, and I had been asked down from New York for tea, the invitation coming in response to a letter I had written him about a study I was making of his work. It was raining hard, and by the time I reached the big Georgian house on Stockton Street after walking from the train station, I was very humid indeed.

Not tall, but slender and mobile, Mann appeared much younger than his sixty-four years. We sat down in a large, sparely furnished living room, and as he turned to address me, he would cock his head a little to one side. I told him of my interest in the relation of disease to artistic creation, and he said he thought it strange that a young American should be concerned with such a *German* idea. Since my work had something to do with both philosophy and literature, I asked him how much deliberate use he had made of metaphysical ideas in composing his masterwork *The Magic Mountain*. His reply was that critics tended to overestimate the part played by the intellect in a writer like himself, but that he believed a work of art could and often did contain a metaphysical idea—though it was not necessary that the reader or even the artist at the moment of creation be aware of what it was. Then in came his wife, Katia, a small, friendly, bright-eyed woman, her graying hair brushed up in the German fashion. Tea was poured, sandwiches and cakes were brought, and we talked of Germany, the war, Mann's current writing projects, and the doings of his children.

A year later, when another invitation for tea came, Mary was invited too. Mann was charming to her; he reminded her of the actor Clifton Webb. Once again we talked of *The Magic Mountain*, and Mann expressed pleased surprise at the novel's steady popularity in the United States. Meanwhile, he and my wife were having a quiet little contest to see who would get the last of certain small cakes for which he seemed to have a particular liking. As we got up to leave, Mann disappeared up the stairs and came down a moment later with a copy of his new novel, just published in Stockholm—*The Transposed Heads,* a tale based on an old Indian legend he had heard from Heinrich Zimmer, who, with his family, was in fact soon to be our neighbor in New Rochelle. As Mann inscribed the book for me, Katia was showing Mary a fur-lined coat in the hall closet—her very favorite winter coat. She had brought it from Europe, which they had left a little more than two years earlier, after Hitler came to power. They would not return to Europe for twelve years.

Katia Mann had much to do with the conceiving of *The Magic Mountain,* and Mann often told the story. His wife of seven years had a weakness of the lungs, and in 1912 went to the Waldsanatorium in Davos for a cure. (It is now the Hotel Wald Bellevue, about halfway between the Dorf and the Platz.) Mann stayed with Katia for three weeks, and while there, gathered "my own strange impressions of it," as he later wrote. After he returned to their Munich home, his wife sent him letters with details of the sanatorium routine and about the odd characters who turned up at the place. When he had finished *Death in Venice* in 1911, Mann had begun to think about composing a counterweight to that gloomy tale, a novella about a Candide-like young man of good North German family who has a romantic attraction to death—another very German idea. The young man would visit a tuberculosis sanatorium, where the physical facts of disease and death would contrast grotesquely with his high-toned expectations of romantic death. Mann began to write the story in 1912, interrupted it in 1915 to write essays on World War I, picked it up again in 1919, and finally finished it in 1924. It was published at the end of that year—not the modest novella originally planned, but a two-volume, twelve-hundred-page, world-championship novel.

From the time of its publication to the present *The Magic Mountain* has sold extraordinarily well, particularly in the German original and in English translation. *Der Zauberberg* appeared in Germany in December 1924, and although Mann's publisher put the date 1925 on the second printing of 10,000 copies, all were sold before Christmas. By the end of 1925, *Der Zauberberg* had sold 50,000 copies in the expensive two-volume printing. A cheaper, one-volume edition brought sales to nearly 100,000 by the end of 1927, and six years later 155,000 German copies had been sold. (In Germany, *Der Zauberberg* ran second in popularity to Mann's *Buddenbrooks,* which by 1945 had sold well over a million copies.) English, American, Dutch, Polish, Swedish, and French translations of Mann's Davos novel had all appeared by 1931.

Reviews of *The Magic Mountain* in Europe were for the most part highly favorable, though some critics thought the work too dialectical to be called a novel at all. The Swedish writer Fredrik Böök, whose vote was influential in awarding Nobel Prizes for literature, considered *Der Zauberberg* an "artistic monstrosity," and when Mann received the prize in 1929, the citation (it hangs today on the wall of the Thomas Mann Archive in Zurich) stated explicitly that the prize was given "above all" for *Buddenbrooks,* the four-generation saga of a Lübeck merchant family that so closely resembled Mann's own. In France, André Gide, always friendly to Mann, paid the Davos novel careful tribute, citing it somewhat opaquely as "truly not comparable to anything." Years later, Jean Cocteau was less cautious in his praise: *"La Montagne magique* is a book which is part of my system; its ink runs in my veins."

In this country where the novel appeared in 1927 in Helen Lowe-Porter's translation, reviews were mostly enthusiastic, although an occasional critic found Hans Castorp a boring young man, and there were the usual regrets about what was lost in translation. Ludwig Lewisohn, our testy onetime next-door neighbor in New Rochelle, put the doubters in their place, calling Mann's king-sized novel "one of the greatest and most moving books of our time, a book to which no reviewer can do justice. It is a novel from which each must draw whatever he is able. He who draws nothing is impossible." To date Mann's American publisher, Alfred A. Knopf, has sold nearly half a million copies of *The Magic Mountain.*

"What a movie it would make!" I thought upon finishing the novel for the third time. The year is 1907, the year of the Triple Entente. Hans Castorp, a young German engineer, comes to visit his cousin Joachim at a Davos sanatorium patronized by affluent European bourgeoisie. Hans's planned stay is for three weeks, but he remains seven years when a moist spot shows up on his lung. He falls in love with Clavdia Chauchat, a Russian patient with "Kirghiz eyes," and the progress of his disease and his love are carefully correlated. Two tubercular professors, Settembrini and Naphta, one a rationalist Italian and champion of Western freedom and democracy, the other a Marxist Jesuit inclined to terrorism, fight over Hans's soul. But in a dream that comes to him in a mountain snowstorm, Hans refuses to follow either mentor, or to surrender his humanity to an infatuation with death. Earlier, at the sanatorium, he has wooed his Isolde on Carnival night in high-toned French. She departs, later to return with a Dutch millionaire, whose pearls she wears. Seeing that Clavdia and Hans have been lovers, Peeperkorn gallantly kills himself to step out of their way, but somehow his suicide brings the affair to an end. At a sanatorium séance, the ghost of the now-dead cousin Joachim appears in the uniform of the approaching 1914 war. Humanist and Jesuit take up pistols in a

Dostoyevskyan duel over their conflicting ideologies, and the clerical terrorist turns his weapon on himself. From dreamingly contemplating his own Wilhelm Meisterish self-development, Hans is knocked to his feet by the events of August 1914. His seven-year dream ended, he will act, will pick up the sword of the fallen Joachim. Singing bits of Schubert's "Der Lindenbaum," he goes to almost certain death with a German student regiment advancing through Flanders.

What a movie, indeed! Mortal coughs on the sound track, snowy Alpine vistas, the corpses of the tubercular dead sliding down the Schatzalp on toboggans, perhaps Oskar Werner as sleepy-eyed Hans Castorp. The idea had in fact occurred to others earlier. Shortly after World War II, Alexander Korda bought the movie rights to *The Magic Mountain* for a mere twenty thousand dollars. His brother Zoltan was to be director, Mann's son Klaus a collaborator on the screenplay. (Thomas Mann himself, with his brother Viktor, had once written a film script of *Tristan und Isolde,* but nothing came of it.) At cocktail parties, film actresses began to talk about who would get the female lead. Unbelievably, Jayne Mansfield was mentioned, and Gregory Peck's name came up as a possible Hans Castorp. In the end the project was shelved. Peck went off to play Ahab in John Huston's *Moby Dick.* In Hollywood only a footnote remained: after band leader Artie Shaw had gone long-hair and was playing Mozart's Clarinet Quintet instead of "Begin the Beguine," he and Ava Gardner were divorced. "He made me read books," Miss Gardner told the judge in court. "He made me read *The Magic Mountain.* I thought I'd never finish that damn book!" The sympathetic judge gave Miss Gardner her decree.

In length and art, *The Magic Mountain* unquestionably stands first in that odd genre, the sanatorium novel. In 1894, twelve years after the discovery of the tuberculosis bacillus, Beatrice Harraden published an Alpine sanatorium novel, *Ships That Pass in the Night.* The story is not well equipped with medical apparatus, but it does touch delicately on the relation between disease and the erotic. Mann's own early novella *Tristan* (1903) pokes cynical fun at two eccentric patients falling in love over the piano score of Wagner's music-drama. Hermann Hesse's novella *Guest of the Cure* (1924) parallels Mann's larger work in certain respects, but the "guest" has arthritis, not TB; Mann read it while writing the last part of his supernovel and noted the similarities with approval. A. E.

Ellis's *The Rack* (1948), a poor man's *Magic Mountain*, portrays the unhappy lot of a group of tubercular veterans of World War II stuck in a sanatorium high in the French Alps, where the management cheats them out of their daily ration of butter.

Today, with the success of chemotherapy, both the morbidity and the mortality of tuberculosis have declined steeply, and Alpine sanatoriums devoted exclusively to that disease are nearly extinct. Now surviving Davos cures shelter tuberculosis patients together with sufferers from a variety of other respiratory diseases. The career of the private Alpine sanatorium for tuberculosis alone lasted hardly more than fifty years, as did the literary genre it inspired. But *The Magic Mountain* has more than survived.

On my own first visit to Davos in 1945, there were still a few tuberculosis sanatoriums left. Still in uniform (the European war had just ended), I stopped at a hospital for tubercular children and fell into conversation with a visiting Austrian physician. Hearing of my interest in Mann's Davos novel, the doctor told me a strange story. Not far from Lucerne, he said, there lived a man who thought he was Hans Castorp. A German, a man in his sixties, in poor health as the result of a cerebrovascular accident, the man was otherwise rational enough, though rather a recluse, living alone save for an elderly housekeeper, who took care of him. The physician—I think his name was Dr. Silvermann—had visited the eccentric. Despite his years and obvious ill health, the man's face had a ruddy, youthful appearance, the doctor said. His right arm was disabled, presumably the result of the stroke. Dr. Silvermann accepted the Hans Castorp identification, and asked the man how he had gotten out of the 1914 war alive. The man said he had survived a smashed knee on the Somme and the removal of part of a lung damaged by gas. He said that Dr. Behrens, head physician at the Berghof sanatorium in *The Magic Mountain*, had been dead twenty years. Behrens had been forced to retire from medical practice because of psychotic depression. Settembrini, the Italian humanist, had died in August 1915 and had been interred in the Davos hillside cemetery near the Dorf. "Castorp" claimed that he himself had had the humanist's body removed to Italy after the war at his own expense, and had it buried in a cemetery near Padua, Settembrini's native city. Indeed the poor fellow was full of news. Clavdia Chauchat had been shot by the Reds in the Caucusus. She had gone there after the Revolution to join her

husband, a White Russian official. They were both killed. Clavdia, he
said, struggled as they forced her toward the ditch, and she stood up
in the snow to receive the bullets with half her clothes torn off. At
that point, Dr. Silvermann got up to leave. "Castorp" was agitated,
his face had gone gray, his bloodshot eyes protruded, and his palsied
chin shook. His housekeeper said, "Herr Castorp, it is time for your
rest."

"Poor man," said the physician. "An odd delusion. But more
interesting than most, don't you agree, Herr Leutnant?" I agreed.

But then, over the years, I have taught so many students who,
liking *The Magic Mountain,* tended to, as they put it, "identify"
with Hans Castorp, though well short of the psychotic extreme.
Goodness knows, the basic theme of the novel is congenial: the self-
actualization of a young man who opts out of the established social
order, where freedom is only a choice among the six careers one's
parents approve. But some young people have trouble with the book.
It *is* long, and they share Ava Gardner's stern view. Mann's masterly
play with historical and ideological material does not interest the
impatient ones, and they complain that his style is too formal and
long-winded, too grandfatherly—*altväterlich,* as a young woman of
good German family recently described it to me. I used to tell them
that Mann's senatorial periods often parody the formalities of his
native tongue, particularly the language of German burghers; that
it's easier to catch this if they read German. But such impatient
students preferred to "identify" with the absolution-seeking adoles-
cents of Hermann Hesse.

Other people are kept away from *The Magic Mountain* by all
they have heard about the symbolic aspects of the novel and the
representative roles allotted to the characters. In Norman Mailer's
The Naked and the Dead (1948), Lieutenant Hearn remembers his
Harvard days and a professor (obviously Harry Levin) lecturing on
the significance of the number seven in *The Magic Mountain:* Hans
Castorp stays seven years in the sanatorium, most of the major
characters have seven letters in their names, Clavdia Chauchat's room
number is 7, and so on. Hearn remembers the scribbling of notes,
the pious acceptance, then his own interruption:

> Sir, . . . what's the importance of that? I mean frankly I found
> the novel a pompous bore, and I think this seven business is a per-

fect example of German didacticism, expanding a whim into all
kinds of critical claptrap, virtuosity, perhaps, but it leaves me un-
moved.

What annoys readers like Mailer-Hearn is the cathedral-like solem-
nity of so much of the critical treatment of the symbolic and allegori-
cal side of the novel. But such touches as the seven business are to
be taken lightly and humorously, as Mann intended (and, I suppose,
as Levin himself took them *). From beginning to end, the novel is
about magic, and it is no more than fitting that a bit of numerology
should be embroidered onto it. Seven is, after all, a magic number,
and has figured in a wide spectrum of human activities ranging from
dice games to the Sacraments.

One critic who took the seven numerology very seriously is
Charles Neider, who in his essay in *The Stature of Thomas Mann*
asks, "Was it a strange coincidence or even stranger inner design
which caused Mann to reject precisely seven sections of the manuscript, the unpublished sections deposited at Yale?" The truth is,
there are eight sections of the manuscript at Yale's Beinecke Library,
and they are simply early drafts of certain parts of the story. James F.
White has worked up a neat edition (as yet unpublished) from those
manuscript pages which Mann in a moment of generous impulse gave
to an American, Joseph Angell. Little of it differs essentially from
the way the novel stands today. The handling of the next-door love-
making of the "bad" Russian couple on Han's first day at the sanatorium is more explicit than it is in the finished work, and, in
general, there is in the final version more indirection in the render-
ing of Castorp's first impressions. The French in the dialogue between Hans and Clavdia was also improved. One particular touch in
the Yale manuscript is interesting. In the published novel, the Carnival sequence ends with Clavdia's exit. After she pauses at the door
to remind Castorp to return the pencil she has lent him, a subtle invitation to her chamber, she goes out—period. It is a breathtaking
moment. But in the Yale manuscript, Hans remains seated in the

---

* The number eight gave Professor Levin a little trouble in his *The Gates of
Horn* (1963) where he confuses those two octet-lettered German names Schumann and
Schubert. He observes that in Proust's novel *Remembrance of Things Past,* the
narrator's friend St. Loup is killed at the front with a song of Schumann on his lips,
and notes that "when the hero of Thomas Mann's *Magic Mountain* is lost in battle
on the other side, he, too, is singing a lied by the same composer."

salon for seven minutes, then rises to follow her. Now we know the length of a discreet interval.

Even before the novel was published in Germany, word had gotten around literary circles that Herr Peeperkorn, the big Dutch-man who accompanies Clavdia Chauchat on her return to the sana-torium and later kills himself, was drawn from life, the model none other than Gerhart Hauptmann, poet and dramatist. At first Mann backed away from the suggestion, but later he admitted that he had borrowed from Hauptmann more than a few wrinkles from his brow. Hauptmann's imposing physical presence, his alcoholism, his inarticulate striving for ordinary speech were characteristics Mann had noted when he met the dramatist in Bozen in 1923, and he in-corporated them into his Peeperkorn. Hauptmann took offense, and Mann was forced to write him an almost abject letter of apology:

> *Lieber . . . verehrter* Gerhart Hauptmann . . . I have sinned . . . I have offended you. I was indeed, I was led into temptation and yielded to the temptation. The need was artistic: I was looking for a figure who was necessary, whose place in the composition had been thought out long before, but whom I did not see or hear or possess.

In other words, Mann had trouble visualizing the character who would accompany Clavdia back to the sanatorium; the appearance and deportment of Hauptmann solved the problem. Mann went on to say that apart from his use of Hauptmann for externals, Peeper-korn was an entirely fictional creation and one of the most admirable characters in the novel, a fabulous monster whose mighty, stammering personality reduces the intellectuals Settembrini and Naphta to in-significance and silence.

Years later, by the way, the aging Hauptmann succumbed to the flattery of the Nazis and paid confused tributes to Hitler and his program. Klaus Mann, in his memoir *The Turning Point* (1942), mimicked the old poet in somebody's drawing room, champagne glass in unsteady hand, striving to give utterance to his doubtful sympathies:

> Hitler . . . after all, . . . My dear friends! . . . no hard feelings! Let's try to be. . . . No, if you please, allow me . . . objective. . . .

May I refill my glass? This champagne . . . Very remarkable, indeed—that man Hitler, I mean . . . The champagne too, for that
matter. Almost seven million votes . . . As I so often said to my
Jewish friends . . . Those Germans . . . incalculable nation . . .
very mysterious indeed . . . cosmic impluses . . . Goethe . . . Ni-
belungen Saga . . . Hitler, in a sense, expresses . . . As I tried to
explain to my Jewish friends . . . dynamic tendencies . . .

Klaus Mann may well have heard Hauptmann carrying on in this
way, but I suspect that before writing this he reread the Peeperkorn
pages of his father's novel, then made life imitate art.

Another debate arose over the question of the model of Naphta,
the Marxist Jesuit whom Castorp does not like but admits is "nearly
always right." In 1922, Thomas Mann met the literary critic and
theoretician Georg Lukacs in Budapest, and was impressed by the
young Marxist's dialectical skill with arguments of hair-raising ab-
stractness. Most scholars have agreed that Lukacs was the external
model for Naphta, although some have thought the candidacy of the
Marxist philosopher Ernst Bloch should not be ignored. In his
Figures de Lukacs, Yvon Bourdet argued for the identity not only of
the appearance and mannerisms of Naphta and Lukacs but also of
their very doctrines. For Naphta's "Church," Bourdet says, we
should read "the Communist State." But the Rumanian critic
Nicolas Tertulian vigorously contended that Naphta is a pre-Fascist,
an agent of the Holy Office, a clerical reactionary, the exact opposite
of the Hungarian Marxist. But Tertulian did not deny the physical
resemblance.

Hans Castorp has no particular external model. He stands in the
long line of Mann's merchant-class heroes who have a little something wrong with them. (*"Petit bourgeois!"* Clavdia murmurs to
Hans on Carnival night. *"Joli bourgeois à la petite tache humide."*)
First in that line is Mann himself, who could never get over
the contrast between the rectitude and discipline of his Lübeck
forbears—which he determined never to forsake—and his own creative aberration, which he liked to trace to his exotic mother. (*"Ich
habe eine portugiesische Mutter."* Well, half-Portuguese.) Hans's
memory of his schoolboy crush on Pribislav Hippe reflects Mann's
own youthful relations, intense and experimental, with young men
like Kurt Martens and Paul Ehrenberg. And like his creator, Hans

has a passion for learning by experiment. "Er widersteht nicht dem Bösen," Mann says of his Faustian hero. "He resists not evil."

While Mann has been criticized for making Clavdia Chauchat a rather standard *femme fatale,* the author points out that she is only one of many sorts of temptation offered to Hans during his stay on the enchanted mountain. "I should not like to be saddled with the reputation of regarding woman as the one and only seducer," Mann wrote to one of his translators in 1939, adding that Clavdia is seductive not only erotically, but "a little in the intellectual sense as well." Certainly Joachim Ziemmsen, Hans's soldier cousin (by common agreement "the best of the lot up there"), does not approve of her. Joachim's name has a familiar ring, incidentally, and my guess is that it was suggested by Theodor Fontane's "Der alte Zieten," a ballad about Joachim Hans von Zieten, general of hussars, the simple, loyal aide of Frederick the Great who could always be found in battle where the fighting was hottest. Mann once wrote an essay on the author of "Der alte Zieten" titled "Der alte Fontane." As for some critics' disapproval of Mann's bringing back Joachim as a ghost dressed in the uniform of a war which has not yet happened, Mann himself was uneasy about the episode (it originated in a séance he visited in Munich in the early 1920s), and in a letter to Julius Bab he admitted that it is "something that I probably should not have permitted myself." But why not? *Der Zauberberg* is, after all, a story about magic, and the highest (or lowest) aim of magic has always been to raise the dead.

Much has been written about the psychoanalytic side of *The Magic Mountain.* Dr. Krokowski, the official psychoanalyst of the Berghof sanatorium, claims that "all disease is love transformed." Freud did not go quite so far, but as early as 1898 he said, "Factors arising in the sexual life represent the nearest and practically the most momentous cause of every single case of nervous illness." Hans's love for his hyperborean enchantress and his elusive tubercular infection are blended into a unity, a quasimusical *Liebestod* motif that dominates the novel. Hans's seven-year process of self-actualization begins, in fact, when he hears the death-cough of the gentleman rider down the hall and the daytime love-making of the "bad" Russian couple next door. Some critics, inclined to psychoanalytic interpretation, have argued that Mann's Davos novel is a remarkable example of self-administered analysis, with the author's neurosis handled and catharsis achieved by the objectification of his personal conflicts in the warring characters and conflicting ideologies of the tale. It may be, but Freud said, "We forget too easily that we have no right to place neurosis in the foreground where a great accomplishment is involved." Krokowski himself gets more and more Jungian as the novel goes on, and by the time the séance episode is reached, he is proclaiming something very like the Zurich analyst's doctrine of the collective unconscious.

The manuscript of the final version of *The Magic Mountain* was destroyed in the Allied bombing of Munich during World War II, together with most of Mann's notes for the novel. Hitler had become chancellor of the Reich on January 30, 1933. In March, while Mann was staying at Arosa in Switzerland, his children Erika and Klaus telephoned him from Munich about "bad weather" in Germany. Mann's exile dates from that telephone call. (He was not deprived of his German citizenship until the end of 1936.) And on the evening of May 10, 1933, at a square on Unter den Linden opposite the Helmholz University in Berlin, a torchlight procession of students ended with a bonfire and book burning; copies of *Der Zauberberg* were tossed into the flames together with other books— by Mann, by his brother Heinrich, both Zweigs, Einstein, Feuchtwanger, Remarque, and, inexplicably, Jack London. It was reported that Dr. Goebbels looked on approvingly. Yet Goebbels had once been a Thomas Mann fan; his diary records a trip to Lübeck, where he visited the landmarks made familiar by the novel: "I sense the old Hanse spirit and think of Buddenbrooks. . . . The Senate chamber. Those carvings. Work that took a lifetime. I always think of Thomas Mann."

Although Mann's house in Munich was not destroyed by the Allied bombing (the house that burned was that of a lawyer friend to whom he had entrusted his notebooks), it was confiscated by the Reich authorities and converted into a home for unmarried mothers. But first the Gestapo had carefully catalogued and packed up Mann's library, which was later distributed to various military barracks. Some items found their way back years later—Mann's edition of Nietzsche's works (Leipzig, 1894) stands on the shelves of the Thomas Mann Archive in Zurich today, its Gestapo catalogue number inside the covers. Erika Mann had risked arrest to get Mann's *Joseph* manuscript out of the Munich house. But none of the *Zauberberg* material remains, and that is why, of all Thomas Mann's major works, *The Magic Mountain* is the most poorly documented.

It was at the invitation of his publisher, Alfred Knopf, that Mann made the first of those visits to the United States which were to lead to his decision to reside permanently here and to become an American citizen. I saw him at the 1935 Harvard commencement (I was getting my M.A.), where with Albert Einstein, Henry A. Wallace, and some others, he was awarded an honorary doctorate. Boston's legendary Irish political boss James Michael Curley was seated on the platform—to the intense annoyance of certain members of the Harvard Corporation—as governor of the commonwealth of Massachusetts, and when Mann stepped forward to receive his crimson hood from President Conant there was a loud burst of applause from the assembled degree candidates. Curley turned to his platform neighbor Abbott Lawrence Lowell and asked, "Who is Thomas Mann?" Tactfully, the old Brahmin nodded toward the applauding graduates, "He is a writer whom the young people like."

Mann accepted a position at Princeton, where he was to give three public lectures a year, and offer seminars on Goethe's *Faust* and on *The Magic Mountain,* and to live in the house on Stockton Street. (While at Princeton he wrote a lecture on the Davos novel for his students which, revised, was published in *The Atlantic Monthly* as "The Making of The Magic Mountain" and is still used by Knopf as an afterword in their editions of the novel.) But in 1941, he left Princeton for the more congenial climate of southern California. Over the next six years, at his new home in Pacific Palisades, he wrote anti-Nazi polemics, broadcast to Germany for the American government, finished his multivolume biblical saga, *Joseph and His Brothers,* and wrote his last great novel, *Doctor Faustus,* that tragic redoing of the theme of disease and creativity he had worked with such wit in *The Magic Mountain.* After that, sadness and disillusion set in. His son Klaus died by his own hand in 1949. Many of Mann's émigré friends in California were hounded by Red-hunting congressional investigating committees. A 1950 lecture of his own, scheduled for delivery at the Library of Congress, had to be canceled because of suspicions aroused in our government by his visit to East Germany the year before. The Cold War atmosphere of the United States troubled him deeply, and he began to think of returning to Europe to end his days.

While still in Pacific Palisades, Mann wrote me in response to a letter I had sent him describing, among other things, my brief acquaintance with Heinrich Zimmer (by then dead), who had told him the transposed-heads story. In my letter I also told him how much my Barnard and Columbia students were enjoying *The Magic Mountain* in a course on Philosophy and the Modern Novel that dealt with writers from Proust to Nathanael West. At the close of his answering letter, the "writer whom the young people like" wrote:

> Of course the most eloquent tongue would be of no avail if there weren't warm young hearts, thirsting for the good and the spiritual, to respond to it. That they are there . . . is a beautiful comforting sign. I personally am, naturally, quite moved by the news that these striving and receptive young people like to hear about my books, and take pleasure in reading them. After all, we poets are all longing for a little immortality, the sympathy of the young generation for our work is a guarantee that it will survive us for a little while. Please give my kindest regards to your pupils, together with my best wishes for the success of their studies. By that I do not mean just the outward success, but I hope that the devoted study of what great minds, through their suffering, have contributed to the world, may form them into human beings which are able to cope with the difficulties of this confused period of transition.

Mann left the United States in 1952 for Switzerland. He bought a house in Kilchberg, a comfortable suburb of Zurich, overlooking the lake. He lived there with his wife until his death in August 1955.

The Thomas Mann Archive is in Bodmer House, on Schönberggasse in Zurich not far from Doctor Faust Lane, up among the Zurich University and Technische Hochschule buildings. In the archive there is a wealth of interesting material, much of it supplied by Mann's widow, Katia, from Mann's library and files. If you wonder about the external resemblance of Gustav Mahler and Aschenbach of *Death in Venice,* look at the 1911 obituary of Gustav Mahler that Mann clipped from a newspaper; you will find it in his *Death in Venice* working file. If you need a Japanese review of *The Magic Mountain* or a report on how the novel was received in a small Massachusetts town, one of the seventy-two trays of catalogue cards will tell you where to find them in the archive collection.

Mann's notebooks are there, with his jottings of ideas for stories and novels, including extensive notes for the novel *Maya* he never wrote (though Aschenbach of *Death in Venice* did). Typical is a note for a possible story: "Artist marries. His creative gift deserts him. Wife is unfaithful. Creative gift returns." Mann's daily notes from 1933 to 1955 marked by himself, "Without literary value (*ohne literarische Wert*) but not to be opened by anybody before twenty years after my death" were opened at the archive shortly after the Zurich 1975 celebration of the centennial of Mann's birth. By that time Hans Wysling and Marianne Fischer, director and librarian of the archives, had finished their extensive edition of Mann's voluminous writings about his own work, and the first volume of Peter de Mendessohn's life of Mann (itself more an archive than a biography) had appeared.

In May 1974 I sent word to Katia Mann that I was doing some work at the archive and I did not want to leave Zurich without seeing her. An invitation to lunch at Kilchberg followed. The tarnished silver nameplate on the door of Alte Landstrasse, 39, reads "Thomas Mann." Katia Mann was ninety-one years old. More than a trace of her youthful beauty remained, particularly in her bright eyes. She wore a gray dress with black piping, and a double strand of pearls. She was remarkably agile and still a bit miffed that the Zurich police had respectfully lifted her driver's license a couple of years before after what she described as "a little incident." (Her husband never learned to drive a car, but bought his first automobile, a Fiat, out of seventy thousand marks' profit from the early sales of *The Magic Mountain*.) Katia chatted amiably over sherry in the sitting room, with its blooming flowerbox on the window overlooking the lake. The white of the lilies reflected in the glass of the old ceiling-high bookcase from Lübeck. A portrait of Katia's mother hung on the wall and a smaller one of herself as a young girl by Lenbach. Mostly we talked about the comings and goings of her surviving children, and a little about my own. When we visited her at Princeton so many years before, Mary was expecting our first child, Peter. "Tell him I was his earliest acquaintance," Katia said.

She told me how her husband managed to make *her* acquaintance seventy years before. Herr Mann was a passenger on a Munich tram she was riding and she had a fight with the conductor. The fellow was angry with her because she had discarded her ticket on the floor rather than handing it to him, and she let him have a piece of her cultivated mind. Mann knew she was the daughter of Professor Pringsheim, but did not choose that moment to speak to her. Instead he went to a friend, and an introduction to the Pringsheim household was arranged.

Her son, the historian Golo Mann, joined us for lunch. At the time he was living in the Kilchberg house working on his biography of Wallenstein when not traveling or doing political work in West Germany. We talked of the fall of Willy Brandt, another son of Lübeck (Golo said Brandt had lost the confidence of his own party leaders because of his growing indecisiveness), and then the three of us got onto the inevitable Watergate. Katia thought the trouble was that the American political system gives the president too much power; division of responsibility between a president and a prime minister would be a "more sensible" arrangement. Golo showed some annoyance when I mentioned I had looked over those early draft pages of *The Magic Mountain* at Yale. Apparently he did not like the idea of his eminent parent handing them over as a gift. "My father had the weakness," he repeated the word, "the *weakness* to give over the manuscript." The idea of Thomas Mann having any weakness at all startled me into silence.

When I finally took my leave of her, Katia asked me to come see her next time I came to Zurich, "if I'm still alive." I told her she would live for many years, and believed it. The last time I saw her was not in Switzerland, but in Germany, at the centennial celebration of her husband's birthday, June 6, 1975, in his old home town, the Hanseatic city-state of Lübeck. It was a super-Buddenbrooks affair with symphony orchestra and choir onstage (Mozart's Symphony no. 25 and Bach's "Lobet Gott in seinem Reichen") and the inevitable *Vortrag*, "learned discourse," Germans expect at such celebrations—in that case delivered by the writer's son, the late Michael Mann, still on crutches from an injury received when he fell off the platform at Rutgers University where he, I, and others, had read commemorative papers less than two months before. The president of the Federal Republic, the president of the city-state, the burgomaster, and a general of the army lined up to kiss Katia's hand. Then she went back to Kilchberg.

In the beautifully kept churchyard of St. Peter's near Kilchberg's highest point, a vertical headstone marks Thomas Mann's grave. A small slab, flat to the ground, is for his daughter Erika, who died in 1969. Mann's grave is screened by luxuriant shrubbery and covered with flowers carefully planted and tended. I remembered from *The Magic Mountain* how Hans Castorp loved flowers, and how he initiated a series of visits to the *moribundi* of the sanatorium by bringing a pretty hortensia in a little pot to a girl who was going to die. I looked around at a gardener who was watering plants nearby, and asked him in my very odd German what were those lovely flowers growing over Thomas Mann's grave. No, not the geraniums, those other ones. He said they were hortensias.

PHILOSOPHY I

"You can put on your pants now."

The doctor sat down at his desk and wrote something on my form. He was a commander, an older man than the lieutenant who had picked up the nodule some weeks earlier at my annual physical. As the new chief of urology, he had only recently been transferred from the medical facility at Newport to the Naval Hospital, Submarine Base, New London. He spoke with a Vermont accent.

"Let's see, your age nearest birthday . . . ?"

"Sixty-five."

"Well, Dr. Brand did the right thing in sending you to see me. There's definitely a nodule there on the prostate. It's not large—about 15 grams, I'd say. But in cases like this I want to lay all my cards on the table. More than 50 percent of nodules like yours turn out to be cancerous."

"What do I do now?"

"We'll arrange for a biopsy, with X-rays first, including kidneys, and cystoscopy. If it's malignant, we can start cobalt treatment right away. You can probably arrange through the Navy to have treatments at some civilian hospital nearer you. You wouldn't want to come all the way up here from Long Island for that."

"What about surgery?"

"Usually not at this stage. Cancer of the prostate can be controlled. There are several kinds of treatment, some of them quite successful. If we operate now, we'd be using the last thing we have to fall back on. But we'll see when we take a closer look at it."

At the desk outside, they made the appointment for the examination ten days later. The corpsman told me it would take all morning and gave me a sheet of instructions about preexamination diet, laxatives, and other unlovely things. Before I left, I made reservations at nearby Groton Navy Lodge for the night before the examination. The naval facility is called U.S. Submarine Base, New London, but it's really in Groton, on the other side of Connecticut's Thames River.

On the 150-mile drive back to Bethpage, I had time to think about it. It was prostate cancer that killed the philosopher Ludwig Wittgenstein. I remembered it from Norman Malcolm's memoir of his teacher and friend, a little book I had ready many times, and regularly assigned to my students in introductory philosophy. He died in 1951. From England, Wittgenstein had written Malcolm at Cornell that the diagnosis had been made by the doctors at Cambridge. He said there was a drug—some hormone, I think—that could control the disease so he could live on for years. But he lasted only about a year and a half. Wittgenstein refused to die in a hospital and asked his physician, Dr. Bevan, to take him into his house so he could die there. Just before the end he said to Mrs. Bevan, "Tell them I've had a wonderful life."

So what was I to do? I had never been hospitalized in my life. Here it was, early fall, the academic year just begun. Suppose an operation were necessary, what about my classes? In case they had to keep me in the hospital after the examination, I'd have to make arrangements with my colleagues in the Barnard philosophy department to take over my courses or find someone who could. Then, things would have to be dealt with at home. But that wouldn't be so hard. Mary would handle things well, I had no doubt of that. No, it was those silly courses that bothered me. In twenty-nine years at the college, I had not been absent for illness more than six days. This foolish concern with courses at such a moment must be a protective device of mind to block personal fear.

When I got home I waited for a quiet moment over a cup of tea to tell Mary. She listened, then went out to the kitchen to put something into the refrigerator. When she came back, she put her arms around me and said, "Don't you worry. I know you're going to be all right."

Next day at Barnard, I told Sue Larson, now chairman of the department, having just relieved Mary Mothersill, who had done the chore for eleven years, one less than my term. Sue said that everything would be taken care of and not to worry about the courses. I assured her that before I went back to Groton, I'd bring to her office all my file folders with course outlines, reading lists, and recent tests. Classes went along routinely, my teaching of them neither better nor worse than usual. Using the men's room one day before lunch, I noticed my urine was tinged with blood.

Now a question began to bother me; sometimes it seemed foolish, sometimes not. It was this. Faced with illness and death, did a philosopher—a philosopher *today*—have the duty to behave any differently than a psychologist, poet, geologist, or historian in like circumstances? Of course, I knew I wasn't really a philosopher, only a teacher of philosophy; yet I couldn't disown my discipline or its history. An ancient tradition laid it down that a philosopher should not fear death but face it courageously. Plato tells us in his *Phaedo* that Socrates spent his last hours discussing death with his students. He tried to persuade them that a philosopher should not be afraid of death but welcome it. Then he drank off the cup of aconite handed to him by the weeping jailer.

No doubt the account is highly idealized. Plato absented himself from the execution, and wrote up the scene at least twelve years afterward. Still, Plato's lines on the death of his teacher have echoed down the ages: "Such was the end, Echecrates, of our friend; concerning whom I may truly say, that of all the men of his time whom I have known, he was the wisest and justest and best." In the ancient world, philosophers of every school pointed to Socrates's farewell to life as the model of how a man ought to die. In modern times too. In Victorian Jowett's great translation of Plato's works, Socrates stands as a martyr like Jesus Christ, only much more sensible. Conan Doyle's Dr. Watson mourns the apparent death of Sherlock Holmes with Plato's lines, barely paraphrased. And more recently when S. M. Ulam, discoverer of the mathematics of the H-bomb, heard that physicist Enrico Fermi had died, he wept and thought about Plato's story of the death of Socrates.

But it was easy for Socrates to face death with serenity, for, if Plato's account is true, the old man believed that when we die our soul, freed from the material body that for a lifetime has dragged it down, rises to a transcendent state of beatific vision. Death liberates us from the bonds of the flesh, the limitations of matter. Immortal by its very nature, the soul, our real self, soars once more to the realm of True Being from whence it came, and if we have lived worthily, soul will have lost all desire to rejoin a mortal body in this world, half-real, object of sense-perception but not of knowledge. The early Christian Fathers adapted Plato's account of the separable and immortal soul to their religious belief in Christ's teaching that His Kingdom was not of this world.

But who believes this today? Certainly not the philosophers. Plato himself knew that what he was telling in the *Phaedo* was a myth, a truth in story form, and it is not at all clear that the historical Socrates actually believed in personal immortality. Nor did the ancient Stoics, who cited Socrates as a paradigm of how a man should live and die. They thought God was Nature, death a spark rejoining that eternal Flame. Anyone who seeks to know the true causes of things will have no trouble keeping a stiff upper lip in facing death. So too that modern Stoic, Benedict Spinoza, the Amsterdam lens-grinder. Hume as well—David Hume of Edinburgh, who died in 1776, the year the American colonies declared their independence.

Hume thought we could know, really know, only two sorts of things: those true by definition and those true by virtue of some matter of fact that can be tested by sense observation and experience. Everything else, including what we may find in high-flown books of metaphysics or theology, could only be sophistry and illusion. Arguments for the existence of God left him unimpressed. Some years after Hume's death, Dean Paley, his contemporary, said that we know of God's existence from the orderly and lawlike character of the universe. If, finding a watch on a desert island, a reasonable person would conclude that an intelligent designer rather than blind chance produced it, how can we doubt that the universe, a mechanism infinitely more marvelous than a watch, was made by some

Supreme Intelligence. But Hume had already criticized such arguments. The analogy was bad. Seeing a house, a rational human will rightly conclude that an intelligent being made it. But that's because we've had experience of both houses *and* house-builders. We have had absolutely no experience of universe-makers. As for the human soul and its alleged immortality, Hume said we cannot even prove the existence of a *self* apart from that bundle of sense-impressions and memories we know through experience and which, for reasons of convenience, we call "I."

But skeptic though he was, philosopher Hume met death with the same fortitude and good cheer as did Plato's idealized Socrates. He died of cancer at the age of sixty-five ("Your age nearest birthday? . . .") and says of his illness:

> In spring 1775, I was struck with a disorder in my bowels, which at first gave me no alarm, but has since, as I apprehend it, become mortal and incurable. I now reckon upon a speedy dissolution. I have suffered very little pain from my disorder, and what is more strange, have, notwithstanding the great decline of my person, never suffered a moment's abatement of my spirits, insomuch that were I to name the period of my life which I should most choose to pass over again, I might be tempted to point to this later period. I possess the same order as ever in study, and the same gaiety in company. I consider, besides, that a man of sixty-five, by dying, cuts off only a few years of infirmities; and though I see many symptoms of my literary reputation's breaking out at last with additional luster, I knew that I could have but few years to enjoy it. It is difficult to be more detached from life than I am at present.

Very different from the cheerful Hume, Ludwig Wittgenstein lived most of his life close to the border of mental illness. Yet that pair of philosophers, two centuries apart, influenced the course of a philosophical tradition that has dominated England and America almost to the present day. In his early book, the *Tractatus*, Wittgenstein seemed to be arguing for a variant of Hume's doctrine, advanced by the sophisticated apparatus of modern formal logic. He thought that Whitehead and Russell's encyclopediac *Principia Mathematica* had set forth the logical forms of whatever could be stated in language. There remained only the job of filling in the variables taken from "whatever is the case." That is to say, the world. Apart from that, there is no more to be said. "Whereof one cannot speak, thereof one must be silent."

But Wittgenstein—handsome, intense, the very Platonic Idea of the Tormented Genius—could never rest in what he had achieved. He found that his earlier doctrine was far too simple and broke with it to search for new strategies in the struggle of philosophy to rescue mind from the confusions of language. Some reports of that struggle, courageous and despairing, appeared in *Philosophical Investigations* after the philosopher's death in 1951.

Wittgenstein had no religious belief, yet admired theologians like Augustine and Kierkegaard. They didn't attempt to prove the existence of God by reasonable argument, but made the leap of faith. Part of the last year of his life he spent with Elizabeth Anscombe, wife of Peter Geach. The Geaches had become Roman Catholics.* Wittgenstein said he could not possibly bring himself to believe all the things they believed, yet as Malcolm noted, that was not so much a criticism of their belief, as an observation of his own incapacity for belief. For all his logical and linguistic strictness, there was a touch of the mystic about Wittgenstein. Sometimes he wondered about the existence of the world; why should there be a world in the first place, indeed, *why should there be anything at all?* Philosophers of the old

---

* Elizabeth Anscombe, professor of philosophy at Cambridge, visited Barnard and Columbia in the 1960s and 1970s both for formal papers and informal discussions with philosophy faculty and students. Small group colloquies with her were often intense, hands held to brows with anxiety lest one should utter a Mistake. In a lighter moment at Mary Mothersill's apartment, I was surprised to find that Miss Anscombe had never heard of the cult of the Fourteen Auxiliary Saints, though her daughter Barbara, who was present, bore the name of one of them and knew that her name-saint was patron of miners and artillery men and since the fourteenth century had been traditionally invoked for protection against lightning and sudden death.

An old church dedicated to the Fourteen Holy Helpers stands (or used to) not far from the Ring in Vienna, native city of her teacher and friend Wittgenstein. Some gossips said that Anscombe and Wittgenstein had been lovers, though this was doubted by those who claimed that Wittgenstein's sexual drives were homoerotic. In preparing his book *Wittgenstein* (1973), W. W. Bartley III investigated the period 1918–27, the "Austrian decade" of Wittgenstein's life when he withdrew from philosophical activities, and concluded on the basis of his findings that Wittgenstein was a "homosexual given to bouts of extravagant and almost uncontrollable promiscuity," that throughout his life he was tormented by intense guilt and sufferings to such a degree that he felt himself as one damned and already in hell. With finely controlled fury, Elizabeth Anscombe wrote to the *Times Literary Supplement* challenging Bartley on nine counts of allegations made with no evidence adduced beyond hearsay.

religious traditions had been struck by this strange wonder; they thought there must be a God to account for there being something rather than nothing. But Wittgenstein could not understand the idea of a Creator.

Though he left religion to others, there was something religious in Wittgenstein's utter commitment to his work, the seriousness with which he took it, his sense of philosophy as a calling, a vocation, a duty from which even death could not release him. He believed that all of us have a duty to do whatever we can as well as we are able, never sparing ourselves, never allowing ourselves even a little easy-goingness in the matter of career. To do philosophy was to make an absolute demand on oneself and one's talents.

But what if one's capacity should fade away, one's power give out? Like composer Adrian Leverkuhn of Thomas Mann's *Doctor Faustus,* Wittgenstein feared that one day he might lose his talent, and in that case life would not be worth living. For the philosopher who said, "An expression has meaning only in the stream of life," life itself then would have lost its meaning.

There are two "meanings" here—meaning in language and meaning in life. The classical tradition of philosophy, still at home on the continent of Europe, concerned itself more with the second— meaning in human life. British-American philosophy, on the other hand, tends to stress the importance of meaning in language. In this context "meaning" refers not just to the sense of natural languages like English or Chinese, but to meaning in any form of communication, including the technical languages of mathematics and symbolic logic. In our time, there is a new awareness of the various ways in which language is inextricably mixed up with how we see the world, how we experience it, how we interpret it. Especially since World War II, many sciences—not only philosophy, but anthropology, psychology, linguistics, and others—have raised fundamental questions about the role of language in various forms of human communication. The fact that Wittgenstein, Oxford linguistic philosophy, structuralism, and Chomsky's transformational grammar became intellectually fashionable does not mean they are not important.

Noam Chomsky's linguistic theories challenged the old empiricist explanation of language ability. That tradition held that everything we know about the world comes to us by experience from the outside. But Chomsky suggested that a child's early mastery of the complexities of grammar and syntax in his own language—Chinese or English—cannot be explained simply by the child's experience of words coming at him or her from the outside via parents, siblings, or playmates. The naïve Englishman of the story who thought little French children amazing because they learned to speak that foreign language so young is really intuitively right. Language ability *is* amazing, so much so in fact that Chomsky concluded that language ability must be *innate*. We are all born with the capacity to deal with the complexities of grammar. Our ability to put words together in correct grammatical and syntactical form,

> The girl is singing.
> Is the girl singing?
> The cake is in the box.
> Is the cake in the box?

to understand what is said to us, to speak to others so they understand us, is related to an inner "deep structure" characteristic of the human mind, an innate capacity of that mind to form rules of language in the course of acquiring knowledge. Later Chomsky softened his claim that the meaning of a sentence is determined by its deep structure and gives more weight to the influence of surface structure. But to the larger question—How is it we humans know so much?—he still gives the reply: Because in a sense we already know it. Universal grammar is an innate, built-in feature of the human mind.

People often grumble that philosophy and linguistics and all that stuff are just too technical. Maybe it's all right for intellectual gymnasts who like to fool around with words, but it doesn't teach us anything about reality or how to live. That is an old complaint. Ancient Athens accused Socrates of getting his reputation by cleverness with words. In the Middle Ages, philosophers found all their arduous labor dismissed as *vox et praeterea nihil*—words and nothing else. It's hard for people to understand that philosophy and its allied disciplines must be technical, but that technicality doesn't mean that's all there is to it. Kant's *Critique of Pure Reason* is very hard to read, even for Germans. Yet it was, as its author claimed, a Copernican revolution in the theory of knowledge. It's not easy to teach and sustain the level of abstraction that technical philosophy requires. People would rather read stories and plays. Look at Sartre and Camus—they write things you can *read!*

Yet while Jean-Paul Sartre was publishing stories and plays, at the same time he wrote *Being and Nothingness* in the awful jargon of the German philosopher Heidegger. Later, in his *Critique of Dialectical Reason,* he developed a Sartre-Marxian vocabulary that was even worse. Sartre had no interest in linguistic philosophy; he confessed that reading Wittgenstein bored him. That's because he was a son of the Continental tradition of philosophy, very different from the English—a classical tradition that had remained more friendly to the old-line metaphysics, more interested in constructing, however technically, a philosophy of human existence. Sartre's key concept of the *Project* is a notion not too far from what we might call "the meaning of life." There's another point of difference between the two traditions. Postwar philosophy on the continent of Europe had far more political theory and political activism packed into it than the work of the British-American linguists and philosophers of language. Sartre did not have to make the jump from theory to act that Chomsky did when he threw himself into the anti–Vietnam War cause.

Wittgenstein liked to think of philosophy as a battle to rescue intelligence from the bewitchment of language. He did not believe it was the job of philosophy to discover new facts, but to arrange and clarify our muddled ways of talking about facts already there. That way of describing the task of philosophy—a way already pointed out by G. E. Moore, Wittgenstein's sponsor at Cambridge—opened a path followed thereafter by contemporary philosophy in Britain and the United States. Today, though his powerful presence is still felt, Wittgenstein is no longer accorded the uncritical reverence bestowed on him for so many years. Reversing a fifty-year-old trend, younger British philosophers now look to the United States, where prestige names in philosophy include, besides W. V. Quine and Nelson Goodman, who have been around a long time, Donald Davidson and Sol Kripke, the latter a sort of Bobby Fischer of philosophy who published his first technical paper while still in high school and whose brilliant and interminable rambles pack the house at any meeting of the American Philosophical Association.

These are some of the reasons why it's hard to say—in thirty words, no more no less—just what philosophy is. When people ask you what you teach and you say philosophy, they often murmur, "Oh," and change the subject. Sometimes they think the word refers to something else. When our Mario was a little boy in the third grade, his teacher one day asked the class what their daddies *did*. One child said her father worked for Grumman's, another said his father was a fireman in New York. When Mario's turn came, he said, "He's a teacher."

"That's nice, Mario. What does he teach?"

"Philosophy."

"Oh no, dear, you mean *psychology*."

Sometimes in a bar a stranger will ask me what I do for a living. When he hears the word *philosophy,* he may push his glass nearer and say, "You want to know my philosophy of life? Well, I look at it this way," and so on. I never make fun of this. If my bar mate believes that philosophy has something to do with broad guidelines one sets oneself in living one's life, he is in accord with the idea of the task of philosophy held by most classical moral philosophers, including Socrates, even though their guidelines may not have had much in common with my importunate friend's. So I listen to him, however fuzzy his opinions, and, if it turns out that he does not take his life rules from *psychology,* as Mario's teacher probably thought well-educated people should do, I buy him a drink.

Philosophy began with the first scientists long ago in ancient Greece. They tried to explain the world and the way things happened by the natural rather than by the supernatural. Not gods and spirits, but by fire, air, water, or tiny particles of these they called atoms. Observing the way physical events interacted, those ancient philosopher-scientists concluded that there must be some ordering factor in the world, a rationale that suggested Mind. In his old age Socrates took more interest in human action than in physics. He thought that mind, intention, purpose, were better causal explanations of human action than mechanical mixtures of physical elements, and turned philosophy to moral and ethical matters. A good man should live justly, according to the universal law of right binding on all. The essence of Good, goodness itself, transcended the promptings of individual desire to look out after oneself and to get the better of the other fellow. A wise human should seek knowledge, not resting content with the ordinary beliefs that pass for knowledge

—particularly in a democracy where one man's opinion is thought to be as good as another's.

Socrates' great pupil Plato concerned himself with science and mathematics as well as moral and political philosophy. Expanding his teacher's doctrine of a universal moral law, he postulated an invisible world of True Being of which this world is but a poor copy. The realm of Being is made up of the Forms, the Platonic Ideas, changeless models of the many, and changing things of the world of sense. The Forms are the only objects of real knowledge—not their feeble images in this transient world we apprehend through our senses.

Aristotle, the Macedonian, studied on and off at Plato's Academy in Athens for twenty years. Like Plato, he believed there were two kinds of being, mutable and immutable, inferior and superior, and that our world belonged to the first category—though he didn't think it as poor a show as Plato did. Aristotle said that God, an unchanging Being, is prime mover of the world. Otherwise the cosmos would be an infinite series of things moved and moving, none of which had the power of self-causation—which would be awkward, scientifically speaking. As for the Platonic Ideas, Aristotle saw no need for them to have a separate existence in some divine invisible realm. Why not simply say that Plato's universals are the forms of things—the general character of objects that enables us to identify them as trees, humans, stones, stars, or whatever?

When he opened his own school in Athens, the Lyceum, Aristotle had textbook notes prepared on just about everything—physics, astronomy, biology, zoology, psychology, metaphysics, logic, rhetoric, ethics, political science, and drama criticism. His work on embryology alone would have won him an ancient Nobel Prize were it not for the rising anti-Macedonian feeling in Athens (Aristotle had tutored King Philip's son, Alexander the Great) that in the end compelled him to leave the city in a hurry. He said he'd go so that Athens would not have the chance to sin against philosophy twice.

When Alexander took over the Greek world, Athens lost her independence, and when the young conqueror died, his general Ptolemy made the Egyptian city named after his dead king into a new center of culture, with a great library and institute of advanced studies. In Hellenistic Alexandria, philosophy became more mystical, in Athens more ethical. Though the Greek founders of the Stoic and Epicurean schools had searched deeply into the physical causes of things and constructed ingenious cosmologies of fire or atoms, their successors concentrated on the moral philosophies associated with those traditions. They defined Philosophy as the Guide to Life. (The initial letters of that definition are Phi Beta Kappa).

Epicureans held that pleasure was the highest good. They had a reputation as pig-philosophers, since their founder Epicurus had once said that the pleasures of the stomach were most intense. Actually the Epicurean communities recommended simple lunches of bread and wine, reserving the accolade of highest pleasure for friendship and philosophical-scientific discourse in agreeable natural surroundings. A garden would do nicely, and cultivated ladies were welcome. Not so different, after all, from the Ideal exalted by G. E. Moore in his *Principia Ethica,* moral Bible of the Bloomsbury group —aesthetic enjoyment and personal affection.

The Stoics' temperament was more austere. They believed that Nature is an expression of divine Mind, that its order and self-sufficiency provide us with a moral model to imitate. If we follow Nature in the Spirit of Science we will be in the right. Nature's law-like character tells us that the way to the Good is the way of Reason. One who understands the causes of things will not complain about matters beyond his will to control, but will accept what fate brings him. Such a man will neither be unduly elated by good fortune nor cast down by ill. He notes everything, marvels at nothing. Should his house burn down, his wealth be stolen, even if wife or child die, he will not say he has lost them, only that he has restored them, given them back to Nature whence they came. When we ourselves die, we simply return to Nature, which brought us forth, as a child to its mother. Evil—what *appears* to us as evil—cannot harm the wise and just man. His will, his inner being, his real self is invulnerable, inviolate. In the storms of life, he will be secure; nothing can touch him. And he will broaden the sense of his own worth to encompass humanity; he is a citizen of the world, and all men are his brothers.

A bit of Stoicism colors nearly all philosophy, and touches our ordinary language as well. "To take things philosophically," derives from the Stoic idea of *apathia,* the refusal to be upset by what we cannot control. Even poor mad Nietzsche took the Stoic concept *amor fati* as his own: to know one's fate and accept it with love.

Zarathustra embraces his destiny, willing to have his life, for all its suffering, played over again *da capo,* from the beginning. The dancing prophet's vision reveals the Eternal Return—"We know," the animals say to him, "that you teach that all things eternally return and ourselves with them." But that was a commonplace of Stoic cosmology. That other mad genius, Wittgenstein, experienced moments of luminous certitude, quite like the Stoic tranquility. He wrote that sometimes he had "the feeling of being *absolutely* safe, I mean the state of mind in which one is inclined to say, 'I am safe, nothing can injure me *whatever* happens.'" The tradition of such consoling epiphanies goes back to Socrates, who said, "No evil can befall a good man." The religious counterpart is Saint Teresa's faith that if we love God, as John the Evangelist wrote, nothing can harm us—"Let nothing trouble thee; let nothing frighten thee!"

In Rome under the Emperor Nero there lived a slave named Epictetus who managed to study philosophy. On obtaining his freedom from a generous master, he became a teaching Stoic. Years of his life coincided with the reign of Marcus Aurelius, the Roman emperor who was also a Stoic philosopher. In *The Phenomenology of the Spirit,* Hegel illustrates his famous dialectic of master and slave by these two ancient Stoics, so different in earthly status, so alike in power of Reason. The relation between master and slave unfolds in a dialectical way, says Hegel. Forced to live by his own work, the slave develops a certain self-reliance or independence. But the freedom of the master, who finds himself dependent on the slave, is relatively diminished. In the relation between Marcus Aurelius, the philosopher-emperor, and Epictetus, the philosopher-slave, Hegel sees an archetypal example of the master-slave raised to the highest level of self-consciousness. The Antonine emperor was a Stoic, and to the Stoic, all men, masters and slaves, are brothers. Thus in the dialectical process of Reason, Hegel believed, slavery is cancelled and humanity exalted.

I first heard of Epictetus at Boston College from Père de Mangeleere, our professor of French. ("Who wrote ziz meeserable letter? A peasant from ze peat bogs of Ireland?") Reading from the *Pensées* one day in class, he paused in his explication of the text to remark how closely Pascal's thoughts resembled those of old Épictète. How near the pagan philosopher had come to the spirit of Christ! Curious, I dug out a library copy of Epictetus's *Discourses* and the digest of them called *Enchiridion*. Impossible! All my sympathy with Père de Mangeleere could not make me put up with it for a moment. A windbag! An ancient Polonius, sententious, full of wise saws. No fascinating metaphysics, no subtle theory of knowledge. Just bald moral exhortation, wise-old-owlish advice about not letting our happiness depend on things not in our control—repetitious insistence that the only things always in our power are our self and our own personal will. Could Epictetus bear toothache with patience? Suppose his beloved daughter died; would all his philosophy avail him in that pinch? I thought no more about Epictetus and, save indirectly through Hegel, neither he nor his moral philosophy entered my thoughts or teaching for more than forty years. But then a news item brought him back to me.

PHILOSOPHY II

ॐ In the fall of 1975 when I was waiting for the day of my biopsy examination at Groton, I noticed a small piece in the *Times* about some aviation admiral getting a backlog of decorations that had piled up during his seven years' confinement as a prisoner of war in North Vietnam. A Navy flier, he had been shot down over enemy territory. According to the newspaper story, the officer (he had just been promoted from captain to rear admiral) had been tortured over extended periods, but he had not broken. He had refused to do the will of his captors who wanted him publicly to denounce the United States and to abase himself in various ways. Must have been a long time, that seven years. But what really caught my eye was a sentence stating that the admiral, James B. Stockdale, credited the philosophy of Epictetus with helping him hold out. Curious as to what the man could possibly have found in that old coot to sustain him in his seven-year ordeal, I wrote for his address to Ainslie, then a Navy ensign at the U.S. naval base, Yokosuka, Japan. She wrote back that Stockdale was at present commander of the Pacific Fleet's Anti-Submarine Warfare Wing at San Diego. There I sent a polite letter of inquiry: How did the admiral happen to come across the philosophy of Epictetus?

What was there about that philosophy that helped him through his long captivity with unbroken spirit? Admiral Stockdale replied promptly and at some length:

> I was honored to receive your inquiry about the comfort and strength philosophical readings gave me throughout my 7½ years in prison. Perhaps I can best explain how this came to be with a rather rambling chronology.
>
> I came into the Navy as a Naval Academy Midshipman in 1943 at the age of 19. For the next twenty years or so I was a rather technically oriented person. I was a seagoing destroyer officer, an aviator, a landing signal officer, a test pilot and academic instructor at the test pilot school, a many-times-deployed fighter pilot and ultimately a squadron commander of a supersonic F-8 Crusader outfit.
>
> In 1960 I was sent to Stanford University for two full years of study in politics/history/economics, etc., in preparation for later assignments in politico-military policy making. I loved the subject matter, but noticed that in many courses my interest would peak at about the time the professor would say, "We're getting into philosophy—let's get back to the subject." I had more than adequate time to get the expected master's degree, and suggested to my advisor in my second year that I sign up for some courses over in the philosophy corner of the quadrangle. He was dead set against it—thought it would be a waste of my time. He said, "That's a very technical subject—it would take two terms to learn their peculiar vocabulary." Finally, after I persisted, he said, "It's up to you."
>
> It was my good fortune on that first morning that I wandered through the halls of the philosophy department, gray-haired and in civilian clothes (of course), to come by an open office whose occupant looked me in the eye and asked if he could be of help. When I told him that I was a graduate student in the humanities with no formal philosophy background he could scarcely believe it. When I told him I was a naval officer he asked me to have a seat. He had been in the Navy in WWII. His name was Philip Rhinelander. . . . As a Harvard lawyer he had practiced in Boston for 15 or 20 years before Pearl Harbor, volunteered for war service at sea, and thereafter took his Ph.D. at Harvard under Whitehead. After tours as a dean at Harvard and Stanford, he was back in the classroom at his own request. He was in the midst of his two-term "personal" course: The Problems of Good and Evil. This he had built upon the lessons of the Book of Job ("Life is not fair"). He offered to let me enter the course, and to overcome my shortcomings of background, to

give me an hour of private tutoring each week. What a departure from the other departments! (In some, Ph.D. candidates sat outside their advisor's office for hours on end awaiting a ten-minute conversation.) I loved Rhinelander's class, and particularly our hour together each week. I remember how patient he was in trying to get me to realize the full implication of Hume's *Dialogues on Natural Religion* (I still have page after page of notes on that). . . .

As we parted after our last session, he reached up to his bookshelf and said something like, "As I remember it, you are a military man —take this booklet as a memento of our hours together. It provides moral philosophy applicable to your profession." It was the *Enchiridion*.

That night I started to peruse my gift. I recognized nothing that applied to the career I had known. I was a fighter pilot, an organizer, a motivator of young aviators, a martini drinker, a golf player, a technologist—and this ancient rag talked about not concerning oneself with matters over which he had no control, etc. I thought to myself, "Poor old Rhinelander—he's just too far gone." Nevertheless, I read and remembered almost all of it—if for no other reason than that it was given to me by the man I had come to worship as the most complete human being I had ever met. . . .

About three years after I had said goodbye to "poor old Rhinelander," while in the midst of my second combat tour against North Vietnam as a Wing Commander, I pulled off a target one September morning in the midst of heavy flak when all the lights came on (fire warning, hydraulic failure, electrical failure, etc.). As I sped over the treetops it became immediately apparent that I had lost my flight controls—by reflex action I pulled the curtain and ejected —and was almost immediately suspended in air 200 feet above a village street, in total silence except for rifle shots and the whir of bullets past my ear. So help me in those fleeting seconds before I landed among the waiting crowd I had two vivid thoughts. (1) Five years to wait (I had studied enough modern Far East history and talked to enough Forward Air Controllers in the South to fully appreciate the dilemma of Vietnam—I turned out to be an optimist by 2½ years). (2) I am leaving that technological world and entering the world of Epictetus.

The world view of the stoics, Professor Rhinelander had joked, was that their environment was a buzz saw in which human will was the only salvation. I was to spend over four years combatting a veritable buzz saw (until the torture and extortion machine was set in idle in the late autumn of 1969) and over three more years of simple deprived detention of the sort one would expect in a primitive, hostile country. Over four years were to be spent in solitary confinement, nearly half of it in leg irons. Throughout, until 1970, every effort was to be made to break my will, to make me a cat's paw in tinhorn propaganda schemes. Real or fabricated "violations of the established regulations for criminal's detention" (e.g., tapping on the walls to another prisoner) would result in torture, with the end aim of sequential (1) confession of guilt, (2) begging for forgiveness, (3) apology, and (4) atonement (signing an antiwar statement). A similar sequence would be set up with *particular* gusto if I were found to be exercising leadership of others via the tap code ("inciting other criminals to oppose the camp authority").

The situation was thus framed in the above context. I was crippled (knee broken, eventually to become rigidly fused by nature; shoulder broken, partial use of arm); alone, sick (weight down fifty pounds); depressed (not so much from anticipating the next pain as from the prospect of my eventually losing my honor and self-respect); and helpless except for will. What conditions could be more appropriate for Epictetus' admonitions? As a soldier, I had bound myself to a military ethics:

> "Remember that you are an actor in a drama of such sort as the author chooses—if short, then in a short one; if long, then in a long one. If it be his pleasure that you should enact a poor man, see that you act it well; or a cripple, or a ruler, or a private citizen. For this is your business—to act well the given part; but to choose it belongs to another."

I was crippled:

> "Sickness is an impediment to the body, but not to the will unless itself pleases. Lameness is an impediment to the leg, but not to the will; and say this to yourself with regard to everything that happens. For you will find it to be an impediment to something else, but not truly to yourself."

I was dependent on my extortionists for life support, and soon learned to ask for nothing to avoid demands for "reciprocity";

> "Whoever then would be free, let him wish nothing, let him decline nothing, which depends on others; else he must necessarily be a slave."

I could stop my misery at any time by becoming a puppet; was it worth the shame?

> "If a person had delivered up your body to some passer-by, you would certainly be angry. And do you feel no shame in delivering up your own mind to any reviler, to be disconcerted and confounded?"

Relief from boils, heat, cold, broken bones was "available" for the asking—for a price. What should I say?

> "If I can get them with the preservation of my own honor and fidelity and self-respect, show me the way and I will get them; but if you require me to lose my own proper good, consider how unreasonable and foolish you are."

Epictetus was not the only valuable philosophic memory in my predicament: Job (Why me . . . Why *not me?*), Descartes's bifurcation of mind and body, and many other readings were invaluable.

It is important to note that I am speaking *only* for myself. Some of my prison mates had more doctrinaire religious concepts which served them well, some drew resolve from their concepts of political virtue, and so on in a broad spectrum of varying levels of sophistication. Thoughts of God and country helped me, too—but my "secret weapon" was the security I felt in anchoring my resolve to those selected portions of philosophic thought that emphasized human dignity and self-respect. Epictetus certainly taught that.

This has been a much longer explanation than I had planned, but I am enthusiastic about the wonders a man in your profession and discipline can bring about in the lives of people in need. I wish I had the qualification to be in your shoes, teaching in a good school. From first-hand experience I am committed to the position that the study of moral philosophy is a particularly relevant part of education. And though education, as one of my favorite quotations reads, may be but an ornament in prosperity, it is a refuge in adversity.

I showed the letter to three colleagues. One read it without comment. Loren Graham found in it an illustration of what he had noticed in other areas such as his own field, the history of science. Certain writings, he said, that play very large roles in the lives of individuals are frequently writings which would not appear at the top of rigorous academic reading lists. He mentioned Ernst Schrödinger's *What Is Life?*, a semipopular piece cited by several prominent molecular biologists as being one of the most important intellectual influences on their work. In Stockdale's case, he thought, an experience that probably would not have happened at all if his education (including his philosophy courses) had undeviatingly included only what was academically most rigorous turned out to be more important to his ability to preserve his ethical and intellectual integrity than anything else. Ernest Nagel, whose philosophical renown does not come from his celebration of military virtues, wrote me, "The man's fortitude is amazing. I'm overwhelmed with admiration for his strength of character in enduring without spiritual surrender the suffering that was inflicted upon him and the serenity of mind with which he recalls those years." *

From Epictetus down through the ages a long line of moral philosophers have taught that serenity in suffering can be achieved only if one can give *meaning* to enduring it. In "What Is the Meaning of Ascetic Ideals," Nietzsche said the problem of suffering lies not so much in suffering itself, but in its *senselessness*. So, to handle it at all, people try in various ways to find significance in it. Some use suffering to excuse themselves; others as a rope around the neck of the strong to drag them down to their level. Still others meet suffering as a challenge to overcome, to transcend the limitations imposed by it. Nothing great, Nietzsche said, can come into being except *in despite*. In the human capacity for suffering lies the possibility of transcendence, of going beyond. Nietzsche, who lived with pain as his daily companion, believed that the position of a being in the hierarchy is in direct proportion to its capacity to suffer. Not that suffering is good in itself; it is the response to it, the meaning we impose to deal with it, that counts. Wittgenstein agreed. He remarked to Malcolm that he thought the measure of a man's greatness would be in terms of what his work *cost* him.

What is the meaning of life? Positivist philosophers hold that the question itself is meaningless. But, granting a little looseness, we can understand what people are trying to get at when they ask that large age-old question. Of course, there is no one single meaning. But the human mind, by its very nature, wants explanations of things, reasons why things happen as they do. When Job questioned God about his woes, it was not the suffering but the apparent meaninglessness of it that bothered him. It did not make sense; he did not

* On March 4, 1976, in Washington, D.C., Admiral Stockdale was awarded the Congressional Medal of Honor by President Gerald Ford.

deserve this; it was not fair—for he was a just man. What was the meaning of all the evil that had been dumped upon his head? He wanted a reasonable explanation. But God avoids a direct answer. He could have explained that Job's sufferings came from a trial of strength, a test agreed on by God and Satan to see whether Job could remain steadfast in his faith. That answer Job would have understood. But instead God asks: Could Job create the universe? Could he make a hippopotamus? In brief, Job, don't compare your puny powers with Mine. Understood? The Danish eccentric Kierkegaard reminded Job's sympathizers that God had commanded Abraham to sacrifice his only son. What did *that* mean? As in the case of Job, it meant simply that the human, the creaturely, the finite, are incommensurable, even ethically, with the infinite.

For the better part of two thousand years, a Christian world found transcendent meaning in God and a supernatural destiny. We are but travelers, *viatores,* in this vale of tears. Earthly life is pain, relieved only by a few moments of passing joy. But there is meaning in our suffering, and that meaning cannot be grasped apart from knowledge that our true end and purpose is not this life but the Kingdom of Heaven. Except for God's grace, Augustine said, we humans could not possibly escape the penalty of time and death— the annihilation entailed by finitude. Thirteen centuries later, in the first glory of modern science, Pascal wrote that we know the universe will crush us (and there's a certain grandeur in being able to *know* it) save for the goodness of God. By ourselves, we can do nothing.

That tradition lasted a long time. In 1951 François Mauriac set down his final testament of belief; at sixty-five years of age, he thought he had little time to live—a surgeon had removed a cancerous vocal chord:

> In the 66th year of my life, I believe as I did when I was a child that life does have meaning, direction, value; that no suffering is ever pointless, that each tear counts, each drop of blood, and that the secret of the universe is contained in Saint John's "Deus caritas est"—God is love.

Despite his official prediction of his own imminent demise, Mauriac lived nearly twenty years more, picking up a Nobel Prize for literature on the way. (Yukio Mishima, who tried to give supreme meaning to his life by ending it in the ritual gesture of disembowelment, said that it was his reading of Mauriac that taught him to write a novel.) Mauriac never forgot the feel of his native region, the countryside of the *Landes,* the pines, the hot sun, the metal sky. In his old age he thinks of a hare, hiding between two clumps, the color of his fur blending with the earth on which he crouches. The hare feels relief when he hears the barking of the dogs die away in the distance, and "if he is an old hare capable of knowing God, then the form in which he lies thinking becomes a shelter where he prays."

But suppose one does not believe in God or that life has a transcendent meaning. The Ages of Faith did not continue unbroken down to our day, when for the first time in the history of the world the dominant culture is agnostic. A contradictory tradition has always existed, though it did not move freely until great changes—scientific, religious, political—had begun to work in modern society. Before Christ's birth, the pagan poet Lucretius tried his best to free men from fear of death and punishment in afterlife by telling them that there isn't anything up there or down there for us after we pass. Reality is composed only of physical atoms. For all our fine minds and aspiring hearts, we are but complexes of material particles that have come together by chance. If there are any gods, they too are made of atoms and take no account of our small concerns. The universe we inhabit for so short a time is itself destined to plunge into ruin:

> *The ramparts of this mighty world*
> *Shall fall on every side*
> *And in splintered fragments crash to wreck.*

Nearly 2,000 years after Lucretius's death, his modern disciple Bertrand Russell had a moment of terrifying solitude, something like that of an earlier mathematical philosopher, Pascal, frightened by the infinite spaces of a silent universe. But for the skeptical Englishman there was no balancing thought of infinite goodness, no key to the enigma in God's grace:

> Brief and powerless is man's life; on him and all his race the slow, sure doom falls pitiless and dark. Blind to good and evil, reckless of destruction, omnipotent matter rolls on its relentless way; for man, condemned today to lose his dearest, tomorrow himself to pass

through the gates of darkness, it remains only to cherish, ere yet the blow fall, the lofty thoughts that ennoble his little day; disdaining the coward terrors of the slave of Fate, to worship at the shrine that his own hands have built; undismayed by the empire of chance, to preserve a mind free from the wanton tyranny that rules his outward life; proudly defiant of the irresistible forces that tolerate, for a moment, his knowledge and his condemnation, to sustain alone, a weary but unyielding Atlas, the world that his own ideals have fashioned despite the trampling march of unconscious power.

There's richness for you! I prefer Shakespeare's Macbeth when he learns his wife is dead. Doomed himself, the trapped king sees life's meaninglessness in terms of the brevity of human existence, the contrast between the living man who acts as if his life is important, as if what happens to us, and what we do about it, counts. It counts for nothing:

> *Tomorrow, and tomorrow, and tomorrow,*
> *Creeps in this petty pace from day to day,*
> *To the last syllable of recorded time;*
> *And all our yesterdays have lighted fools*
> *The way to dusty death. Out, out, brief candle!*
> *Life's but a walking shadow, a poor player*
> *That struts and frets his hour upon the stage*
> *And then is heard no more: it is a tale*
> *Told by an idiot, full of sound and fury*
> *Signifying nothing.*

Suppose there is no God or divine ordering of things; suppose that life has no significance that transcends this world. People ask what meaning in life can we find if we accept this denial of supernatural destiny.

Bourgeois humanism found the answer in the Idea of Man. Since the eighteenth century, political thinkers and social reformers dedicated to reason and enlightenment replaced faith in God with faith in Man. You and I will die, but our fellow citizens who come after us, men and women loyal to the ideals of science, progress, and democracy, will carry on the torch. Our founding fathers, heirs to the European Enlightenment, believed this. So did the post–Civil War progressives and their philosopher John Dewey, who held that the value of a democratic society may be judged only by its success in serving the good of each of its individual members. So did William Faulkner who took the title of his best-known novel from Macbeth's despairing lines on the meaninglessness of life. In his Nobel Prize speech of 1950 Faulkner said Man Will Prevail—although over *what* he did not specify.

But to communism, faith in Man, the humanist ideal, counts for little so long as it is tied to the welfare of bourgeois capitalist democracy. Life's meaning can be found only in revolutionary fraternity. True revolution liberates the masses, not the master; it frees the workers, not bourgeois industrialists. To so many of the educated classes of a world disillusioned by the murderous 1914–18 war waged by the "educated" capitalist nations of the West, the Bolshevik revolution seemed to promise hope of man's redemption. According to Marx and Lenin, History, itself, moves on the side of the Revolution, its material forces inexorably thrusting forward dialectically, crushing outmoded institutions, creating a world in which the humble masses, long in servitude, will be exalted and come to power.

But then the Revolution, like Saturn, began to devour its own children. Stalin's tyranny was more merciless than the Czar's. Yet he died at last, and the Revolution became cautious, middle-aged, respectable. One wore a good business suit and did not appear on the street with a pencil tucked behind one's ear. The Soviet Union learned to fear the capitalist democracies less than its new Marxist-Leninist neighbor in the East, Mao's China.

Existentialism appeared to have a new and dramatic answer to the problem of life's meaning, high-toned enough to become the intellectual fashion of the West immediately after World War II. Jean-Paul Sartre took no stock in the humanist ideal, the Idea of Man. "Hitler came too close to winning," he said, "for me to put my trust in men 200 years from now." He acknowledged the truth in Dostoyevsky's claim that if there is no God, some awkward questions have to be faced. He faced them. There is no God, no transcendent meaning in the universe, no rational scheme of things *already there*. Meaning in a human life comes from the individual person who decides what to do with it. That's the heavy burden of freedom. Each of us is free to choose what we shall do, and the sum of our acts is what we are. Our individual choice imposes meaning on the flux of existence in which we are caught. Meaning—in the sense of the meaning of a lived life—never exists *a priori*. Only after the fact. That most of us go along with the crowd, choosing prepackaged lives, proves only that we have chosen to live that way. We are, each of us, *thrown* into existence. We have nothing to say about it. That is the basic irrational fact. Confronting that reasonless given, what patterns of meaning we choose to shape our lives are up to us. Men and women create themselves. Each of our acts, freely chosen, is a brush stroke on our self-portraits. Only when the brush is laid down at the moment of death will the portrait be complete. Then we are all Essence. But we exist no more.

Sartre later modified his doctrine of individualistic freedom to give more room to Marxist stress on the heavy role played in our lives by the material and social circumstances into which we are born. But he never surrendered his conviction that in the end each of us must assume responsibility for what we turn out to be. Flaubert's social milieu made him a bourgeois; there was nothing he could do about that. But he gave back to that social environment something more than what it pressed in upon him—he was Flaubert. Genet's environment made him a thief and he was a thief—but he made himself a poet. "I believe," said Sartre, "a man can always make something out of what has been made of him."

Albert Camus had little faith in Revolution. Too often the Idea ended by betraying itself in act. He broke with his friend Sartre over this. Camus found his ideal Man of Revolt not in the political revolutionary but in the artist. Dostoyevsky, Melville, Kafka—each had the power to create in his art another world, a rival to this one. (Earlier Malraux had that idea.) The human condition is *absurd,* a mixture of contradiction and the comic. We humans aspire to the eternal; yet we suffer and we die. The human heart longs for some resting place that transcends the limitations inseparable from what life inexorably deals out to us: time and death. Yet in the struggle to discover meaning in the universe, we find that it is indifferent to our fate, which is annihilation.

Camus did not care much for technical philosophy: for him the most important philosophical problem was suicide. Or, in William James's version of the question: Is life worth living? Camus answers by offering a new humanism, one without shallow optimism, a humanism of courageous disillusion. Dr. Rieux knows that his medicines are useless against the Plague; yet he works day and night to fight it, knowing that the disease will withdraw when it wants to, not before. Sisyphus knows that his rock will always roll back down to the foot of the hill; yet he continues to push it up again. They are absurd men. But with Camus, the word *absurd,* applied ethically, bears praise. Like Pascal's "thinking reed" the absurd man and woman stand higher than the mindless universe about to annihilate them because they *know* they will be crushed by it, and the universe knows nothing of this. If we raise to consciousness our knowledge of our inevitable fate and refuse to reconcile ourselves to it, the refusal constitutes what Camus calls revolt. The lucidity that accompanies such revolt is greater than hope of transcendent meaning, since that hope is founded on self-deception:

> One of the only coherent philosophical positions is thus revolt. It is a constant confrontation between man and his own obscurity. . . . It is not aspiration, for it is devoid of hope. That revolt is the certainty of a crushing fate, without the resignation that ought to accompany it. . . . That revolt gives life its value. Spread out over the whole length of a life, it restores its majesty to that life. To one devoid of blinkers, there is no finer sight than that of intelligence at grips with a reality that transcends it.

In short, there's courage and nobility in knowing we're licked—and fighting back anyway. In the manner we choose to fight back dwells the meaning of our life. Camus cites actor, Don Juan, conqueror, artist as examples of those who stand in revolt against their inevitable defeat. For they try to cram a hundred lives into the single one they have to live. Even Sisyphus must find some satisfaction in his eternal task of pushing his rock up the hill. Here Camus waves the old banner of amateur moralists from Shakespeare to Kazantzakis: it's more fun to chase than to enjoy, our worth lies not in victory but in our fight for it. "The struggle itself towards the heights is enough to fill a man's heart," says Camus. "One must imagine Sisyphus happy."

Jacques Monod, Nobel Prize-winning biochemist and amateur philosopher, so admires Camus's Sisyphus that he puts him at the head of his *Chance and Necessity* (1970) along with the dark saying of the old atomist Democritus, "Everything existing in the Universe is the fruit of chance and of necessity." For Monod, scientific or "objective" knowledge is the only source of truth. He knows all about that profound ache in our hearts for transcendent explanations. That's something we've inherited from our evolutionary ancestry, the origin of all myths, religion, philosophy, science itself. That's why today we are torn between the old animist need for transcendent explanations of the meaning of the universe and our uncomfortable knowledge that science is true, that organic life is a beautiful, complex mechanism formed of physical particles that have come together by chance in the course of the immense evolutionary history of our planet. In an access of Gallic eloquence, Monod deals with those who still believe that a trans-material key to the enigma exists:

> For the first time in history a civilization is trying to shape itself while clinging desperately to the animist tradition to justify its values, and at the same time abandoning it as a source of knowledge of truth. For their moral bases the "liberal" societies of the West still teach—or pay lip-service to—a disgusting farrago of Judaeo-Christian religiosity, scientific progressism, belief in the "natural" rights of man and utilitarian pragmatism.

So adieu to all that. Monod then proceeds to demolish the illusion that there is any difference between Mind and that half pound of matter we call the human brain. But the illusion is so deeply ingrained in us, he says, that it would be impossible now for us to live without it. Surprisingly, he believes in Soul. Why should we have to live emotionally and morally without it? "What doubt can there be of the presence of the spirit within us?"

Spirit in this sense includes the Pascal-Camus consciousness of our inevitable annihilation. But no need to be downhearted about it. There is a certain joy in knowing what the score is, and science even today is just beginning to disclose the mysteries of the universe, great and small, "the two infinites" as Pascal called them—the great world of galaxies, incredibly remote from us, and the subatomic realm where flash strange entities like quarks, some of which have the property of "charm." There is so much yet to know and so much fun in searching for it. As the Stoic Seneca said, "One life, fully lived, is enough."

Postwar existentialism gave no really new answer to the question of the meaning of human life. Camus updated Stoicism without the Stoic's belief in the rationality and benevolence of Nature.

Sartre's affirmation of our individual power to choose, to act, to *make* ourselves in a universe without God dramatized an agnosticism familiar to the nineteenth century. Victorian poets experienced alienation, a feeling of shock and estrangement in the wake of loss of religious faith that accompanied scientific and technological advances, the evolutionism that marked that century's second half. In "Dover Beach" Matthew Arnold expresses this fear of meaninglessness by his metaphor of the "darkling plain where ignorant armies strive by night." W. E. Henley thought life was darkling enough, but insisted nevertheless that we are free to determine our own life-direction, though we know not what lies at the end of the path we have chosen:

> *It matters not how strait the gate,*
> *How charged with punishment the scroll,*
> *I am the master of my fate;*
> *I am the captain of my soul.*

Bad poetry, perhaps, but it spoke for many intelligent men and women of more than a century ago who found themselves deprived of the faith of their fathers. For life's meaning they could only turn inward toward themselves as they redefined the old Stoic virtue of self-reliance.

A danger in such inventories of high-toned talk about the meaning of life may be to suggest that life-meanings are the preserve of poets or intellectuals, discoverable only by philosophers or moralists —that a life must be meaningless unless there is Deep Thinking done about it. But that is not true. Don't be taken in by Socrates' old saw that the unexamined life is not worth living. I've seen too many people who enjoyed life to the full go roaring drunk to their own funerals without ever having wasted a moment in self-scrutiny. Lives of countless people who don't stand out from the crowd can be, and so often are, full of meaning—meaning they themselves choose or accept, though perhaps unaware they have chosen or accepted. For simple and complicated souls alike, most of us select patterns of order, hence of meaning, and impose them on the flow of our lives without thinking much about it. A human life described in terms of growing up from childhood, going to school, falling in love, marrying, bringing up children, working at a trade, planting and harvesting, going drinking, bowling, or playing chamber music, baking pies for the family or for the Methodist church social, visiting the grand-children or waiting for letters from sons and daughters far away— such lives may have far more meaning than those of bored people who bitch about the meaninglessness of it all, and run to pop therapy books by doctors who tell them they don't love themselves enough. We cannot say that a life has no meaning simply because it is routine, measured out in doing the same thing over and over again. Heartbeats recur, and so do the seasons, and so does the cycle of birth and death.

I like to read Walt Whitman (he was born in West Hills, just five miles from where we live; the little farmhouse still stands just off Route 110, overshadowed by the sprawling suburban shopping mall named after him). I don't mind his laundry lists of suspenders and ironing boards, his interminable catalogues of routine jobs, the everyday coming and goings. For he saw meaning in them and in the lives of those who had to do with them:

A song for occupations!
In the labor of engines and trades and the labor fields I find
  the developments
And find the eternal meanings. . . .
The carpenter dresses his plant, the tongue of his foreplane whistles its
  wild ascending lisp
The duck-shooter walks by silent and cautious stretches
The deacons are ordain'd with cross'd hands at the altar. . . .
The crew of the fish-smack pack repeated layers of halibut in the hold,
The paving-man leans on his two-handed rammer, the reporter's lead
  flies swiftly over the notebook, the sign-painter is lettering in blue and
  gold. . . .
The floor-men are laying the floor, the tinners are tinning the roof, the
  masons are calling for mortar,
As the fare-collector goes through the train he gives notice by the jingling
  of loose change
The one-year wife is recovering and happy having a week ago borne her
  first child, . . .
The clean-hair'd Yankee girl works with her sewing-machine. . . .
The living sleep for their time, and the dead sleep for their time,
The old husband sleeps by his wife, and the young husband sleeps by
  his wife. . . .
The wife, and she is not one jot less than the husband,

The daughter, and she is just as good as the son,
The mother, and she is every bit as much as the father.

Walt had a sense of meaning and value open to ordinary lives. Others have touched on the theme: Hopkins with his praise of all trades, their gear and tackle and trim, his Christ who can reeve a rope with the best of them; Thornton Wilder, sentimentally, in *Our Town;* Camus's stranger who couldn't care less, yet notes pools of brightness under the street lamps, a girl's tanned face, a silver bangle. But nobody could come up to Walt for sheer quantity of inventory of meaning in ordinary things and lives.

Unlike Pascal, Whitman was not scared by those infinite spaces, and tried to find meaning in the cosmos itself. For him, a key to the enigma exists, each tear counts, each drop of blood:

And I say to any man or woman, Let your soul stand cool and composed
before a million universes. . . .
I do not doubt that the orbs and systems of orbs play their swift sports
through the air on purpose, and that I shall one day be eligible to do
as much as they, and more than they,
I do not doubt that passionately-wept deaths of young men are provided
for, or that the deaths of young women and the deaths of little children
are provided for. . . .

That's Walt reassuring himself, talking himself out of his doubts about possible annihilation by death. His transcendentalist faith tells him he is as limitless and immortal as the universe, yet he can't help worrying a bit about the fate of that unique and wonderful Self of his—grown old and sick, soon to die in that upstairs room on Camden's Mickle Street, he shivers a little:

Soon to be lost for aye in the darkness—loth, O so loth to depart!
Garrulous to the very last.

Earlier he had consoled himself with the thought that at least there has been *this* one bright crowded life:

O soul, we have positively appeared—that is enough—

So he starts to pack his gear:

Embrace thy friends, leave all in order,
To port and hawser's tie no more returning . . .
Depart on thy endless cruise old Sailor.

At Grez-sur-Loing, blind and paralyzed, Frederick Delius had Fenby's help in finishing his last compositions. In *Songs of Farewell,* he sets Whitman's lyrics of parting to music for chorus and orchestra. In the last song, at the line:

> *Depart on thy endless cruise old Sailor,*

the chorus echoes, "Depart!" *pianissimo* as the orchestra brings the work to a close with a slow rocking theme in the cellos and basses, fitting the long swell of the open sea facing the voyager on his last sailing.

The new naval hospital at Groton crowns the top of a high hill from which you can see the gray-black submarines in the river below and the city of New London across the twin bridges. Mary and I sat in the small waiting room in urology. We did not have to wait long before my name was called. I followed the technician down the hall to a room where the biopsy would be done, took off my clothes, put on a green paper gown, and got up on the chrome and black vinyl table. First, the pyelogram had to be done, an injection followed by a complete set of X-rays. Minimal food intake and a laxative the previous day had been required so they could see everything clearly in the X-rays from the kidneys on down. The technician was a corpsman, first class.

"Are you allergic to lobster? Crab? Any fish?"

"No, why?"

"The fluid I'm going to inject has a sort of fish base, and some people react to it. You'll get a metallic taste in your mouth and start feeling warm."

I lay there motionless after the injection, waiting for the feeling of warmth and the metallic taste. Neither came.

"Feeling all right? Now for this first picture I want you to turn just slightly on your side to the right. No, this way. Move your knee up. Good. Now hold it right there." The machine buzzed. The corpsman pulled the slide out and slammed another in.

"Now, this way. Can you slide down a little?"

After each X-ray picture he would bang out of the room with the plate, then come back after a while for the next round. That went on for half an hour while I stared at the overhead light, a translucent white square about four feet by four.

After a longer-than-average wait for the technician to come back, I heard hurried footsteps approaching. The door opened, and the urologist himself came into the room holding a sheaf of enormous black-and-gray X-ray pictures.

"These X-rays show something very interesting. See here." He poked one under my nose as I hoisted myself up on my elbow.

"Look, there's your prostate. Now see those small white spots? Those are stones. There's the one that made the nodule Dr. Brand found."

"Is that good or bad?"

"Good. There's no malignancy. These are not like kidney stones. They won't hurt you. We just leave them there. Once in a great while they may cause an infection, but that's unusual."

"What about that blood in the urine I told you about?"

"That's from my mashing around your prostate when I examined you the first time. Now to confirm that these are just stones, we'll do a cystoscopy, but not a biopsy, unless you want it." I didn't want it.

Cystoscopy involves threading a thin metal tube with a tiny light up the genitourinary tract while they peek through the other end to see what's in there. I held my breath and said, "Ouch!" frequently. Two doctors took turns looking. They were stones all right. Finally they let me off the table and I got dressed, cheerfully bloodying my shorts.

Mary was waiting in the urologist's office, looking at the X-rays and listening to him giving her a lecture on the subject. She turned to me and whatever tenderness may have been eroded by nearly forty years of marriage came flooding back and her face was that of a beautiful young girl.

"You must feel wonderful," she said, as we drove back down the hill. "Don't you feel relieved?"

"Oh, yes. I got away with it this time," I said. "But . . . it's the beginning."

We went for a drink and lunch at the club on base, and decided not to go home but to drive over to Newport and spend a day or two there. Ainslie had prepped at the officers' candidate school in Newport before the Navy sent her to Japan, and we still had some tokens left in the car for the toll bridge with its lovely view of Narragansett Bay.

JUST FOR TAKE-OFF

₰ Ainslie saw me off at Haneda Airport, Tokyo. We had visited her favorite coffee shops in Shinjuku, offered a prayer for the war dead at Yakasuni shrine, bought a small print by Hiroshige showing Asakuna temple in the 1850s. Then we went walking in the hill country of central Honshu, stopping overnight at farmhouses that provided meals and lodging for hikers. The futons were comfortable to sleep on, but the breakfasts tended to raw egg and fermented bean curd. At Kisofukushima I had my first earthquake, a small one that sounded like a truck full of old iron crossing a bridge. We finished off with a pleasant week at a beach near Shimoda, where the swimming was good.

Now as Pan Am Flight 800 (New York via Fairbanks, Alaska) prepared to move out to the runway, the purser paced up and down the aisles of the well-filled 707. Would anyone be willing to hold a baby during take-off? Along with six or eight other passengers— only one other man—I held up my hand. Almost instantly each of us was handed a Korean baby. Mine was a tiny girl screaming bloody murder.

The babies were Korean orphans in the care of three missionaries and a Peace Corps volunteer aboard the plane. There were ten infants plus four tots and a couple of older Korean children helping to care for the younger ones. All were bound for foster homes in the United States.

Enduring a drumfire of angry kicks on my midriff during take-off, I discovered from my charge's laminated wrists that her name was Sung Ae Park, that she was seven months old, had all her shots, and was bound for the home of South Carolina foster parents. Her dress carried the name of her orphanage. Her diaper was (at that moment) quite dry.

After take-off, Sung Ae's indignation subsided somewhat and she began thoughtfully, to pull threads out of my shirt collar. I concluded that it was the moment to manage a charming smile and to restore the baby to her rightful custodians. But not so fast! Did I really want to hand lovely Sung Ae back so soon? Wouldn't I like her company for just a little while longer? My attention was invited to the poor missionaries trying to take care of two or three babies at once. Had I not noticed those kind stewardesses running around frantically with all those bottles to heat, as well as having to attend to the wants of the one hundred-plus passengers?

I looked at Sung Ae on my lap. She was glaring at me, obviously working up to a bellow of rage. A warm bottle was placed in my hand, and I was told that if I were just to give it to her, she would stop crying at once. Sigh of resignation on my part, bottle accepted and shoved into Sung Ae's avid mouth. A clean diaper was gently draped on my shoulder ("In case she wants to burp, you know") and my supplier moved down the aisle *pour encourager les autres*. The only other male baby-holder had already handed back his baby, claiming with absolute accuracy that he had done his duty.

For twelve hours I held Sung Ae in my arms or laid her to sleep on the seat beside me. (There was forty-five minutes' relief at Fairbanks when the adult passengers for New York were allowed to take the cold Alaskan air outside during refueling. Sung Ae was in great physical shape. She had remarkably well-developed leg muscles (the better to kick with) and tremendous lung capacity. Since she quickly stopped yelling the moment she had access to a bottle, I found myself constantly signaling, "Bottle, please—quick!" I also discovered that Sung Ae did not burp as other babies I'd encountered in the course of my paternal career. (Patrick, the youngest of our six, is now a college senior.)

Sung Ae simply did not burp at all. After each two-ounce slug of milk or formula, I held her up against my left shoulder with encouraging pats on her small back. No response other than outraged screams and a vigorous tattoo of feet on my stomach. Finally I gave up. Though she must have consumed the better part of four bottles of milk and/or formula during the long flight, Sung Ae traveled the nearly seven thousand miles from Tokyo to New York absolutely burpless.

To her credit, it must be said that Sung Ae did not regurgitate one atom of what she so greedily consumed. My shoulder diaper was superfluous. Not so the other. I managed *that* well enough, having changed diapers for my own offspring in the old days. Sung Ae's were not the disposable kind with tapes but cloth ones like the sort I remembered. Except that nowadays the pins are different. Those big white safety clasps seemed to get in the way of the opening and closing procedures I was familiar with.

For diversion, Sung Ae liked to be taken for an occasional stroll, so from time to time I trudged up and down the aisles with her as she turned her small inquiring head from side to side. Once I glanced bitterly into the first-class section at the one and only Korean baby being held there. Everybody else in first class was having a great time, what with filet mignons sizzling and champagne corks popping. "How do you think those first-class people got where they are?" an economy class fellow-passenger commented. "Not by volunteering to hold Korean babies."

As the plane banked into its final turn over Kennedy Airport, plexiglass window flashing blue from the sea below, Sung Ae worked herself up to a final paroxysm of rage, beating up on my bruised ribs for the last time. When the engines whined to a stop after landing, I thought I might at least have the privilege of handing her over to her new parents, who had never seen her. Nothing doing. The missionaries thanked me and I was allowed to carry Sung Ae off the plane and into the terminal. But at that point a well-muscled immigration officer took her from me. "Sorry, sir, you have to go through customs. I'll take her from here." I hope he got a good boot on his ribs.

Would I do it again? Would I volunteer to hold a baby, with all the kicks and screams and that final moment of frustration?

Well, maybe just for the take-off.

It's fun to do some things over again, though it sometimes takes a little courage. Especially if you're thinking of life itself. But if poor Nietzsche was willing, why not?

So that was Life? Very good. Let's play it over again from the beginning. Take it from the top. *Da capo!*

ABOUT THE AUTHOR

Joseph Gerard Brennan is Emeritus Professor of Philosophy, Barnard College, Columbia University. When not traveling, he continues active teaching as lecturer in philosophy, Hofstra University. He is married to Mary McLeod Brennan, and they have six children: Peter, Colin, Ainslie, Nicholas, Patrick, and Mario.